TREKKERMAN

Walking the World's Best Trails

Ric Samulski

Wasteland Press
www.wastelandpress.net
Shelbyville, KY USA

Trekkerman:
Walking the World's Best Trails
by Ric Samulski

First Printing – December 2012
ISBN: 978-1-60047-814-7

Printed in the U.S.A.

0 1 2 3 4 5 6 7

To those who walked before me—

Alfred Wainwright
Paul Petzoldt
Colin Fletcher
John Muir
Finis Mitchell
Orrin Bonney

"Persons attempting to find a motive in this narrative will be prosecuted; persons attempting to find a moral in it will be banished; persons attempting to find a plot in it will be shot."

By Order of the Author
Mark Twain, *Adventures of Huckleberry Finn*

Pre-Amble

It never occurred to me until about a decade ago that it would be possible to actually undertake the trekking adventures that follow. I had heard of some of the places and trails, but the concept of doing these treks, hikes, and walks seemed out of reach, so I typically did not dwell on them. On one occasion, I remember picking up an adventure magazine and lambasting the publication for describing trips that seemed to be nothing but adventure fantasies.

'Who the hell can afford to go hiking in the Himalayas?' I remember mumbling. 'Here's another article about trekking some mountain trail halfway across the world. What are the odds that most hikers would ever do that?' and 'These treks are way too difficult for me and most other people.'

But my cynicism proved to be ill-founded. Most of the solo treks that I undertook cost me less than a few thousand dollars. Itineraries that seemed initially complex when first investigated usually were less than intimidating when they were actually implemented. It's important to keep the advice of Chinese philosopher Lao-tzu in mind when planning a far-off trek. "A journey of a thousand miles must begin with a single step," he told us twenty-five centuries ago. That's still good advice.

That first step is usually the purchasing of an airline ticket. Like jumping into the pool, once you take the plunge, the rest will follow. All of these adventures abroad occurred when I was beyond sixty years of age.

There were a few times when my body was challenged, but no matter how long the track or how steep the trail, I always managed to get over the pass and complete the trek. It's not about the legs and lungs. It's what's in your heart and head that counts most. Accepting the fact that you'll experience nasty weather, bad food, lousy accommodations, and sore muscles makes the going easier. "Embrace it. Embrace it." a trekking companion reminded me whenever I complained.

Purchasing that airline ticket may be the initial, tangible step in beginning a trek to a distant continent, but confronting your own mortality probably comes first. Accepting the fact that there's a good chance an assisted care facility may be in your future should be all it takes to get you going. You will long remember the things you see and the people you meet, but to do that you've got to get off the couch and get on your feet.

Good old Lao-tzu spent most of his adult life working in a library. One day he saw the light, walked out of the library for good, and hit the road. He was last seen leading his water buffalo off into the horizon. Of course, unlike Lao-tzu, you'll probably want to return home. But maybe not....

Acknowledgments

I extend my appreciation to those who hiked with me on these treks either in their entirety or for brief stretches along the way. Most were younger than I and, in consideration of my advanced age, allowed me to set the pace of both the day's hike and the conversation. Jose Maria Luis walked a large chunk of the Camino de Santiago with me, and I will long remember his humor, engaging personality, and insights into Spain. Thanks to Australian Morgan Laplonge who accompanied me along every kilometer of the West Coast Way and the Torres del Paine Circuit. His wit and demeanor eased the pain of every uphill slog and bottomless bog.

Thanks to Detroit Tiger fan Susan Giffin who provided vital editorial and formatting expertise. Susan maintained her professional approach to the task at hand even when I revealed to her my life-long affection for the San Francisco Giants. (The two teams met in the 2012 World Series.)

The sketch on the front cover and the sketches at the beginning of each chapter were drawn by artist Brandon Marr who captured the essence of each of my treks. Brandon moved to Wyoming in 2012, working at the Great Outdoor Shop in Pinedale. During that first summer, he also found the time to complete Wyoming's "Triple Crown" by climbing each of the state's three iconic peaks—Gannett, the Grand Teton, and Devils Tower. No small achievement.

Thanks also to Fred Pflughoft of Pinedale. His numerous successful photographic and writing achievements helped motivate me finally to sit down and put something on paper.

My wife, Rosemary, was instrumental in seeing this project through. From the beginning, she encouraged me to undertake whatever great trek was next on my list. We did two treks together—Ireland's Dingle Way and England's Coast to Coast Walk. With the possible exceptions of sailing a boat or putting up a tent, there's no tougher challenge to a marriage than hiking day after day together across muddy meadows in a driving rainstorm. Thankfully we're still together, even though we inexplicably carried only one umbrella. Over the years, she has also accompanied me on countless backpacking trips into the Wind River Range and shares my love for those mountains. Rosemary also provided valuable editorial and research support by helping with my frequent requests for historical and literary material. If the needed book was out there, she brought it home. In addition, Rosemary's computer skills are far superior to mine, and she always came to my rescue when I faced technical obstacles.

Contents

Illustrations

By Brandon Marr

Front cover artwork

Wyoming's Gannett Peak from Bonney Pass

The West Coast Trail, Vancouver Island

The West Highland Way

The Camino de Santiago

Mount Fitz Roy

Fiordlands Track

Taking a Break on the Dingle

Along the Annapurna Circuit

Rosthwaite, Cumbria

Finis Mitchell

1

The Great Treks of the World

"Just show up at the trailhead and follow
the German girl ahead of you."

"We're not just talking about it," Ben told me as we backpacked in Yellowstone National Park ten years ago. "We're out here doing it." Although forty years my junior, we shared a love of mountains and the backcountry. Ben and his buddy, Jeff, were employed in summer jobs, clerking a "four days on and three days off" schedule at The Great Outdoor Shop in Pinedale, Wyoming, on the edge of the Wind River Range. I worked there part-time, shuttling hikers to trailheads, and became impressed by the zeal the two young men showed in climbing and hiking the mountains of northwest Wyoming. I quickly developed a respect for their adventuring accomplishments that summer.

"What did you guys do this time?" I asked them.

"We climbed the Grand Teton," one of them answered.

"What's up this week?"

"We're going for Gannett Peak, and we're not just talking about it."

They liked to poke fun at hikers and climbers who spend lots of time discussing their adventure plans but not much time actually implementing them. "We're walkers not talkers," Ben told me. Sure enough, when I saw them again later that week, they showed me photos of the two of them standing atop Wyoming's highest mountain, ice axes in hand.

That's what they did all summer. Jeff and Ben had the fever. Those two guys might have climbed more peaks and hiked more wilderness trails that season than I had done my entire life. I was honored when Jeff asked me to join him for a Yellowstone trip late that fall.

The two young men did not return to climb and hike in the Wind Rivers the next summer. They died climbing Mount Rainier in June 2002. According to the *Seattle Times,* the two climbers were last seen at 13,000 feet, ascending the mountain with light daypacks. Their tent was found the next day at 11,000 feet. Their bodies were found at 12,000 feet, and they appeared to have slid down an extremely steep slope. According to a park ranger, they reached the summit and were descending when they fell.

Ben Hernstedt, twenty-five, from Tigard, Oregon, was a graduate of Boston College and spent two years studying at the Sorbonne in Paris. Jeff Dupuis, twenty-one, of Big Flats, New York, was a student at Syracuse University and had recently been elected president of the Bob Marshall Club, a wilderness outing group.

Late in my life, I adopted their mantra to "not just talk about it." Maybe it would be good idea to spend less time on the couch.

The true test of the long-distance walker is if offered a ride, would he accept it? One suspects that Saint Paul the Apostle kept looking over his shoulder for an oncoming chariot as he trekked across Macedonia. But who could blame him? Christianity was becoming all the rage, and he was anxious to get the word out. Besides, sandals offered little in the way of arch support.

Walking for the sake of walking is a relatively recent phenomenon. John "Johnny Appleseed" Chapman, for instance, walked through much of

America's upper Midwest but was motivated by the desire to sow apple seeds. Super-environmentalist John Muir may have been one of the first Americans to trek for trekking's sake. In 1867 Muir, a Scottish immigrant, left Indiana headed for Florida. "I walked from Louisville a distance of 170 miles and my feet are sore," he told readers early on in his *A Thousand Mile Walk to the Gulf*.

His publisher must have realized that there wasn't much interest in long-distance trekking. The book didn't hit the bookstores until 1916, two years after Muir's death. He was just too far ahead of his time.

Muir, along with Henry Thoreau, Aldo Leopold, and Wallace Stegner, was one of the giants of the wilderness movement and helped provide the impetus resulting in the creation of America's designated wilderness areas. The actual wilderness system didn't officially happen until 1964 with the passage of the Wilderness Act. Today, hiking in those wilderness areas is an avocation for millions, although long-distance trekking isn't restricted solely to those areas.

In 2011 a Canadian, Jean Béliveau, fifty-six, claimed to have completed the longest uninterrupted walk around the world. Béliveau left Montreal in August of 2000 on his forty-fifth birthday. He showed up again in Montreal in October of 2011. His girlfriend, Luce Archambault, flew off to see him each year at Christmas. "I'm his Penelope, and he's my Ulysses," she said.

Arguably the most famous, modern, long-distance American walker is Colin Fletcher. Fletcher emigrated from Wales to the United States in 1956, started walking, and never quit. In 1958 he walked from one end of California to another. Then in 1963 he walked the length of the Grand Canyon and wrote about it in his 1968 bestseller, *The Man Who Walked Through Time*. His *The Complete Walker* was published the same year and has been revised numerous times. The book covered almost every single aspect of backpacking from tent repairs to shoelaces, backpacks to long johns. You can tell if someone's a genuine backpacker, he said, if they've cut off most of the handle on their toothbrush.

The two books were widely read, and Fletcher became the iconic guru of backpacking and long-distance walking. Fletcher was the first person to walk the entire length of the Colorado River from its headwaters in Wyoming's Wind Rivers to the Gulf of California. He explained his love for his avocation in the opening paragraph of his *The New Complete Walker*:

> "I had better admit right away that walking can in the end become an addiction, and that it is then as deadly in its fashion as heroin or television or the stock exchange. But even in this final stage it remains a delectable madness, very good for sanity, and I recommend it with passion."

Fletcher, who died in 2007 at the age of eighty-five, lived long enough to see thousands follow in his footsteps, taking on a variety of long trails across America. Those with only a mild interest in trekking are familiar with well-known trails like the Appalachian Trail (2,100 miles), the Continental Divide Trail (3,100 miles), and the Pacific Crest Trail (2,600 miles). But new long-distance walks are popping up all over the place. There's South Carolina's Palmetto Trail, Alabama's Chief Ladiga, and even the less-traveled Robert Frost Trail in Massachusetts. Even Edward Abbey's eco-terrorist, George Washington Hayduke, has a trail named in his honor in Utah and Arizona. Abbey would be happy. The Four Corners area was his first love and the setting for his infamous *The Monkey Wrench Gang*.

Around the turn of the last century, I started shuttling backpackers to various trailheads in the Wind River Range. I had been backpacking in the Wind Rivers for nearly thirty years, and it was fun to be involved with people who shared my interest in these special mountains. My seasonal part-time job opened my eyes to the fact that lots of people came from across the country to hike my mountains. They came from Texas, New England, California, and wherever. Once in awhile there were Europeans.

"What the heck are you doing here?" I asked a solo backpacker from France. "You guys got the Alps."

"Yeah, but they're crowded, and expensive. And these mountains are supposed to be very nice. Some friends of mine from France were here last year, and they said I should come."

Then there was the little old lady from Oregon whom I met standing at the Green River Lakes trailhead at the northern end of the range one mid-August afternoon. I stopped and offered her a free ride back to Pinedale.

"Thanks," she said. "I just finished walking the range and was hoping to get a ride into town."

"You walked the entire ninety miles?" I asked.

"Yes."

"It's fifty miles back to town from here. How did you expect to get there?"

"Don't be silly," she teased. "Who's not going to pick up an eighty-two-year-old woman?"

On the ride back, she told me that it took her about twelve days to walk the Continental Divide Trail through the range.

"I've wanted to do it for a long time. It's been on my list. But I've got a few more to go. There's so little time and so many places."

"What else have you done?" I asked

"Well, last year I went to Nepal and did a trek there. It was my third trip to the Himalayas."

I was aware of the treks in the Himalayas, but that's the first time I actually met anyone who had been there and done it. When I asked her to tell me more, she rattled off places like a Sherpa.

"There are three or four that are really popular. You can do the Everest base camp or do the Annapurna Sanctuary or the complete Annapurna Circuit. There's also one called the Royal Trek, but lots of people prefer Pakistan's Karakoram and Hindu Kush areas. I have a friend that went there a couple of years ago, and she loved it."

"Aren't those big-time trips expensive?" I asked. "Don't you have to hire guides and go on some sort of catered trek?"

"Listen," she said looking right at me. "It's no different than here. These places are well known. Lots of people are doing these treks. Save your money and do it yourself. You don't need a guide. Get the *Lonely Planet* book for the area, then just show up at the trailhead and follow the German girl in front of you."

She scribbled some of the destinations on a piece of paper, along with her e-mail address. "E-mail me if you want more information, but I won't respond right away because I'm a retired librarian and don't have lots and lots of money, so I use the library's computer in Portland."

With the possible exception of the nun in fourth grade who told me I would face eternal damnation if I didn't go to confession, even though I had nothing to confess, few people had motivated me more in such a short time.

'Is this what I'm supposed to be doing with the rest of my life?' I asked myself after dropping her off at a motel in Pinedale. If I was going to knock off some of these exotic treks, I'd better get after it. At sixty years of age, the clock was ticking.

Then there was the kid from Ohio who couldn't have been more than twenty.

"What brings you to the Wind Rivers?" I asked him.

"I'm here to walk the range from one end to the other," he told me.

"How'd you find out about them? I don't suppose there are lots of people from Ohio your age into backpacking out here in the West."

"It's in the book," he said.

"What book?"

"*The Great Treks of the World.* Walking the length of the Wind River Range is listed as one of the world's best treks."

As with the little old lady from Oregon, it was a seminal moment, or at least it got me thinking:

> "Something hidden. Go and find it. Go and look behind the Ranges –
> Something lost behind the Ranges. Lost and waiting for you. Go!"
>
> *Rudyard Kipling*
> *1865-1936*

Kipling may have been a little overly dramatic, but it seemed like a good idea to do a little investigating. Sure enough a quick check of Amazon.com turned up ten or fifteen books about great treks. The list included *When Mountains Live: Twelve Great Treks of the World, The World's Great Adventure Treks, Classic Hikes of the World, Trekking, Great Walks of the World, Walking the World's Most Exceptional Trails,* and even *The Trekking Atlas of the World.* The list went on, but after four decades tramping across the Wind River Range, it dawned on me that maybe I should go walking somewhere a little more exotic than the Rocky Mountains.

Bucket lists have been around since the ancient Greeks started recounting the twelve labors of Hercules. Cleaning the Augean Stables and slaying the nine-headed hydra are no longer in fashion, but lots of older people, especially men, have taken up the challenge of checking off a list of somewhat irrational accomplishments before they lie down for good.

The lists are endless. Some choose to play the world's greatest golf courses; others chase bird species. Tracking down birds may seem anal, but it offers the opportunity to travel and provides plenty of mental stimulation. Most important, it can be done outside. Birding (not "bird watching" anymore) can be challenging and competitive.

Ornithologists estimate there are about 10,000 species worldwide. Numerous individuals have recorded some 7,000 species on their life list, and there's always someone out there trying to break the one-year North American record. Bird expert, Ken Kaufman, saw 671 species in 1973 and wrote about it in his *Kingbird Highway*. Kaufman's record didn't last long. Sandy Komito checked off 745 North American species in 1998, and his bird odyssey became the subject of a book, *The Big Year,* by Mark Obmascik. (A movie of the same name, starring Steve Martin, was a financial bust.) Since you asked, the record for most species seen in a single twenty-four-hour period is 385, set in Panama in 1985.

Over the years, my criteria for activities that constitute a valid use of one's leisure time has become less stringent, and for me practically anything that gets one off the couch is time well spent. Didn't some guy write a book about attempting to watch a baseball game in every major and minor league park before he died?

One of the more strenuous bucket lists involves attempting to climb the highest point in each of the fifty states. There's even a club. The Highpointers organization was founded in the early 1980s by Jack Longacre; its members rendezvous each year to reminisce, reconnoiter, and recognize those who have made it to the top of each state. In 2010 the

Highpointers convened on Mississippi's Woodall Mountain (806 feet). The 2012 gathering was scheduled for the slopes of Oregon's Mt. Hood.

There are a couple of books out there on the highest points in the United States, from Alaska's Denali (20,320 feet) to the lowest high point Florida's 345-foot Britton Hill. Try *Highpoints of the United States* by Donald Holmes, which details the logistics of each summit including elevation gains, trailheads, and access points. Most are simply walkups, but a few, like Denali, are major mountain-climbing endeavors. After Denali, the toughest are Washington's Rainier (14,410 feet), Montana's Granite (12,799 feet), and Wyoming's Gannett (13,804 feet). Climbing Gannett, for instance, is not simply about climbing the actual mountain. Just getting to the base of the mountain requires a two-day, sixteen-mile hike from the trailhead. Iowa's Hawkeye Point (1,670 feet), on the other hand, is in the middle of a farmyard and "climbers" are encouraged not to litter when making the drive through the cornfield.

Not surprising, there are all kinds of recognized categories from the youngest person to accomplish the feat to the oldest. Then there's the first couple and the first person to do them all in one calendar year. Arthur Marshall is credited with being the first person to climb the highest point in each state. He finished in 1936. Of course it was easier back then; there were only forty-eight states. The organization's Web site even keeps a list of those who have climbed all fifty. In June 2011 some 214 individuals were credited with accomplishing the feat.

"It's entirely an honor system," Longacre replied when questioned as to the credence of those claiming to have stood atop the nation's fifty highest points. "We believe you." There's no record if anyone ever asked him why Highpointer members feel a need to climb every mountain. We can only assume that if asked he would have replied in the spirit of Everest's George Mallory, "Because they're there."

Any list of the world's greatest walks by its very nature has got to be a subjective opinion, and the list varies with the author. Nonetheless, a few appear repeatedly. And lots of people seem to be checking them off right and left. Here are a few:

Europe

The Tour du Mont Blanc in France, Italy, and Switzerland
A classic walk around western Europe's highest mountain: Ten days or more trekking across glacial ridges and through three cultures. Bonjour!

The Haute Route from Chamonix to Zermatt
A high-altitude traverse through the heart of the Alps: A panorama of 14,000-foot peaks, including Mont Blanc and the Matterhorn. Allow two weeks.

The Grand Randonnee (GR5) from Geneva to the Mediterranean
Wind through remote valleys of the Alps, along the French–Italian border. Chamois, ibex, and France's first national park.

The Camino de Santiago across northern Spain
A medieval trek so good Hollywood made a movie about it (*The Way*). From the Pyrenees to the Atlantic coast with plenty of red wine and olives. Four hundred miles if you do it all.

The Dolomites of the Italian Alps.
Walk through Europe's most dramatic mountains, including the historic Via Ferrata (Iron Way) used by the military in WW I. A UNESCO World Heritage site.

The GR 20 along Corsica's spine.
Rugged, with isolated villages. Allow two weeks to do the entire Traverse. One hundred twenty miles from Calenzana to Conca.

The British Isles

Ireland's Dingle Way

Take a week to walk the Dingle Peninsula, the westernmost point in Europe. Leave your tent at home. It's a pub every evening and a B&B every night. Delightful but take an umbrella. Is that Maureen O'Hara at the end of the bar?

England from Coast to Coast

Touch your boots in the Irish Sea at St Bees on the west and in the North Sea at Robin Hood's Bay on the east—a 200-mile trek through the English countryside, including the Lake District.

Scotland's West Highland Way

Leave your tent at home for this rugged and picturesque trek along the bonnie banks of Loch Lomand and the Scottish Highlands. These are serious mountains and so is the whisky.

South America

The Ausangate Circuit of Peru

A week long arduous circular trek through Peru's skyscraping Andes: Not for the faint of heart. Rent a guide with a mule to carry your stuff.

Torres del Paine Circuit and Mt. Fitz Roy, Chile and Argentina

These two are on every list of great treks. You can day hike to the base of Fitz Roy, but the Paine Circuit requires a serious commitment of at least eight days. It's all about the Great Grey Glacier, Cerro Torre, and the Paine Towers. Take your tent. This is a hardcore backpacking experience

Inca Trail, Peru

A spectacular trek via an ancient trail through the high Andes to the lost city of Machu Picchu. The classic Inca Trail is only forty-three k's long and full of tourists. A guide is required, and the minimum per person is $500. (The Peruvians know a good thing when they see it.)

Asia

Lycian Way, Turkey

The track takes you along Turkey's southwest coast for some 300 miles along ancient roads, mule trails, and wooded paths.

Mount Kailash Kora, Tibet

"The world's best walk," according to the Walkopedia Web site. The two- to three-day thirty-mile experience takes the trekker around Tibet's most sacred mountain with Hindu and Buddhist pilgrims.

Annapurna Circuit, Nepal

Another classic hike on every list. The twelve-day trek circles the iconic Himalayan massif through mountain villages and over the 18,000-foot Throng La Pass. It's as much a cultural as a mountain experience with Hindu temples and Buddhist monks. Most trekkers hire a porter.

Africa

Mount Kilimanjaro, Tanzania

More of a climb than a trek. About half those beginning the ascent don't summit. It's the highest mountain in Africa and the highest "free-standing" mountain in the world (19,340 feet). Allow six to eight days.

Down Under

Routeburn and Milford Tracks, New Zealand

The well-known Milford Track labels itself as the "Finest Walk In the World" past waterfalls, through exotic flora in Fiordlands National Park. The Routeburn is a three- to four-day traverse of the southern Alps. You can take a tent, but the rain can be so severe, staying in the huts is almost mandatory.

North America

John Muir Trail, California

An extended backpack of some 200 miles along the spine of California's Sierra Nevadas—John Muir's "Range of Light." Bears! Although more of a nuisance than a threat.

Wind River Range Traverse, Wyoming
It takes seven to ten days to walk from one end to the other. All things considered, it may be the finest backpacking experience in the world. Don't miss the Cirque of the Towers and spectacular Titcomb Valley.

The West Coast Trail, Vancouver Island, Canada
A special experience along the beaches and headlands of British Columbia's Pacific Coast. Arduous. There are ladders to climb, mud up to your knees, and all the while the surf is pounding and seals are barking. About forty miles and it can be tough to get a permit.

Buckskin Gulch and Paria Canyon, Arizona, Utah.
Maybe the world's most unique backpacking experience. It's only about twenty miles from the Wire Pass trailhead to the finish at the Paria Ranger Station, but along the way you'll pass through one of the world's finest slot canyons. At times your backpack will scrape the canyon's walls. Try to get a permit into "The Wave" when you're in the area.

There are plenty more places, of course. You could be the first person in your neighborhood to trek the Haraz Mountain in Yemen or climb to the top of Norway's Preikestolen and look down on the Lyse fjord. There's also South Africa's Fugitives' Trail, and one guided adventure company offered an 800-mile Antarctic voyage from Elephant Island to South Georgia Island on the edge of Antarctica, culminating in a thirty-two-mile trek across the spine of South Georgia, duplicating Sir Ernest Shackleton's feat in 1916. Take your mittens.

The three popular long-distance trails with which most Americans are familiar rarely appear on any list of great treks. Apparently the Appalachian Trail, the Pacific Crest Trail, and the Continental Divide Trail are too mundane to make the grade or maybe just too long. Some may be surprised to learn that the famous Kalalau Trail along the Nepali coast on the island of Kauai, Hawaii, is not mentioned here. The trail along the coast was long considered one of the world's premier hikes with panoramic views, tropical rainforests, lush valleys, and waterfalls. Unfortunately crowds, helicopters, and naked drunks have caused even *Backpacker* magazine to remove it from its "Best Trips Ever" list and include it instead on its "Lemon List of Hike's We'd Like to Forget" list.

You can get started by contacting any of the myriad of outdoor adventure companies offering guided expeditions to here and there: National Geographic Expeditions, the Sierra Club, World Expeditions, REI, Mountain Travel Sobek, or any listed in the ads in the back of *Outside* Magazine. Soon color catalogs will arrive at your home, filled with photographs of beautiful people sipping wine while gazing at bucolic landscapes. Just having the catalogs lying around the house will be good for your self-esteem, and your friends will be very impressed.

"Gee, are you guys going to India?"

"Well, we're kind of thinking about it."

These guided trips are expensive. In December 2011 the National Outdoor Leadership (NOLS) was charging over $4,000 for a thirty-day course in the Wind Rivers. Adventure outfitter, The World Outdoors, wanted $2,798 for an eleven-day trek in the Dolomites. That price for their trips included food and lodging but not airfare to Italy. Mountain Travel Sobek asked slightly more than $4,000 for their guided Tour de Mont Blanc, not including your flight to Geneva.

Even if you don't sign up for a trip, these catalogs can be useful. Pick out a couple of trips, contact them, and they'll send you a specific day-by-day itinerary. Once you start walking, you'll discover you're doing the same trail, eating the same food, and staying in the same hut or hotel for at a much lower cost. You'll even find yourself walking and socializing with them. And you won't have to wear a silly name tag. On every single trek I undertook, no guide was needed, and a map was an amenity not a necessity. The little old lady from Portland was right. "Just follow the German girl ahead of you."

One more suggestion: *The Lonely Planet* Web site chat room can be helpful. There are lots of people that have done what you're about to do, and they'll give you excellent tips on hotels, huts, hostels, shuttles, restaurants, border crossings, and even medications. Unless you're headed for Mars, someone's been there before and can provide lots of advice. Summitpost.org is also an excellent source of information on international trips. It offers detailed reports on climbing the world's great mountains and serious treks through the Andes, Alps, and Himalayas. *Backpacker* magazine also has a Web site that provides interaction between hikers, especially those focusing on the contiguous United States. There's not much action on the international thread, however.

"If you're not doing nothing,
how are you going to know when you're finished?"

Click and Clack, the Tappet Brothers

Trekking with a commercial outfitter may bring some piece of mind and ease the hassle of some logistical challenges, like getting to your hotel from the airport or actually finding the trailhead, but it's not really necessary to spend the money. In addition, no outfitter can provide you any special protection against wilderness trekking's most common hazards—bad weather and insects. Midges in Scotland can be terrifying, sand flies in New Zealand are voracious, and the hordes of mosquitoes that swarm around backpackers in the early summer in the northern Rockies can make you wish you had taken up needlepoint.

There are, however, legitimate dangers in the wilderness. Statistically the chances that you'll be attacked by a bear or become stuck in a narrow canyon for 127 hours and have to cut your arm off like Aron Ralston did are pretty slim. Backpackers do become lost, mostly because they decide to wander off the trail and over the hill to see what's on the other side. Despite over 400 single pages of single-spaced writing in his *The New Complete Walker*, Colin Fletcher didn't give any advice about what to do if you are lost. He did, however, offer this often-repeated, sage advice: "Let someone responsible know where you're going and when you'll be back."

It's also a good idea to sign the register at the trailhead, assuming there is one. In the United States, many backpackers may be under the impression that those registers are routinely read by Forest Service or National Park personnel. That's doubtful. But in the case of an emergency, they can be useful for search-and-rescue operations. The main purpose of trail registers, however, may be to provide an opportunity for backpackers to vent their frustrations with public lands policy, under the naïve assumption that some government bureaucratic actually cares what you think and has a modicum of actual authority to implement your suggestions.

The USFS also figures that if you record your concerns at the trailhead, you'll have vented your frustrations and be less likely to bother them by coming into the office in person. Here are a few comments taken over the years from a trailhead register in the Wind River Mountains:

> "Why is the trail over Jackass Pass not maintained?"
>
> "The bear boxes at Big Sandy Lake are filthy and filled with rodent droppings."
>
> "Get the sheep out of the wilderness."
>
> "The sign at the base of Hailey Pass has been lying on the ground for four years."

> "Get the cows out of the wilderness."
>
> "How come there's a fee at the trailhead to park? I paid my taxes."

On the other hand, some comments can make one wonder if certain people should be allowed in the wilderness:

> "We saw two guys with guns hunting right in the wilderness."
>
> "Found at Deep Lake, Canon EOS Rebel camera. Black. Please identify."
>
> "Jim, we've gone on. Meet you at Dad's Lake or Shadow Lake. If we're not there, we went on over the pass."
>
> "How come there's no bridge over Washakie Creek? We had to get our feet wet."

Negative reactions at seeing the lack of improvements in designated wilderness areas are not surprising. Many confuse wilderness areas with national parks, although the parks often have large areas designated as "wilderness." Generally speaking, motorized vehicles are prohibited in wilderness areas, although some have improvements such as bridges and even pit toilets. The building of bridges in U.S. wilderness areas is generally accepted, but a small minority opposes the placing of improvements within wilderness areas. "If it's a true wilderness, how can there be bridges?" is the argument.

At a U.S. Forest Service public meeting a number of years ago, I was taken aback when an elderly man argued against people being allowed into designated wilderness areas.

"Humans should stay out," I remember him saying. "Wilderness areas should be restricted to birds, amphibians, and four-legged animals only." His was an extreme view, but it had certain validity.

Hearing gunshots in a wilderness area also surprises some backpackers. They're confusing wilderness areas with national parks. The hunting of big game is a common activity in all wilderness areas of the American West, and whether you like it or not, it's perfectly legal to disrupt the quiet of a serene mountain meadow by repeatedly blasting away with your handgun at some imaginary beast.

The introduction of the new satellite spot locators like the Spot Satellite Messenger and the Personal Locator Beacon have proved their worth by saving lives, or at least allowing rescuers to reach backpackers who think they are in life-threatening situations. The issue over the devices, however, is that many people with simple strains and sprains can just hit the Spot's "help" button activating an expensive rescue operation whether it's justified or not.

It's not the fear of getting lost, however, that causes the most apprehension among backpackers in Canada, Wyoming, Montana, Idaho, and Alaska. It's bears. Especially grizzly bears. No amount of statistics regarding the actual number of bear attacks in relation to the number of backpackers can overcome the irrational paranoia of an otherwise intelligent and educated adult about to start hiking in the Greater Yellowstone Ecosystem.

During the past decade, the USFS and U. S. National Park authorities have done an admirable job of putting the fear of death into the minds of hikers. BE BEAR AWARE signs and myriad recommended procedures to avoid bear/human encounters not only have reduced the number of encounters but also have resulted in many hikers developing an excessive fear of being attacked. The authorities argue that their policies may save not only the life of a hiker but also the life of a bear that would be put down because it had lost its fear of man.

That's not to trivialize the possibility of an attack. In July 2010 two people were injured and one person killed by a three-hundred- to four-hundred-pound female grizzly in a national forest campground east of Yellowstone National Park near Cooke City, Montana. According to the Montana Fish, Wildlife and Parks Department, during the night the bear made three separate attacks on three different tents. Kevin R. Krammer, forty-eight, of Grand Rapids, Michigan, was found dead at the campground when authorities arrived. The other two victims were treated for severe bites but survived. Descriptions of the attack by campers who reported it said it sounded like a Hollywood horror movie.

"We weren't sure what it was," Don Wilhelm said when he and his wife heard the first screams. "We thought maybe teenagers were yelling." Wilhelm told authorities that they tried to go back to sleep, but a few minutes later, the bear was tearing into the tent of a woman next to their site. "First she said, 'No!' Then we heard her say, 'It's a bear! I've been attacked by a bear!'" Paige Wilhelm said.

The Wilhelms ran to their vehicle and turned its headlights on the woman's tent. "And we could see her there, kind of half in her sleeping bag. I don't remember seeing any tent," Don Wilhelm said. The couple, along with their nine- and twelve-year-old boys, drove through the Soda Butte Campground, blowing their horn and warning other campers. According to the couple, they saw a truck leaving the campground with a third victim who had been bitten in the leg, trying to fight off the bear by punching it in the nose after it entered his tent.

Don Wilhelm returned to the campsite of the woman who had been attacked and helped bandage her wounds. The Wilhelms did not learn that Krammer had been killed in the attack until later that morning.

"Everyone appears to have followed all food storage regulations," a Fish, Wildlife, and Parks spokesman said. "No food was found in the victims' tents." Authorities then prepared a trap for the rogue bear the next evening. "We set up tents as they were the night before, and the bear that returned didn't just sniff the tent, she destroyed it," Warden Sam Sheppard said. The bear was captured and euthanized.

There were two other grizzly attacks resulting in human fatalities in 2011 in Yellowstone National Park. In July Brian Matayoshi, a fifty-seven-year-old pharmacist from California, and his wife were attacked while hiking the Wapiti Lake Trail. According to the Park Service, the couple was just over a mile and a half from the trailhead when they spotted a grizzly with two cubs about a hundred yards away. They retreated, but the bear chased and attacked Brian Matayoshi and killed him. It then attacked Brian's wife who played dead. It lifted her off the ground by the backpack she was wearing, dropped her, and then left the area.

Despite the ever-present fear of a grizzly encounter, hikers are extremely unlikely to experience an attack. According to a report by Christine Peterson in the Wyoming *Casper Star Tribune,* "Nearly seventy percent of people injured by grizzly bears in the past decade were hunters." That's because hunters, by their very nature, walk quietly through remote areas early in the morning and in late evening. That's exactly what one should not do if they want to avoid bears.

Statistics aside, more and more hikers are carrying bear spray. The jury's still out as to the effectiveness of bear spray, especially when you factor in the odds of being able to un-holster the canister, remove its safety tab, and discharge it before the bear hits you. By the way, don't discharge the canister too quickly. The spray won't travel more than a few feet, especially if there's a sturdy breeze. Think like a minuteman at Bunker Hill. "Don't shoot until you see the whites of their eyes."

Bear attacks, which are frequently instantaneous, give the bear's victim little time in which to act. One school of thought even holds that spraying the chili pepper stuff will only further aggravate the bear. But frequent TV late night guest Jack Hanna of the Columbus (Ohio) Zoo is a proponent of bear spray. While vacationing with his family in Glacier National Park in 2010, Hanna came face to face with a mother grizzly and two cubs and sprayed one of the cubs when it charged. The cub fled.

Maybe nowhere is the fear of a grizzly attack more evident than on the trails of Grand Teton and Yellowstone National Parks. On any given day, it's virtually impossible to find any hiker without a can of bear spray. Even on extremely busy trails like Grand Teton's Cascade Canyon Trail, nearly every party of day-hikers is armed with the canisters. I actually saw one lone day-hiker going up the canyon with bear spray in hand and the safety clip removed; he was obviously a victim of "death by a grizzly attack" paranoia. Chief beneficiaries of this paranoia are the manufacturers of the spray, which can range from $25 to $50. The beautiful thing for the manufacturers is that only a few of the canisters are ever actually used. And in the rare event that the spray is discharged to thwart an attack, the customer is either satisfied with its effectiveness or dead. There are few complaints.

The bear spray phenomena reached some sort of apex in the summer of 2011 when a tourist inside the visitors' center at Grand Teton National Park sat on his bear spray canister, causing it to discharge, resulting in the evacuation of the facility. EMT personnel were called and medical treatment was provided to those affected by the powerful pepper spray. Park officials issued a subsequent warning that the safety clip on the spray should be removed only in the event of an actual bear attack. Duh!

Since it is illegal to carry bear spray on airplanes, scores of perfectly good canisters accumulate in airports in the Greater Yellowstone area all summer. In an attempt to discourage hikers from disposing of their bear spray irresponsibly, the Yellowstone Park Foundation and Montana State University have developed a device that removes the pepper spray and the propellant and then crushes the canister. Apparently nobody has yet thought of simply redistributing perfectly good canisters. You can be certain the manufacturers of bear spray would be less than enthused about that idea. For those seeking the ultimate protection from bear attack, there is another option.

Thanks to the National Rifle Association and George W. Bush, loaded guns are allowed in most national parks including those in Glacier, Yellowstone, and Grand Teton. There are, however, restrictions on the actual discharging of weapons. Under our convoluted legislative process, the right to bear arms in our parks was tied to the "Credit Card Accountability Responsibility and Disclosure Act of 2009." The rule was implemented in the final days of the Bush II administration, and despite legal challenges is still on the books. You can now stand among the throngs watching Old Faithful with a loaded rifle on your back. We all should feel safer.

Colin Fletcher offered a simple, if naïve, solution to the bear issue. "We carry insect repellent, why not bear repellent?" he said in his *The New Complete Walker*. "Something neutral or pleasing to a human nose but obnoxious to a bear's. Just spread or spray the mixture on your tent or pack bag and then go fishing all day without a bear worry in the world." He presumably was talking about black bears. He was more realistic when it comes to grizzlies. Fletcher recommended the usual, innocuous, bear-thwarting tactics like bells, stones in a can, and singing loudly but also suggested a more formidable defense against a grizzly attack. "Walk alertly and carry a big gun."

Bear-proof food canisters are now required in Grand Teton and Rocky Mountain National Parks. They are not required in Yellowstone and Glacier National Park, but hanging one's food from bear poles at the designated campsites is required. Bears are an issue in only two areas (the Wind Rivers and the West Coast Trail) described in this book.

Scotland may not have bears, but it does have poisonous snakes. The adder (*Vipera berus*) is found across most of mainland Scotland, except in the far north and the Western Islands. Maybe St. Patrick drove them out of Ireland into Protestant Scotland as some sort of Catholic retribution. Their bite is rarely fatal, and I never saw one.

I'm not certain if they're dangerous, but we looked for Yetis as we walked the Annapurna Circuit, and except for a shadowy glimpse one night after drinking lots of local Nepalese apple brandy, we never had a good look at the mysterious Himalayan creature. I suppose if they're cornered, a Himalayan snow leopard could be a threat to humans.

Far bigger threats to your health may exist out there in adventureland, however. Although there are no required vaccinations to enter Nepal, for instance, it might be a good idea to consider getting a shot for hepatitis A, which is transmitted through contaminated drinking water and food. The Web site for the Center for Disease Control and all travel clinics makes recommendations for specific countries. I got a typhoid shot too and was talked into getting a rabies booster by the inoculation technician at my friendly travel clinic. "There are lots of stray dogs in those countries," he said. (Unlike the United States, I guess.)

I also took along some Diamox for altitude sickness, which I used. Make sure to include an anti-diarrhea medication like Ciprol in your usual assortment of over-the-counter medications. Sanitation habits in Nepal can be nonexistent. On mountain treks in the Himalayas, you'll probably see more Yetis than bars of soap. Take your own. Trekking abroad is a big investment in time and real money. Getting sick during a trek is a huge bummer.

Developed campsites in the back country of Patagonian Chile usually had signs saying that the tap water was *AGUA POTABLE,* but I didn't believe them. I always played it safe by using my MSR pump. Not everybody did, however. During my Annapurna trek in Nepal, my day usually began by heading to the local village water pump and straining the water for the day's walk through my pump. The sight of me using the strange device typically put a few puzzled looks on the faces of the Nepalese women and children who simply filled up their jugs and headed home.

Three trips described in this book are hardcore backpacking experiences that required me to carry all of my food and equipment on my back for a week or more. When Colin Fletcher began his trip through the Grand Canyon, he started with a pack weighing just over sixty-six pounds. In this day of ultra-light backpacking, his list included many items that many backpackers would consider superfluous now. Trekkers doing the CDT, PCT, and the Appalachian Trail, who pride themselves on carrying packs weighing as little as twenty pounds, would be horrified at Fletcher's list, which included two cooking pots (4 oz.), binoculars (14 oz.), a sheath knife (6 oz.), four empty canteens (2 lbs. 7 oz.), air mattress (1 lb. 14 oz.), backpack (4 lbs. 14 oz.), a coil of rope (1 lb. 14 oz.), 35mm camera and tripod (2 lbs. 14 oz.), and maps (12 oz.). His Italian hiking boots hit the scales at 4 lbs. 12 oz. Times have changed, of course. Interestingly, Fletcher did not take a tent when he did his famous Grand Canyon trek. He carried only a 9'x 5' polyethylene sheet. In his *The New Complete Walker*, he expressed disdain for tents.

> "Under most conditions, the best roof for your bedroom is the sky. This commonplace arrangement saves weight, time, energy and money. It also keeps you in intimate contact with the world you are presumably walking… Without a roof, you wake directly into the new day."

Further reading reveals, however, there are certain conditions like a snowstorm when a tent becomes "desirable."

After years of involvement with other backpackers, I have come to the conclusion that most backpackers carry *weigh* too much heavy stuff. I am a proponent of the new "flyless" tents, and for the past few years have carried a GoLite Eisenhower Tunnel. It weighs less than three pounds and is roomy enough for two. Being flyless causes moisture to condense on the interior ceiling, but the tradeoff of less weight versus condensation is worth it. Most backpackers carry sleeping bags that are far too heavy. "My bag's good to zero," I've heard hikers say proudly. Exactly why they feel a need to carry the extra pound or two of sleeping bag filler puzzles me. Summertime backpackers are simply not going to experience those kinds of temperatures, and if they do, they'll walk out in a hurry the next morning. Carry a lightweight summer bag and wear a pair of long johns for sleeping.

Just as puzzling are backpackers who carry two shirts, two jackets, and an entire guidebook of the range or national park they're hiking rather than making a photocopy of the pertinent pages. Most men inexplicably carry their wallets, apparently thinking there's going to be an Applebee's over the next ridge. Car keys should be left hidden under the bumper or fender. It's guaranteed you won't need them during the hike. Sensibly more and more backpackers have figured out that unless you're actually doing some serious mountaineering, you don't need ankle-high leather boots.

In recent years, the use of trekking poles has become more commonplace. Trekking pole advocates argue that it's silly to have your body's second strongest muscles dangling by your side doing nothing to help propel you forward. One trekking pole hiker told me that use of the poles can reduce stress on the legs by 20 percent. That may or may not be true, but I found them to be almost a necessity to keep from falling on the wet, slimy track of the West Coast Trail. They are also invaluable in helping to keep your balance when descending a steep slope or rock-hopping across a mountain stream. Don't leave home without 'em.

And God forbid you'd consider backpacking without your cell phone! If given a choice, many guys would rather leave their reproductive tool in the car at the trailhead rather than their T-Mobile Prepaid-Nokia 1661 cell phone. "I only have one bar!" a backpacker once exclaimed in apparent terror when I shuttled him to a remote trailhead. Imagine what happened when he actually walked a few miles along the trail and discovered he had "No bars!" I thought the reason people went into the wilderness was to get away from civilization. But I'm old.

Over the years, I concluded that older backpackers are more likely to complete their entire trek as planned. They've backpacked before. They've experienced the monotony, the rain, the pain, the bugs, the exertion, the wet feet, and the bland food many times. They know what to expect.

Youthful backpackers, particularly those in their early twenties, can be surprised by the vicissitudes of backpacking. They've got plenty of strength but may lack the heart. A few years back, I shuttled two young husky guys from Indiana, equipped with heavy packs loaded with gobs of gear. They told me they intended to traverse the ninety-five-mile length of the Wind River Range and had been planning it all winter.

"Lots of people are doing that now," I remember telling them. "You young guys shouldn't have any trouble."

Not three days later, I saw them walking down Pinedale's main street and asked them about their sudden reappearance out of the mountains. "There were just too many mosquitoes," they told me. That was it. All the planning, all the gear, all the expense, all the travel from Indiana was out the window. I'm convinced that long-distance backpacking and trekking is more about the heart and the head and less about the legs and the lungs.

And there seems to be more and more people in their fifties and sixties out there taking on challenging treks, whether in the remote corners of the world like the Himalayas or in the United States.

"I'm worried that backpacking is losing its appeal," Linda Poulson, who with her husband, Rex, owns the Great Outdoor Shop, told me. "Most of the people we see in the store are older." She may be right.

"Cycling and mountain biking has replaced backpacking for this generation," another Pinedale storeowner observed. There may be some truth to that, although the amount of young hard rock climbers and mountaineers heading up the trail seems to be increasing.

The number of miles one should reasonably expect to walk in a day obviously varies with the individual. Regardless of the shape you're in or the quality of the boots you're wearing, a dull pain begins to set in after about ten miles of even a mild, undulating trail. God did not design the body to walk more than ten miles. Often the amount of altitude gained is a bigger factor than distance covered. On the Paine Circuit in Chile, there were days when the terrain was so constantly ascending that we were exhausted after only six or seven miles. The track along Ireland's Dingle Way or Spain's Camino de Santiago was relatively level, however, and knocking off fifteen miles in a day was reasonable.

My inability to speak any other language but English while traveling and trekking abroad proved to be more of an inconvenience than a hindrance. Canadian Marshall McLuhan had it right decades ago when he predicted that the technological revolution in communications would ultimately create a global village. As far as I could tell, that day is here. Hotel clerks figure out that it's a room you're after, not a beer. Bartenders know you want a beer, not a room, and waiters know that you're looking for a bathroom when you get up from your table in the middle of the meal.

In Spain and Patagonia, I relied heavily on the phrase "*Por favor, estoy buscando*" (Please, I am looking for…). That phrase, along with my best guess of the Spanish version of the appropriate noun, usually resulted in a helpful response. Despite thinking my Spanish was perfect, locals usually recognized that I was a typical mono-linguistic American and replied in near-perfect English.

Even in faraway Nepal, there's no need for a Nepalese phrase book. Most service people spoke some basic English, and just repeating the overused hello, goodbye, thank you greeting of "*Namaste*" would usually get you by, or at a minimum, you'd get a smile.

With all respect to McLuhan, the global village had not yet arrived in many parts of Scotland. A simple request for directions would often result in an incomprehensible reply like, "I dinna ken fare caur birl efter awee. Gae straecht. Hast ye back." Upon hearing this type of answer, you should immediately abandon all hope of understanding the helpful but unintelligible Scot. Offer a polite "Thank you" and proceed down the trail, being grateful that at least you're not lost in Ireland where English is a term that refers only to the spin on a billiard ball.

I purchased travel insurance for my trip to Nepal. It covered all kinds of things, but I never had a great deal of confidence that in the event of a crisis, the insurance outfit would actually pay anything. When hiking in the back o' beyond, the fear of a ruptured appendix, gallbladder attack or other medical calamity was always in the back of my mind. Along the Annapurna Circuit, there were a few helicopter pads presumably used for rescue purposes. Reluctant to risk fate, no trekker in my group ever had the courage to inquire as to the procedure for summoning a helicopter and if payment via credit card had to be assured first. Would the insurance company reimburse the rescued trekker? Better get a receipt for your helicopter ride on your way to the emergency room in Kathmandu.

Trekking alone in remote areas sounds risky. But with a couple of exceptions, I was never actually all by myself for very long on any of these international backcountry adventures. If you don't happen to fall into a group before starting out, there's usually someone not far behind. Only on a couple of occasions did I feel a bit intimidated by my surroundings and was happy to have company.

Crossing the 18,000-foot Thorung La Pass in Nepal was one of those times. We started in the darkness of early morning with headlamps, and the altitude slowed my pace considerably. The trail was snow packed and steep on both sides. If I fell, it was doubtful the line of people ahead and behind me would have made much difference as to my fate, but at least there would have been someone to point out the location of my cadaver far below.

Patagonia's John Garner Pass on the Paine Circuit was also somewhat of a moment of truth. There was no danger of falling, but the pass was windswept and spitting snow. It was a very isolated place, and, after all, I was sixty-eight years old. It was reassuring to have two friends along. (Just in case they needed my help.)

It can be difficult to find a partner to go backpacking or trekking. Feel fortunate if you have a dependable, compatible, and uncomplaining companion. Upon returning from any of my solo overseas adventures, I often became the recipient of two repeated prevarications from friends. "You should have told me you were going. I would have loved to have gone." This is an absolute fabrication that implied that your buddy enjoyed the outdoors and could handle long, tiring hikes over difficult terrain in bad weather. Most likely nothing could be farther from the truth. If he had initially said he would go with me, he would have come up with some lame excuse halfway through the planning stage to avoid actually going. "You know, it's my mother's birthday that month, and I can't miss that. Besides, my knee has been bothering me."

Snow job number two is "Gosh, I've always wanted to go there." For some reason, this was the typical reaction when I said that I had just returned from New Zealand. It seemed everybody wanted to see New Zealand but only a few actually ever went. If they always wanted to go, why haven't they? The free coffee every morning for senior citizens at McDonald's must be too good to pass up. Perhaps they are unaware that one day they will be dead. Guaranteed.

All in all, not finding a trekking partner is not a reason to stay home. Rather it may be a reason to go. When you're traveling alone, you have the comfort of knowing you have only one person to worry about being happy – yourself. There's never a disagreement over the itinerary, food, budget, or lodgings. That said, I was glad when my neighbor, Bob, told me he was going with me on the Annapurna Circuit. It was motivational. The more I thought about the sixteen-hour flight from Los Angeles, the logistics of the layover in Bangkok, the political unrest in Kathmandu, and the lengthy high-altitude trek, the colder my feet became. Then there was some sort of State Department warning about traveling to Nepal in the first place. They said it might be dangerous.

"What about the Communists?" Bob asked me.

"Communists? What Communists?"

"Maybe you should start thinking about becoming one if we're going there," he suggested. "The Communists are trying to take over the country."

"Really? The only Communist I ever wanted to meet was Lenin. Is he still stuffed and mounted in a glass case in Moscow?"

"I think so, but he was a Russian. In Nepal, they're real Asian Communists." I decided to go anyway but was happy Bob would be there to protect me from the Communists. We went. We weren't just talking about it.

2

West Coast Trail

Neap tides, ebb tides, mud, and ladders

Vancouver Island, B.C., Canada
47 Miles

Americans, being uniquely provincial, may be surprised to learn that one of the great treks of the world can be found just over the U.S. border on Vancouver Island. The West Coast Trail is a jaunt along Canada's rain-soaked Pacific coast (129 inches of annual precipitation). Numerous sources referred to it simply as "The World's Greatest Walk." That opinion may be open to debate, but it is certainly unique. After all, what backpacker can resist the call of walking along miles of sandy beach, tide tables in hand, in the shadow of towering Sitka spruce while the surf of the planet's largest body of water crashes at their feet?

And, who doesn't like Canada? A nation that's given us Dan Aykroyd, Buffy Sainte-Marie, Donald Sutherland, and Thomas Chong (yes, that Chong) must be doing something right. Instead of an anthem filled with "bombs bursting in air" and "rockets' red glare," they simply "stand on guard for thee." Canadians celebrate Thanksgiving in October and in some provinces drink draught beer with a little white line at the top of the glass, insuring the customer of receiving more actual beer than foam.

Ignoring their own self-imposed metric system, the professional football teams play on a 110-*yard* field, and Canadian Football League teams have perplexing names like the Blue Bombers, Alouettes, and Argonauts. Despite a playing field longer than those used to the south, each team is allotted just three downs rather than the NFL's four. Then there's something called "the rouge." Few Canadians can actually explain the rouge. It seems to have something to do with punting, but only the Canadian prime minister knows for sure.

The West Coast Trail (WCT) is seventy-five kilometers long (.62 x 75= 47 miles, give or take a meter). Each kilometer is marked, thus allowing the trekker to know how many muddy k's he has behind him and ahead of her. Most hikers allow six or seven days to complete the hike. There are miles of sandy beaches and miles of mud along the track. The thick of the forest and copious rainfall makes slogging through large muddy pools unavoidable. If you don't like wet feet and calf-high mud, don't do the WCT.

You will need a permit to walk the WCT, which is in the Pacific Rim National Park Reserve. In an effort to guarantee a true wilderness experience, the number of persons allowed to begin the trek on any day is restricted by Parks Canada. Only sixty hikers are allowed to begin the trek daily during the "reservation only" season, which runs from June 15 to September 15. Forgetting their traditional quest for a true wilderness experience, backpackers beginning the trek as a group seem to hang together throughout their walk and erect their tents close enough each evening to eliminate any hope of solitude. Every day ends with a camp on the beach and the opportunity to share whiskey, chocolate, and the trials of the day's adventure. The WCT can be very social.

Parks Canada charges about $150 for the privilege of walking the West Coast Trail. Ouch! "The most expensive hike in Canada," one Internet blogger said. In Canada? I'd argue that it's the costliest in North America. (As of 2011, the minimum fee for doing the forty-five-kilometer Inca trail into Machu Picchu is nearly $500. That may be the Guinness record. Backpacking into Machu Picchu on your own without hiring a licensed guide/outfitter is prohibited by the Peruvian government.) Americans would be outraged if we had to pay a hefty fee to walk the Sierra's High Route.

I bought my permit on the Net and had no trouble getting it. Maybe the fact that I was going in September made the process easier. Sources say the permit can be difficult to get in prime time.

My connections from Seattle's airport to the northern trailhead at Bamfield on Vancouver Island were tight. I rescued my backpack from the baggage merry-go-round and caught the bus downtown. Mount Rainier was visible through the window of the bus. It seemed I was the only passenger enthralled by the vista. The others must have lived in Seattle and had become bored with the massive snow-capped volcano. I allowed myself a few minutes to walk through the city's famous Pike Place Market. Unfortunately there was no time for seafood chowder at the iconic Athena Café. I did take the time to watch the fishmongers toss salmon back and forth. The aerial display is apparently a marketing tool meant to entice tourists watching the flying fish to actually purchase an entire salmon. Exactly what the tourist is supposed to do with the fish when they get back to their hotel is never discussed during the transaction.

It was about a mile walk from the Pike Place Market to the *Victoria Clipper* ferry terminal. The passengers-only ferry makes the run back and forth between Seattle and Victoria, B.C., two or three times a day, depending on the season. The trip takes about three hours. Fearing the boat would be fully booked, I had bought a round-trip ticket on-line. It wasn't necessary. There were empty seats both going and upon my return trip ten days later. It was relatively expensive. In 2011 a round-trip ticket was $127.

The trip through the islands of Puget Sound and across the Strait of Juan de Fuca was spectacular. It was a cloudless day. When the sun is shining, this is a place that makes one wonder why the whole world isn't living here. The Olympic Mountains can be seen across the strait to the southwest, and Mount Baker appears to the east. I hadn't realized it was such a dominant peak. I dug into my backpack for my camera to photograph the scene. It wasn't in its usual location. I unloaded my entire pack on the ferry floor. But it was gone. Then I remembered that I had taken the camera out of my pack to charge the battery at my son's home in Salt Lake City. Apparently I failed to grab the camera before I departed for the airport. I promised myself not to let the carelessness eat on me. 'It'll probably be raining every day anyway,' I rationalized as I walked out of the enclosed passenger area to enjoy the sun-splashed deck.

Most of the passengers on the *Victoria Clipper* were American senior citizens. The majority were headed to Victoria to take in some of the provincial capital's tourist attractions like Butchart Gardens, the Royal London Wax Museum, the Royal British Columbia Museum, and sip high tea at the Empress Hotel. The tea thing is a big draw, despite its outrageous price, which can approach $70 or more for two. To rationalize its high cost, the tea experience also included watercress sandwiches, scones, and preserves. What a deal!

I adopted a haughty attitude as I inspected the ferry's senior citizen passengers. 'How can they give up on life so soon?' I asked myself. 'There's not a West Coast Trail trekker among them.' But you can bet every one of them remembered to bring their camera.

The maze of channels, islands, inlets, and bays in this part of the world presented a huge challenge to early European explorers who first sailed along the coast of British Columbia and Washington. The list of early eighteenth-century sea captains, who explored these waters, includes little-known ones like the Russian Alexsey Chirikov, a Spaniard with the elaborate name of Juan Francisco de la Bodega y Quadra, and the more famous James Cook. Some contend that England's Sir Francis Drake wandered around here as early as the 1570s. England's George Vancouver circumnavigated Vancouver Island in the last decade of the eighteenth century and claimed the place for Britain.

Of course, Juan de Fuca's name gets the attention of every pubescent junior high boy even if he doesn't have a clue as to what Juan actually did. Surprisingly Juan's real name was Ioannis Fokas. He was a Greek sailor, in the mold of Odysseus, employed by Spain to explore this part of the world at the end of the sixteenth century. During its Golden Age, Spain was not adverse from employing foreigners. Ferdinand Magellan, the world circumnavigator, was Portuguese, but he sailed for Spain. History's sources are murky when it comes to actually authenticating Fokas's discovery of his strait's namesake. Regardless, British sea captain Charles Barkley (no relation) sailed into these waters in 1787 and officially ascribed the discovery to Fokas, and thus his name became permanently attached to the strait.

Ultimately the sheltered safety of Puget Sound and the Strait of Georgia between Vancouver Island and the mainland of North America began appearing on maps. The trick for ships sailing along the coast was to determine exactly where to turn east into the Strait of Juan de Fuca to find the protection from the high seas of the Pacific that it offered. Ships that guessed incorrectly would often end up on the beaches and rocks of the west coast of Vancouver Island. Remnants of some of these wrecks can be seen by those walking the WCT.

The *Victoria Clipper* pulled into Victoria Harbor. I had some concerns about clearing customs. My cornucopia of dried foods, a liter of whiskey, chocolate bars, dried salami, bug spray, tubes of Vaseline, assorted pills, and backpacking sundries might get the negative attention of customs officials.

Knowing that I would not land in Vancouver until evening, I had no time for grocery shopping for my trek. My shuttle bus from Victoria to Bamfield left at 6:00 a.m., thus I did all of my shopping before leaving home.

"Why are you entering Canada?" the customs officer asked.

"I'm walking the West Coast Trail," I answered.

"Have a good time," he replied. He seemed to be aware of British Columbia's most famous walk.

A day of flying and ferrying left me ready for the sack, but there was one item I could not take on the plane or through Canadian customs. I needed a couple of propane fuel canisters. I hustled past Victoria's overstated, touristy waterfront district with its Empress Hotel, the Royal British Columbia Museum, and provincial parliament building. Horse-drawn carriages stood ready to carry tourists around to see the sights for those too lazy to walk. I made a mental note to take in the museum after my trek. Despite my earlier cynicism regarding traditional sightseeing, the museum and its totem pole collection has an international reputation.

The more conventional retail business section popped up a few blocks from the waterfront. It was nearly 9:00 p.m., but luck was with me. After a few directional questions to strangers, I stumbled upon an outdoor store, acquired the fuel canisters, and located the hostel where I had reserved a bed. It was somewhat shabby, but the assistance of the young man at the desk in finding the West Coast Express bus station made up for its tackiness. "It's right behind the Empress Hotel," he told me.

I was relieved. The bus was to leave at 6:30 a.m., and I had been somewhat concerned about wandering around a strange city very early in the morning, looking for the terminal. I climbed the hostel's stairs, flopped on my assigned lower bunk, set my alarm, and slept.

The bus terminal was exactly where it should be. I had a reservation. As of this writing, the round-trip ticket on the West Coast Trail Express was $133 Canadian dollars. A small group of five or six backpackers was waiting for the bus to depart. We were all there for the same reason. These would be my companions for the next eight days. The bus turned out to be a van, and we piled in, anxious to get our adventure underway.

Urban Victoria quickly turned into wild British Columbia. Paved roads soon became gravel. Rustic cabins and fishing lodges were visible through the trees. We made a stop at Port Renfrew, the southern terminus of the WCT. This is where we would meet the van in a little over a week for the ride back to Victoria.

The WCT may be hiked in either direction. My guidebook was Tim Leadem's *Hiking the West Coast of Vancouver Island.* I was going to hike from north to south beginning at Bamfield. You can also access the northern trailhead at Bamfield by driving or taking a bus from Victoria to Port Alberni, then catching a ferry to Bamfield.

We drove through a thick forest interrupted by occasional clear cuts from timbering. Over the generations, this forest had been heavily logged. While researching my trip, I was advised by a blogger on the *Lonely Planet's* Thorn Tree chat room to avoid the WCT altogether.

"Despite the appearance of a pristine wilderness, there is sometimes only a narrow band of standing trees between the trail along the beach and a huge clear-cut just beyond," he said. He recommended the twenty-two-mile Nootka Trail farther north up the coast of Vancouver Island. But during my walk, I didn't see any evidence of logging. For me, it had every aspect of a wilderness adventure. Pristine, isolated, and wild with that special "Where am I?" feeling.

We took a lunch stop at a small café and then the van rolled on. Despite a light rain, the mood in the van was upbeat. Although we were still strangers, a sense of camaraderie developed.

A father and his teenage son from Oregon, Les and Kevin, joined us at Port Renfrew. They had driven up from Portland, ferrying their car across from Port Angeles in Washington then driving to Port Renfrew. They planned on picking up their car there when their trek was over. When it was least expected, a logging truck suddenly roared around a curve in the middle of the road, causing a brief moment of apprehension to the van's driver and his passengers.

"They don't give a damn about us," the driver said. "I used to drive one of those trucks." He explained that avoiding the timber-hauling trucks made his job somewhat stressful. "You have to be careful."

Our bladders began to be tested and a lighthearted but nonetheless serious refrain began among the passengers. "Pee break, pee break, pee break," we chanted. The driver complied by pulling off the road, allowing plenty of room for the passing timber trucks. The two women in our group marched behind the van for a hundred yards or so and disappeared into the bush. The men didn't bother disappearing and unabashedly stood on the side of the road. Our relief stop was punctuated by the appearance of a small black bear, which stood in the middle of the road about a hundred yards ahead. Everyone, including the bear, had a good look before it disappeared into the bush.

Back in the van, I began a conversation with a young man across the aisle. Morgan was an Australian who had recently moved to Vancouver, at least temporarily, he explained. I guessed he was about thirty-five. He was traveling alone. We seemed to hit it off. I don't usually ask many questions when I initially meet someone on one of my far-flung adventures. Who knows why they're there? Divorce? Job loss? Bankruptcy? A doctor's warning that they had just six months to live? Who knows? It may seem odd that a traveler would want to backpack alone in a relatively isolated part of the world. But then, what was I doing there?

Our van passed by Bamfield without stopping. It's about five k's from Bamfield to the trailhead and the Parks Canada Information Center. When our little group stepped inside the small A-frame, an officially dressed Parks Canada information staff member greeted us. She was Indian, but unlike its neighbor to the south, Canada officially avoids the term "Indians." It prefers the term "First Nations People." So I guess she was technically a "First Nations Person." It seemed like a mouthful.

We were each issued our official WCT permits. The First Nations Person proceeded to give a detailed presentation on just what we might encounter on our trek. As expected, there was a lot of emphasis on safety.

"More than a hundred seriously injured hikers are evacuated every season," she told us. As well as the usual cornucopia of ailments associated with any backpacking trip such as hypothermia and illness, the most common injuries are twisted ankles, sprains, fractures, and dislocations caused by a fall. After a couple days of hiking the WCT, I gained a better understanding for the frequency of these injuries caused by slipping and falling.

Actually getting rescued seemed to be problematical. There was a twenty-four-hour cell phone emergency number, but the ranger was a bit fuzzy when it came to the subject of cell phone reception.

"You are more likely to get a signal on the beach rather than up in the forest," she explained. Specific evacuation points, including Tsocowis Creek, Nitinat Narrows, Cullite Cove, and Carmanah Light, along with the kilometer location of each, were listed in a safety brochure. Actual rescues were accomplished with the use of a helicopter or, more commonly, by Zodiac rigid rubber boats. We saw an occasional Zodiac cruising just beyond the surf during our trek but had no way of knowing if it was involved in a rescue operation.

The list of dangers included in the brochure was enough to make Edmund Hillary turn back. Drowning while crossing a stream, underestimating the power of surf or the tide, falling off a ladder, or confronting a black bear—all made the list. Our ranger also threw in something about wolves, tsunamis, and mountain lions for good measure.

"Always purify your water with a pump filter or chemicals," she told us.

"Is it too late to get back on the bus?" Morgan whispered to me.

I gained a respect for the dangers of drinking unfiltered water late in life. For years, I never bother filtering or chemically treating my water while backpacking. To be sure, I was careful to gather my water from a spring or snow melt, but that was it. Then I had a conversation with an ex-Marine who had served in some of the world's most dangerous places like Lebanon and Vietnam. After a horse-packing trip in Wyoming's Wind Rivers, he was infected with giardia.

"I shit blood for a week," I remember him telling me. "It wouldn't go away. It was worse than anything I ever experienced in the Marines," he told me only half joking. Ever since that conversation, I drink only treated water when backpacking.

During that one-hour orientation session, there was no mention of poisonous snakes, grizzly bears, avalanches, or cannibals. Apparently they do not exist on Vancouver Island.

She also gave us some safety tips on using the cable cars across rivers: ("two people at a time"), avoiding falling on the boardwalks ("keep your eyes on your feet"), and climbing the ladders ("loosen your pack, don't look down, and only one person at a time").

We were all issued tide tables. We soon learned that knowing when the tide was due to roll in or out would be important in deciding whether to abandon the beach and head for the higher forest portion of the trail or to attempt to walk around a headland via the beach.

I gave the confusing chart a brief look but couldn't get past the column headings labeled *jour, heure, pieds*. Years ago, the Canadian government, in a spirit of reconciliation with recalcitrant Quebec province, agreed to have lots of official stuff like traffic stop signs, restroom signage, and the ingredients in a box of cornflakes labeled in French. I decided I'd let Morgan figure it out when a moment of decision came. I had seen him finagling with some sort of mini-combination cell phone and laptop on the bus, so I guessed he was smart. He may have been on to me, however.

"Does this have anything to do with flotsam and jetsam?" he mumbled as he looked at the tide table chart.

The safety brochure also had a warning about eating bivalves. "Consumption of clams, mussels, and oysters can result in occurrences of paralytic shellfish poisoning, which can result in death," it said succinctly. I hadn't packed a lemon or Tabasco sauce anyway.

Getting lost while you're walking the WCT is impossible. Bring your guidebook, compass, and GPS for mental stimulation, but you won't actually need them. The trail alternated between the beach or high along the cliffs and headlands in the forest. The trail through the forest was seldom more than a half mile from the beach, and views of the Pacific through the trees were common. The thickness of the rainforest restricts backpackers to the well-marked trail. Potentially confusing shortcuts do not exist. The only person who was ever lost on a beach was Robinson Crusoe, but he was lost the moment he washed up on shore.

Suitably forewarned of all the dangers ahead, Morgan and I walked out the door, shouldered our packs, and headed down the trail. Within fifteen minutes, we became lost. The trail inappropriately disappeared into a muggy bog. Confused, we turned around and headed back toward the information center to make another attempt.

"You got it right," the First Nations Person said. "It goes through the mud."

Unfortunately she was not simply referring to the beginning portion of the trail. The WCT spent a lot of time in the mud, and people had been plodding through it long before Morgan and I showed up.

The Canada Parks WCT trail map's brief narrative on the history of the trail explained that numerous First Nations like the Huu-ay-aht, Ditidaht, and Pacheedaht have been living on Vancouver Island's west coast almost forever. These peoples naturally developed a rough trail and a paddling route system. The arrival of the Europeans over 300 years ago brought in ships and subsequent shipwrecks. The WCT trail map gave brief descriptions of some thirty shipwrecks on the beaches and rocks alongside the WCT. Most of these wrecks occurred at the end of the nineteenth and beginning of the twentieth century. The coast became known as the "Graveyard of the Pacific."

A telegraph line trail was first carved out of forest in 1889, connecting some of the small settlements along the west coast. In 1896, the *Janet Cowan,* a 2,500-ton windjammer out of Cape Town, lost seven of its crew of twenty-seven. They were waiting to be rescued when the ship slammed into the rocky shore. The 1909 crash of the 767-ton *Sequel* claimed the lives of the captain's wife and their three-year-old daughter when it wrecked on Seabird Rocks just off the coast near what is now the north end of the WCT. But it was the 1906 wreck of the *Valencia,* which forced the Canadian government to upgrade the narrow telegraph pole route. Out of 160 passengers and crew, 133 died when the 253-foot iron steamer ground into the rocks. The telegraph line route was upgraded to a lifesaving trail for shipwreck victims and their rescuers. Small cabins were built to serve lifesavers and the survivors of shipwrecks.

The Canadian government's efforts to create some sort of protected status for the area were met with opposition from logging interests. The backpacking boom beginning in the 1960s and the efforts of conservation groups like the Sierra Club ultimately resulted in the trail becoming part of the newly established Pacific Rim National Park in 1973. The WCT is officially referred to as the West Coast Trail Unit of the Pacific National Park Reserve.

By the time we actually got back on the trail, it was early afternoon and raining. We still managed to walk twelve k's, almost eight miles. There was no choice. That was the distance from the trailhead to the first campground at Michigan Creek. It was enough. None of the trail that first day was on the beach but in the rain forest along the headlands and through the mud. My alarm in the hostel that morning had exploded at 5:30 a.m. I was now exhausted.

That first day gave us a harsh realization of what is to come. We had not walked long before we were confronted by our first ladders. The ladders of the WCT trail were part of the iconic character of trek. Never mind the sunsets, the crashing surf, the barking sea lions, or the beaches. Reading about the ladders in preparation for the trek does not prepare the hiker for the actual ladder experience. They lead the hiker from one level of the trail to another. They were significant. There was never just one ladder, but a series of ladders each about fifty feet long. There were as many as five or six in a series at one location, providing access between the beach below and the forest above.

There were somewhere around fifteen sets of ladders along the forty-seven miles of the WCT. At the top of each ladder, there was a small platform where a hiker could catch his breath and ponder who was responsible for convincing them to hike the WCT. Another ladder immediately took off from there. Then another and another. Unlike many of my childhood buddies, I never wanted to be a fireman. It must have been a premonition.

Remember too that while climbing these ladders, a hiker must carry a backpack weighing thirty to fifty pounds. Parks Canada had, however, made certain that they are well constructed, solidly grounded, and perfectly maintained. I can't recall seeing a broken rung throughout the entire WCT. There were plenty of signs reminding hikers that the ladders should be climbed by one person at a time, just in case someone falls. The domino effect should be avoided. Climbing the ladders proved to be a slow and formidable experience for this old man. My fellow hikers broke out their paperbacks and started reading whenever I was the first to start climbing.

Morgan and I arrived at Michigan Creek around 6:00 p.m. The creek is named for the wooden steamship *Michigan*, which had struck rocks in 1883 near where the stream meets the Pacific. The tragedy doubled when the *Mascots* was destroyed by fire trying to salvage the *Michigan*. Nobody died. There were no signs of either wreckage.

By the end of the day, Morgan and I had become hiking companions. After watching the Academy Awards the past few years, it was refreshing to meet an Australian who wasn't an actor. "I don't even look like Geoffrey Rush," he told me. It turned out he was some sort of software/graphic arts/computer specialist. He was an interesting conversationalist, and most important, like me, he was capable of passing the time by discussing the irrelevant and the trivial.

"The time has come," the Walrus said,
"To talk of many things:
Of shoes—and ships—and sealing wax—
Of cabbages—and kings."

Lewis Carroll
1832-1898

Throughout our trip, I never felt I was a drag. I made a real effort to be the first one on the trail in the morning, leaving as much as an hour before Morgan. He normally caught up with me pretty quickly, and we exchanged banter throughout the day.

"Isn't Mt. Kosciusko the highest peak in Australia? How come it's named after a guy from Poland?" I asked him.

"Australia is pretty flat. I didn't think it had a highest peak," he replied facetiously.

"How'd you find out about the West Coast Trail?" I asked him.

"Somebody over in Vancouver told me about it. How about you?"

I explained to Morgan that I was trying to knock off as many of the great hikes of the world before I knocked off and that the WCT was on the list.

"What list?"

I told him about the Web site naming the greatest hikes in the world and some of the treks I had completed.

He seemed a little intrigued by Spain's Camino de Santiago.

"Is it cheaper if you're Catholic?" he asked.

"It's more," I told him. "They're planning to remodel St. Peter's next year, and all Catholics are expected to chip in."

Morgan told me about a couple of long treks in Australia, including the thousand-kilometer Bibbulum Track from Perth to Albany and a couple in Tasmania. I knew that most lists of great hikes mentioned a couple of treks down under, but I didn't know their names.

"Assuming we survive this one, what's your next one?" he asked.

"I haven't done anything in South America, and all the adventure magazines and trek lists always include the Torres del Paine hike in Patagonia," I said. "It's just so damn far, and sometimes the airplane ride to and from these places is the most painful part of the trip. But I do feel I ought to go down there if I want to be a serious world trekker."

Some of our bus mates were already putting up their tents at Michigan Creek when we arrived. David and Sarah, Canadians from Calgary, worked for one of the big oil companies headquartered there. David seemed to take himself pretty seriously. Sarah, his significant other, was an adult flower child with a couple of tattoos and more earrings than ears.

We would spend the next week together, and they proved to be good companions. Sarah had a special knack for pulling chocolates and other candies out of her pack and sharing them. David had a talent for making campfires on the beach each evening. There was always plenty of driftwood lying on the beach at each campsite, and there were no restrictions on fires. The challenge was actually making a fire. Driftwood tended to be big and not particularly suitable for cozy campfires. It was also damp. David, however, had a talent for overcoming these obstacles. We gathered around his campfire each evening.

There were no restrictions on camping along the WCT. You can camp anywhere. Experienced backpackers understand that they should not take that freedom of choice for granted. Because of heavy use, U.S. national parks, like Yellowstone and Glacier, assign backpackers specifically designated campsites for specific dates. It's understandable, but it's a pain in the ass and tends to take away from the freedom-of-the-hills experience. Having the ranger at the national park backcountry reservation office tell you, "On your fourth night, you guys will be in campground area number six" is a wilderness oxymoron. For that reason, I have developed an aversion to backpacking in U.S. national parks. Wilderness areas, typically with fewer restrictions, offer a better alternative.

With that said, we camped at the WCT's developed sites every night during the trek. Clearings suitable for camping along the trail as it passed through the rain forest along the bluff did not exist. And who can resist camping on an ocean beach? Eleven of the thirteen campgrounds designated on the WCT map had toilets and bear boxes. For me, sit-down toilets are not in conflict with a wilderness experience. (Each individual should be entitled to set their own personal wilderness parameters.) We routinely used both amenities.

"Developed sites" may be a bit misleading. There were no other constructed features. Their locations were all specifically chosen on a beach that had a freshwater stream nearby. The beaches were narrow and crowded with enormous logs that had washed ashore over many stormy winters. The high-tide factor also had to be taken into consideration when we chose a tent site. Tents were erected among the washed-up logs, which served as windbreaks, shelving, backrests, and clotheslines.

There was a negative aspect to the location of the toilets and bear boxes. Because of the narrowness of the beaches, tides and storms are always a threat. Therefore these two amenities are usually situated on higher ground, usually on the bluffs above the beach. At a couple of the campsites, the massive surf had deposited numerous driftwood logs in front of the ladders that provided access to the bear boxes and loos. Climbing over the logs and up the ladders to store one's food for the night or to visit the outhouse could be an unwelcome and strenuous activity. None of us took on the task of going up to store our food without volunteering to take anyone else's food with us.

All things considered, my camping experience along the WCT was the most idyllic of my backpacking life. It just doesn't get any better than pitching a tent on a pristine beach on the edge of the Pacific Ocean and watching the sun set over crashing surf. It was all very special.

We woke up for our first full day of walking to a foggy but rainless morning. My guidebook's warnings of frequent rainy weather to the contrary, we never experienced a rainy day on our trek.

"I was planning on it," Morgan said at the end of our trip with a smile. In hindsight, I cannot imagine walking the WCT and fighting constant rain. It would be a miserable experience. The fog of the maritime climate did soak our tents each morning. They were the last things we packed in a near-futile effort to avoid carrying unwanted moisture and hoped the sun's first rays would dry them out

Early that day, we spotted the huge boiler of the wrecked steamship *Michigan* in the surf. Morgan asked me to take his photo alongside the rusty artifact. "This thing will make me look good," he said. Despite the large number of shipwrecks along the WCT, actual wreckage was usually difficult to spot. Decades of pounding surf has broken the ships' remains into tiny pieces.

Our goal that day was the campground at Klanawa River, about nine k's away, or Tsusiat Falls an additional three k's. According to the map, today involved some beach walking, and everyone was looking forward to getting off the muddy, slippery trail through the forest above. But we soon discovered that walking along the shore was not necessarily as idyllic as pictured on the Parks Canada posters promoting the WCT.

This was not a beach in Florida. One or two easy hours often would be followed by lengthy stretches of sand too soft to support the girl from Ipanema, much less an adult backpacker. We learned that the firmer sand was usually found immediately after a wave's retreat. Improperly timing the waves resulted in the ocean lapping your calves. At times, we abandoned the sand for the rocky tide pools closer to the Pacific, but that could lead to dead-ends that forced us to walk knee deep in the ocean.

Still, there was something magical about hiking along the ocean's edge. Colonies of sea lions squatted on tiny rocky islands just offshore. Their barks could be heard above the crashing surf. They were far enough beyond the beach that actually seeing them was challenging. Both California and Stellar's sea lions were supposed to inhabit this part of the coast. California sea lions bark, Stellar's growl. Morgan and I did not hear any growling, but it was tough to tell over the pounding surf. There were supposed to be harbor seals too, but neither of us had binoculars, so identification was difficult.

Headlands butting into the Pacific usually brought any walk along the beach to a temporary end unless a low tide allowed passage around them. We tried to avoid using our tide table chart and instead resorted to watching which way our fellow hikers in the distance were going. If they headed for the ladders, we followed.

"Is it neap tide or ebb tide?" Morgan asked, trying to impress me with his tidal knowledge.

"Do you know the difference?" I challenged.

"An ebb tide is a low tide," he told me. "A neap tide usually happens when there's a full moon or lots of cloud cover."

I figured he was just bullshitting me, but then Australia has a lot more beaches than my Wyoming.

During our trek, we successfully made it around three or four headlands by staying on the beach. Only once did the ocean begin lapping our thighs, causing some consternation. We were a bit puzzled by the incident because we thought we had a handle on the tide table chart. That evening, someone mentioned that they also had difficulty getting the tides figured out.

"We've been surprised a couple of times too," David, the corporate oil guy, admitted. "I think I know what the problem might be. Canada Parks forgot to factor in daylight savings time into its tide tables."

"Well, do we add or subtract an hour from the table?" Morgan asked.

"I'm working on that," David replied.

Finding the point where the trail left the beach and headed up to the bluff was usually easy. Over the years, Parks Canada personnel or hikers had decorated the access with colorful Styrofoam fishing net buoys by hanging them from a nearby tree. The red, white, green, and orange watermelon-sized floats that had washed up on shore were being put to good use. The buoys led to the ladders and the ladders to the forest trail.

A wooden boardwalk extended along at least half of the WCT as it wound through the rain forest. It was an attempt by Canada Parks to help hikers avoid the mud and bogs of the trail. Unfortunately most of the boardwalk was in complete disrepair and presented a significant safety hazard. Boards were broken or simply missing, and at times the broken support boards caused walkways to tilt dangerously. It was very easy to slip and fall. Old exposed nails were frequent.

"No wonder they put so much emphasis on how to get rescued," I commented to Morgan. "This dangerous boardwalk is probably the cause of many of the sprains, twisted ankles, and broken legs. If they'd repair the boardwalk, they could probably do away with the Zodiacs."

During our week of walking, we saw only one trail crew installing a new section of boardwalk; the rest looked like it hadn't been touched in a decade. Of course, building and maintaining an estimated twenty-five miles of walkway is a huge expense, especially considering the remoteness of the trail. Helicopters had to be used to bring in materials. On the other hand, remember that Parks Canada does charge a hefty fee for hiking the trail.

Tree roots also presented a significant challenge. The huge trees along the trail were supported by a spaghetti-like maze of roots, which presented a constant threat. Thank God, I had my trekking poles. The poles were vital in helping me maintain my balance. Morgan did not have any, and he insisted that he didn't need them. I figured he said that only because he didn't have any.

Unlike walking along a mountain trail, a WCT hiker must constantly keep his eyes looking down at his feet whether on the boardwalk or walking through the mud. A missed step could result in serious injury and a Zodiac ride. One's footing required constant vigilance, only disrupted by the occasional banana slug lying in the trail. Most everyone in our group slipped and fell at least once a day.

"Tell the truth," I asked our group of six or seven around the campfire one evening. "Who didn't fall today?"

Only one hiker claimed a perfect day. Sarah, on the other hand, was at the other end of the spectrum. "I fell three times," she boasted. Canadians can be very self-effacing. The cure for the mud that would accumulate from our thighs to our toes was the Pacific. At the end of each day's hiking, we waded thigh-deep into the ocean and washed away the mud.

That day culminated with our first cable car ride. It crossed the Klanawa River. There were five cable cars along the WCT. Each brought a break from the monotony of the hike and an opportunity to use our arms rather than our legs to move forward. There's also a tinch of fear as we hung suspended across a narrow canyon with a river a hundred feet or so below. For better or worse, we placed our life in the hands of Parks Canada.

"Maybe I shouldn't have been so critical about the boardwalk," I said as Morgan and I climbed into the contraption, which was nothing more than a glorified wooden box hanging on a big wire with pulleys.

Cable cars were constructed to haul two backpackers and their packs. The packs went in the middle between the passengers. The car moved effortlessly toward the down-sloping middle of the wire. Then both riders must use the rope to pull themselves up-wire to safety. Tip: If you're in a group, try not to be the first two across. Those who have already made the trip can pull the rope for you, and you can take photos of them doing it.

Two k's later we arrived at Tsusiat Falls and that night's camp. The waterfalls was one of the most picturesque and photographed sights along the WCT. The Tsusiat River met the Pacific by tumbling down the bluff above. The falls were only about thirty feet high, but the effect was magical. Huge logs, washed clean by the surf, punctuated the scene. Below the falls was a small pool, and then the river continued a short distance across the beach to the ocean. No one could resist the opportunity to wade into the pool and stand beneath the falls. The freshwater was cold, but the experience was once in a lifetime. The whole thing struck me as resembling a Paul Gaugin painting of a tropical island in the South Pacific with half-clad Polynesians cavorting on the beach. There were no coconut palms, however, along the WCT. All seven of our camps during our trek were on the beach.

About three or four days into the trek, we were joined by another couple. Ken and Martha were Canadians who live north of Toronto. They were older, like me, maybe in their late fifties or early sixties. They must have started the trek a day or so ahead of us and we had overtaken them. They appeared exhilarated with the experience but, like most of us, hadn't realized just how difficult the WCT could be.

"I wouldn't have agreed to do it if I had known," Martha confided. The next day, we walked with them off and on for most of the day.

Morgan and I were hiking along the beach when we reached a headland thrusting into the sea. We checked the tide chart and decided reluctantly that the tide was moving in, and the best course of action was to head up the ladders and onto the bluffs. A couple of hours later, we made camp. We put up our tents and started helping to gather firewood for that evening's group therapy session, which was always accompanied by whiskey. Everyone seemed to have some sort of fortified liquid tucked into their packs.

Dusk was approaching when someone asked, "Hey, what happened to Ken and Martha? They should be here by now."

Neither Morgan nor I could remember if they were ahead or behind us when we approached the headland. That was not unusual. Although we always felt we were in a loose group, it frequently shuffled itself as individuals took lunch breaks, pee breaks, photo breaks, and rest breaks. But Ken and Martha's whereabouts raised concern. Just when we started to consider heading back down the trail to see if we could find them, they appeared walking along the beach. They explained that they had walked around the headland through the incoming tide. Ken didn't hesitate to admit that they had had a scare by misjudging the tide. At times, the water rose above their waists.

"We took off our packs, just in case," he told us. The packs would have served as life preservers if necessary. In the middle of everything, they had lost their camera to the Pacific.

"We shouldn't have tried it," Ken said with sigh of relief. They were daunted but not defeated. Morgan later sent me a photo CD of our trip when we all got back home, and I sent a copy to Ken and Martha.

Botanists and foresters might not use the term, but for most, the flora along the west coast of Vancouver Island can be described as a rainforest. Much of the forest adjoining the trail was impenetrable. The understory is a jungle. Western hemlock, Douglas fir, and red cedar Sitka spruce dominated the forest. These big trees have long lives. Sitka spruce can reach 200 feet and have a diameter up to six feet.

A giant Sitka spruce was the focus of a major incident in the Queen Charlotte Islands archipelago about 200 miles north of Vancouver Island in 1997. The islands are the homeland to the Haida people. A single magnificent Sitka spruce grew near the town of Port Clements. The tree had a mutation giving it a low chloroform count and its needles a golden color. It had become a cultural symbol to the Haida.

In the 1980s the Haida had led a much publicized fight against the extensive logging on their islands. On January 22, 1997, Grant Hadwin, an unemployed logging engineer, used a chainsaw to make deep cuts into the Golden Spruce. Two days later it fell. Hadwin was protesting industrial logging on the Queen Charlottes. There was a huge outcry over Hadwin's destructive act, and he was ordered to appear in court on February 18, 1997, in Masset, B.C., on the Queen Charlottes. Hadwin apparently feared for his life and decided to travel to his court appearance by kayaking across the Hecate Strait from Prince Rupert on the mainland rather than taking a commercial flight or the ferry.

His first attempt at the crossing on February 11 failed when he was caught in a storm. He tried again on February 13. He was spotted the next day twenty-five miles north of Prince Rupert but never appeared in court and was never seen again. His wrecked kayak was found seventy miles north of Prince Rupert in June 1997. Hadwin simply disappeared. Some believe he may have faked his death.

Author John Vaillant related this fascinating story in his *The Golden Spruce*. I choose to believe Hadwin is living in the Great Northwest with D.B. Cooper, the guy who hijacked a commercial flight near Seattle in 1971 and parachuted into the void with $200,000. In 2010 an agreement between British Columbia and the Haida Nation resulted in the Queen Charlottes being renamed Haida Gwaii, acknowledging the islands as the Haida's homeland.

Morgan asked me to take his picture as he tried to wrap his arms around the trunk of a Sitka spruce on the WCT. His reach was about five or six feet short.

The waters of Queen Charlotte Sound wash the north shore of Vancouver Island. Tidal salt waters of the Sound flow up the Bella Coola River into British Columbia's mainland. It is at the present-day settlement of Bella Coola where the first European reached the Pacific by crossing the Rocky Mountains from the east. Courteous Canadians bite their tongues when they hear Americans extol the triumph of the 1804-1806 Lewis and Clark Expedition that reached the Pacific over the Rocky Mountains from the Midwest. British explorer and trader Alexander Mackenzie accomplished the feat more than a decade earlier. Mackenzie followed the Peace River up the east slope of the Rockies, crossed the Continental Divide, and paddled downstream to a site near the present settlement of Bella Coola, B.C., in 1793. He sampled the salty water, inscribed his name on a rock, turned around, and headed back east.

Lewis and Clark were not the only early adventurers who receive inaccurate adulation from fellow Americans. Most would be surprised to learn that Charles Lindbergh was not the first person to fly across the Atlantic. Two Brits, Jack Alcock and Arthur Brown, flew nonstop from Newfoundland to Ireland in 1919, beating Lucky Lindy by eight years. (Lindbergh was the first to perform the feat "solo.")

By the third day, our trek began to fall into some sort of routine. We were joined by a copyright attorney from Edmonton who was walking the WCT alone. I wasn't sure if he caught up to us or vice versa but he was welcome company. We reached the much anticipated Nitinat Narrows where a First Nations entrepreneur operated a ferry across the river. We hoisted a couple of roped fishing buoys up a tree branch as a signal to the boatman across the river that there were some passengers on the other side needing a ride. The ferry turned out to be a large flat-bottom aluminum boat powered by an outboard motor. The cost of the ferry was included in the Canada Parks trail fee. We had been looking forward to the Nitinat crossing because we had been told that the ferry operator also sold some basic food and beverages. Sure enough, a can of Labatt's could be had for only $6.00. He also sold barbecued salmon steak dinners for the also outrageous price of $23.00. We paid the money.

"It just doesn't make any sense to pass it up," Morgan rationalized. "There's an outside chance we may never get here again."

Nitinat Narrows was also the only place where a trekker could abandon the trail relatively easily. For a fee, the ferryman would motor a trekker up the river and up the length of Nitinat Lake to the dirt road that ultimately leads back to Victoria. Just how the trekker, who had decided to abandon the WCT, got a ride in a vehicle once the boat dropped him off at the road was not explained. Later in our trek, we heard that two trekkers had an apparent falling-out on the trail, and one had abandoned the hike at Nitinat.

We camped five more times before reaching the end of the WCT. We waded or used suspension bridges or cable cars to cross the Cheewhat River and the Cribbs, Carmanah, Walbran, Adrenaline, and Camper Creeks. At one point, the trail passed by the Carmanah Lighthouse, which was built in 1891 and still flashed its warning to ships at sea. But perhaps not for long.

"The government would like to shut us down," the lighthouse keeper told us. He chatted for a few minutes as we walked through the well-landscaped grounds. The keeper was well aware that technological advances were making lighthouses like his obsolete, but he was fighting the trend and was active in some sort of "Preserve Canadian Lighthouses Even Though They Are Vestigial" organization.

Although we did not go inside any of the structures surrounding the actual lighthouse, the facilities looked decidedly comfortable. There appeared to be a guesthouse as well as a very large main home on the grounds. There was also an extensive vegetable garden. Granted, we were there on a warm sunny afternoon, and this lighthouse keeper must withstand countless days of terrible weather each winter. Yet, from my cursory inspection, his life looked pretty good.

"They routinely used to send a helicopter to take us to town," he told us. "Now everything is by boat. I can see the handwriting on the wall," he said indicating he is already mentally preparing for a new career.

After walking nearly eight days, we finally reached the Gordon River trailhead where another ferry ride across the river brought us within two kilometers of the southern terminus of the WCT—Port Renfrew.

"Congratulations, Morgan," I said and offered my hand. "We made it. Thanks for sticking with me."

His reply was pure Australian. "Good on you."

Les and his son finished a couple of hours ahead of Morgan and me and were at the river's edge when our boat reached the dock. They had walked into town and returned with their truck to give us a ride so we wouldn't have to walk the final two k's into Port Renfrew. We piled into the back of the pickup and headed for the Port Renfrew Hotel where everyone gathered on the deck. We settled in for the afternoon. The West Coast Trail Express bus wasn't due for another four hours. We soaked ourselves with Molson's and sunshine on the deck of the hotel, basking in our accomplishment. A group photo was taken. And to top it all off, the copyright lawyer from Edmonton picked up the entire tab. Pretty nice.

We sang a couple of silly songs during the bus ride back to Victoria. We were all proud of our accomplishment and felt heady. The van stopped at the Canada Parks Information Center, and we helped ourselves to some old but free posters publicizing the 100th anniversary of the WCT in 2007.

At the risk of being labeled an ugly American, I asked the ranger why so much of the boardwalk was in disrepair. She gave me the expected bureaucratic response that logistics and money were an issue.

"But it's a national park," I emphasized. "Canada Parks certainly wouldn't allow any trail in Banff National Park to become this poorly maintained."

"Actually the WCT is not in a national park," she responded. She picked up a copy of the trail map we had all carried and pointed to the title— "Pacific Rim National Park *Reserve*" with the implication that a reserve does not benefit from funding at the same level as a national park. I thanked her and sheepishly boarded the bus.

Looking back on the experience, I had not yet attempted a more arduous trek than the WCT. It was very difficult. Except for the ladders, the trail presented little variation in altitude. There were no long, grueling passes, no undulating valleys, and when walking along an ocean beach, a hiker certainly can't complain, "I'm not used to the altitude."

It was late evening by the time the bus pulled into Victoria. Morgan and I shook hands warmly. It had been a memorable trek, enhanced by each other's company. I felt a sense of indebtedness that he found me interesting, or at least entertaining. As we walked along the beach, we had sung Broadway show tunes, disagreed over U.S. foreign policy, and discussed the likes of Thomas Hardy, George Gershwin, and Oscar Wilde.

"Didn't Oscar Wilde write *The Importance of Being Earnest?*" I had asked him. "What's that about anyway?"

"It's about this guy named Earnest who lacks sincerity," Morgan said.

"Really?" I replied. Someday I need to look that up.

It was a melancholy moment as we parted. We realized that that we would never see one another again. We were mistaken.

3

West Highland Way

Bagpipes, Robert Burns, and Ben Nevis

Scotland
95 miles

"Aye, Yank, you've made it this far along. Let me buy you a wee one," a friendly voice offered almost as soon as I walked into the pub. The offer of the drink was as warming as the whisky itself. It had been a cold, wet day. The middle-aged man was part of a group of three Scottish hikers who had passed me on the trail that morning.

I tried staying up with them, but their pace was more than I could handle. They seemed genuinely pleased that an American was doing the West Highland Way.

"Most just want to play a round of golf at St. Andrews, see Loch Ness, then head back to Edinburgh," I think he said. These Scots were a friendly group, but I sometimes struggled to understand them. I spent four nights drinking and having dinner with the trio. They usually hit the trail an hour after me, passed me by mid-morning, and were well into their second drink by the time I showed up at the pub that evening. Every day along Scotland's ninety-five-mile West Highland Way ended in the pub. That's a good thing.

The trek began seven miles north of gritty Glasgow, Scotland's largest city, in the small town of Milngaive and finished in touristy Fort William. Most trekkers walk The Way south to north. You can catch the train to Milngaive where an obelisk in the middle of town marks the start of another of the great treks of the world. Another obelisk marks the other end of the trek in Fort William.

The Highlands of Scotland had been in the back of my mind for a number of years. The West Highland Way usually appears on any list of great hikes. The Scot at the pub was right. I never actually met anyone who had been to the mountainous northwest. The golf course at St. Andrews seems to be the only place any of my acquaintances wanted to go, and that's farther east. The game of golf, of course, was invented in Scotland, deriving its name from one of its first rules, "*G*entlemen *O*nly…*L*adies *F*orbidden." Many people seem unaware too of the largest annual gathering of bagpipes and drums in the world—the Tattoo—which is held each August in Edinburgh. (Check your dictionary. That's what it's called.) You have to be dead not to love the sound of bagpipes and drums. But Edinburgh was not on my itinerary.

Making the commitment to do Britain and Scotland's most famous walk got a huge boost when I actually met two people from Scotland in Pinedale. Pete and Lynne Long had come to Wyoming to do some hiking and climbing in the Wind River Range. I was working at the Great Outdoor Shop again that summer and shuttled them to one of the trailheads. It always reconfirmed my belief that the Wind Rivers were a world-class climbing and backpacking destination when people from Europe or the British Isles made the long trip here. Yet even many Pinedale people have never bothered to hike into the Wind Rivers' Titcomb Valley or the Cirque of the Towers, and here was a couple traveling thousands of miles to see what was in Pinedale's backyard.

Unfortunately for Pete and Lynne, it rained practically every day during their week in the mountains. I felt bad for them. Backpackers and climbers who travel to Wyoming by air usually were more likely to grind out bad weather since they've purchased roundtrip airplane tickets and have little choice. That was the case with these two. The mountains were socked in most of the week, but Pete and Lynne toughed it out through the thunder, lightning, rain, and wet snow that the Wind Rivers threw at them.

"We're used to it," Pete told me when they finally emerged from the mountains. "We live in Scotland." The bad weather had not prevented them from summiting a few lesser peaks including Laturio and A Cheval.

"Wow, I've looked at those two peaks a hundred times but have never climbed them," I told them. They also climbed one of the Wind Rivers' more elegant mountains—Ellingwood Peak.

"We had to spend the night on the mountain during a thunderstorm," Pete told me. These guys were tough.

After a little tour of Pinedale, I invited them up to our cabin for lunch. We talked about mountains, climbing, and Scotland. Pete and Lynne lived in the northwest of Scotland near the West Highland Way in the small town of Ballachulish. With a name like that, how could I resist stopping to see them while doing Scotland's most famous trek?

I had a three-hour layover in Dublin before flying into Glasgow. It was unusual to find three or four seats in the airport waiting area attached together, not interrupted by armrests. Airports seem to make flying as uncomfortable as possible and make an intentional effort to avoid seats where weary travelers can actually stretch out. I seized the moment and was soon asleep. A tapping on the soles of my shoes woke me. It was an Irish cop with a nightstick in hand.

"Could I see your boarding pass?" the officer asked.

"What do I look like," I responded instinctively, "some sort of airport bum?"

"Your boarding pass," he asked again with a little more authority in his voice. Apparently my disheveled appearance and recumbent position didn't fit well with the officer. He examined my boarding pass and returned it to me. "Keep your feet on the floor in the waiting room," he warned. The balance of the trip to Glasgow was uneventful.

Glasgow was not a pretty city. It resembled Chicago of the 1930s. Massive stone retail and industrial buildings dominated the commercial areas. Curved Georgian apartments added a sense of stateliness in the older residential areas. A nineteenth-century industrial superpower, its shipbuilding capacities along the River Clyde helped to make Britain ruler of the seas and a world power. It was during World War II that the Scots resorted to a unique defense in order to protect Glasgow's shipbuilding yards from Nazi bombs. In an attempt to trick the Luftwaffe, the Brits electrified a grid of lights outside of Glasgow to resemble a shipbuilding facility along the River Clyde. There's no report if any of Hitler's bombing missions wasted their payload on the simulation. But it was a pretty creative idea.

"And a woman is only a woman,
but a good cigar is a smoke."

Rudyard Kipling
1865-1936

Walking Glasgow's streets, I stumbled on a military museum dedicated to a nineteenth-century Scottish military unit—The Royal Highland

Fusiliers. I had no idea what a fusilier was, but I knew a pith helmet when I saw one, and this museum was full of them. It wasn't a particularly large museum, but I was enthralled. Show me an American male whose heart doesn't pound at the sight of a Scottish military unit on parade in ceremonial uniforms playing bagpipes, and I'll show you a down-to-earth, sensible guy who's in control of his emotions. That's wasn't me.

This museum brought to mind Kipling's *The Man Who Would Be King*, which featured two former British soldiers, Daniel Dravot and Peachy Carnahan. The two scalawags dusted off their tunics, put on their pith helmets, and proceeded to take over the nebulous kingdom of Kafiristan. We're talking *Zulu*. I loved the discipline, the stiff upper lip in the face of disaster that this genre of movie depicted. I've watched *Zulu* almost as many times as *Animal House,* although the latter film may be little short on the stiff lip and discipline stuff.

Do you remember the scene in *Zulu* that depicted the famous Battle of Rorke's Drift? A handful of brave British soldiers in red tunics were surrounded by thousands of swarming Zulus. Bodies were lying around everywhere. The Fusiliers were out of drinking water. The Fusiliers were out of ammunition. The Zulus had the bases loaded with no outs. Things were looking really bad for the Fusiliers.

Then Stanley Baker turned to Michael Caine and said, "Pardon me, lieutenant, but you've got a dirty spot on your blouse." Wow! No wonder so many of those guys were awarded the Victoria Cross. Never mind the thousands of Zulus. Those guys were worried about their appearance.

I charged into the museum like *The Light Brigade*. The Royal Highland Fusiliers may not have been at Rorke's Drift, but they were at Waterloo and the Crimean War. It was in the Crimean War at the Battle of Balaclava in 1854 that the Highlander infantry routed a Russian cavalry charge, and the

Thin Red Line became a military legend. Those are the guys Kipling was talking about. (Insert sound of distant bagpipes here.)

The museum had tunics, swords, balaclavas, and baklavas. There were plenty of kilts too. And bearskin hats. There was only one employee. He was obviously a retired British vet and carried a serious military demeanor. He was not to be taken lightly. I gathered my courage, fearing, at best, an aloof response to my question.

"Excuse me, sir, but exactly what was the purpose of those big bearskin hats?"

He nailed the question. "The infantry wore them to scare the charging horses of the attacking cavalry. Horses don't like the smell of bears. They rear up. They're difficult to rein."

His reply brought a lot more questions to mind. How heavy are those hats? Where did they get the bearskins one hundred fifty years ago? Did they wear them at the Battle of Balaclava in the Crimean War? Who actually wore balaclavas? The Turks? Are there any bears in Great Britain? Where did they get the bearskin for the hats now? I decided to hold these important questions for another time, put a pound in the museum's donation jar, thanked him, and left. It was a great stop.

A couple yards of woolen fabric with a traditional tartan plaid sounded like a great Scottish souvenir and the perfect gift for mom who, at ninety-six, still had me plant a tree in her backyard last spring. (It's all about attitude.) The kilt store had every fashion item a traditionally well-dressed Scot might need. This was the place to buy your *sporran* (sort of a male purse), *sgian dubh* (knife), and *ghillies* (shoes). The shop had large bolts of woolen and cotton material woven with every clan tartan. There were Clan Innes, MacCurdy, Buchanan, MacLeod, Fraser, and not less than six Stewart tartans.

"What clan are ye'?" the clerk asked.

"I'm not even an Anglo-Saxon. I'm Polish," I replied. I was taken aback because I had forgotten that most who bought the tartan material identify with a particular clan if not in their name then in their lineage. I had not a lick of Scottish tartan in me.

"All my grandparents came over to America from Poland," I said before settling on the Black Watch tartan. It's green. Mom was genuinely surprised when I presented her with the Black Watch tartan when I returned home. But she was a bit puzzled. "It's beautiful," she said, "but we're Polish." We use it as a tablecloth every Christmas.

The next day, I took the short train ride to Milngaive and officially started walking the West Highland Way. I was carrying all my stuff in my backpack, although two or three baggage shuttling services were based out of Milngaive. They'd transport your stuff ahead to your next B&B the entire length of the Highland Way. The disadvantage of that approach is committing to a specific destination each day. I did not make a single advance reservation for my trek. I could have, but that would have entailed knowing where I would end up each night, and I just wasn't familiar enough with the trek. Besides, I couldn't figure out how to dial those Scottish phone numbers, and if I got lucky and someone actually answered, I probably wouldn't have been able to understand the Gaelic on the other end.

I also prided myself on traveling light. Comfortable hiking shoes, a pair of Crocs for the evening, two pair of pants, a couple shirts, a fleece vest, a windbreaker, rain pants, a couple pair of socks, underwear, a camera, guide book, wool gloves, a very light "just in case" sleeping bag, and my GoLite umbrella. Too many people simply carry too much stuff. Where do they think they're going? The moon? Besides, Scotland had Laundromats! And if you really forget to take something you can't live without, Scotland even had stores where you could actually buy clothes. Most important, the West Highland Way is not a traditional backpack. Although a small percentage of people (mostly young students) camp, most stay in B&Bs or youth hostels. Both are scattered along the trek.

There were even a few developed campgrounds with primitive rough wooden shelters inexplicably called "wigwams." (Apparently some Scots had Algonquin roots.) Trekkers can leave their tent and sleeping bag at home. No permit of any kind was required. If you insist on tent camping, there are several no-fee basic campsites along The Way. The route was clearly marked with directional thistle and hexagon signage pointing the way.

Lonely Planet's Walking in Scotland recommended seven days to complete the hike. That time frame doesn't allow for any tempting side trips like climbing Ben Nevis or taking in Glencoe, one of the Highlands' most dramatic mountain locales. *Walking in Scotland* was my only guidebook for the hike, and it was all I needed. Like all the great hikes, there were usually some fellow hikers behind you just in case you needed a little guidance.

My destination that first day was the village of Drymen, twelve miles up the track. It was the last week in April, and the weather was perfect. It proved to be one of the few days that it did not rain on my trek. One advantage of doing the walk in the spring is the absence of midges. Hordes of these legendary insects can plague summer hikers. I never met a midge.

The first miles beyond Milngaive was a country stroll through sylvan Mugdock Wood, past holiday homes, and along Craigallian Loch. Scottish Highlander cattle equipped with heavy red coats grazed peacefully, accenting the pastoral scenery. The scene was a dramatic contrast to gritty

Glasgow, only a few miles behind. Duntreath Castle, standing in a small clearing, came into view.

'God, I'm glad I decided to do this,' I remember thinking. Glengoyne Distillery sat just off the route, but I continued without stopping. The boutique single-malt operation was one of many distilleries in Scotland's Highlands, and for many, they were a destination within themselves. They reminded me of northern California's Napa Valley vintners who, long ago, lost the charm of small makers and purveyors of wines, adopting "tastings" and "tours" as a blatant marketing ploy. But to the Scotch whisky enthusiasts, visiting the distilleries is a not-to-be-missed experience. Like fine wines, there's a compendium of do's and don'ts associated with fine whiskies.

Lonely Planet's Scotland's and Highlands & Islands said the *whisky* in Scotch whisky is always spelled without an 'e.' *Whiskey* with an 'e' is made in Ireland or America. Single malts had become the epicenter of Scotch snobbery. They are produced by a single distillery from malted barley. Single malts have the distinct taste and smell of the distillery that made it. That character is derived from the particular peat smoke, water, and barley used in that distillery. Even the oak barrels used for aging can provide a specific taste. A single malt from the same distillery may not necessarily be identical. Different distillations from the same distillery can have a slightly different character. It's all part of the single malt mystique.

I hooked up briefly with a middle-aged New York couple that was walking the West Highland Way. They had no backpacks and told me they had hired one of the luggage carriers to move their things along the route.

"You mean you're carrying everything you need for the entire walk?" the woman asked me incredulously. There was a subtle demeaning tone to her question. "We would never do that."

Even though I was clean shaven, and my hair was cut short, I got the feeling that they looked upon me as some sort of unsanitary old hippie with no change of clothes who showered only on weekends. We passed the Beech Tree Inn a couple hundred yards off The Way where tourists and locals were dining outside on the patio. It had an upscale look to it.

"We're going here for lunch," she told me as they turned off. I suspected they just wanted to avoid walking with me. An hour or so later, I lunched on a can of peaches with oatcakes and cheddar cheese under a large silver birch.

About nine or ten miles into my first day's walk, the long day, which started in Glasgow, began to take a toll on my stamina. My guidebook suggested Easter Drumquhasle Farm, a couple miles south of Drymen, as a B&B for the night, but I didn't like the look of the place and was lured on by the bright lights of Drymen. It proved to be a mistake. For the only time on my trek, I had trouble finding a room.

"It's Saturday night and there's a big wedding in town," a nice lady at the third B&B I tried told me. I wondered if my casual approach to finding a room each night was a mistake. It was getting dark and I was worried. I returned to the friendly lady and told her that I was in a bit of bind. She made a couple of phone calls and told me that she found a room for me above the Clachan pub. My *Lonely Planet* guidebook said the Clachan "dates back to 1734, making it Scotland's oldest pub." Serendipity! Thirty minutes earlier, I was worried I'd have to sleep under a bridge and now I was staying in a museum. I made it a point to stop by and thank the helpful lady the next morning on my way out of town

An hour beyond Drymen, the West Highland Way began to parallel Great Britain's largest body of fresh water, Loch Lomond, along its eastern shore. The lake is twenty-two miles long and from one to five miles wide. It was magnificent sheet of water. The entire area is within the newly created Loch Lomond and Trossachs National Park. John Muir, born in Scotland, would be happy with the protection the designation offered the area. Because of its proximity to Glasgow, it was loved to death in the summer months. The western shore was overdeveloped, and motorboats and jet skis can spoil the tranquility. That was not my experience. It was April and not yet summer. The crowds were absent.

As I walked, I saw the holiday homes and the busy highway across the lake, but my experience was genuinely tranquil. Normally The Way passed over the shoulder of 1,184-foot Conic Hill before reaching the shores of Loch Lomond at the tiny settlement of Balmaha. Conic Hill overlooked the geologic fault that separated the rugged Highlands from the more sedate lowlands to the south. The path up the mountain is closed during the spring lambing season, so signs rerouted me through a tiny settlement artfully named Milton of Buchanan. Soon the West Highland Way began to hug the shore of Loch Lomond, which was rarely out of sight for the next two days.

Loch Ness, farther north, may have its monster, but Loch Lomond had the melancholy melody that symbolized Scotland. First published as the poem, "The Bonnie Banks O' Loch Lomond," by Andrew Lang, it evolved into the most traditional of Scottish songs.

"O ye'll tak' the high road, and I'll tak the low
And I'll be in Scotland afore ye
for me an my true love will ne-er meet again
on the bonnie, bonnie banks o' Loch Lomon"

The exact meaning of the lyrics is open to a variety of interpretations, but there appears to be genuine consensus that the song has nothing to do with a disagreement between lovers over which route leads to their favorite picnic site. The words have a real basis in history. One interpretation is that the poem involves the hanging of some of the supporters of the Catholic Bonnie Prince who attempted to wrest the throne from the Protestant English king in 1745. A prisoner sentenced to the gallows took the low road, while those spared would take the high road.

It's along this stretch of The Way that I first encountered the three Scots who would buy me a whisky later that evening. They were a hardy threesome, and I was unable to maintain their pace despite my need for conversation. The flora began to change now that I was in the genuine Highlands. Dark purple heather and stands of Scots pine made their first significant appearance. The trail passed a small oak forest labeled Ross Wood on the map and emerged at Rowardennan. The town wasn't much more than a hotel and the Clansman Pub.

Twenty minutes beyond was the Rowardennan Scottish Youth Hostel. Located on the banks of Loch Lomond, the hostel commanded a view of the Loch and was nearly empty. Its external appearance had the look of a manor house. I was to learn that, despite their appeal to younger travelers, Scottish hostels are mostly havens for seniors like me during the school year when the kids were behind their desks. They offered clean beds, private hot showers, a clean kitchen equipped with pots and pans, dinnerware, quiet sleeping, and conversation if desired. All for about $15 a night. I was the only person in my dormitory of four beds—a situation, which was to repeat itself during my Scottish adventure whenever I stayed in rural hostels and avoided weekends. I always made an attempt to seek them out.

But the lure of the Clansman Pub back down the trail was too much to resist. "It's the Yank," my off-again, on-again trail mates chimed and then bought me a whisky. They then proceeded to convince me that the only thing I could possibly eat for dinner was the traditional Scottish fare—

haggis. You won't convince me that genuine haggis is routinely eaten in Scotland, but it's always served when Scots honor their national poet Robert Burns in January. The arrival of the dish is announced to the diners with the playing of a bagpipe and the reciting of Burns's "Address to a Haggis." His meaning is refreshingly clear despite his eighteenth-century dialect.

"Fair fa' your honest, sonsie face,
Great chieftain o' the puddin-race!"

Robert Burns is loved by Scots not simply for his poetry but for his celebration of Scotland and Scottish culture. He captured the Scottish character like Rodgers and Hammerstein's *Oklahoma* epitomized the American West. But Americans are more familiar with his *Auld Lang Syne* than his praise of the haggis.

Reading the haggis recipe might make one think twice before eating it. "Take the liver, lungs, and heart of a sheep and boil them. Then stuff these ingredients along with oatmeal into a sheep stomach." It doesn't even rhyme. On a Burns Night celebration, a dagger ostentatiously slashes the stomach, spilling out the ingredients to the sound of pipes. Tatties and neaps (potatoes and turnips) accent the dish.

My bartender appeared with my haggis surprisingly soon, certainly not long enough to stuff a sheep's stomach. I later saw generic canned haggis in a Scottish grocery store and suspected the cook in the pub's kitchen had a shelf of haggis cans on hand whenever a naïve tourist ordered it. No bagpipes wheezed when my haggis arrived. Their sound was replaced by laughter from my new acquaintances. I ate it.

"Good for you, Yank. Have another wee one."

Despite the fact that Robert Burns took pen to paper more than 200 years ago, with a little effort, the drift of most of his poems can usually be understood. That is not the case with Hugh MacDiarmid, Scotland's most respected modern poet. No serious discussion of twentieth-century Scottish literature can ignore MacDiarmid's lengthy "A Drunk Man Looks at a Thistle," published in 1926. That's high praise for a poem that all literary critics readily admit is extremely difficult to understand. That's because MacDiarmid used a wide range of words and dialects from a variety of geographic locations across Scotland. Take a crack at the opening stanza of "A Drunk Man," and you'll get the idea.

"I amma fou muckle as tired deid dune
It's gey and hard wark coupin gless for gless
Wi Cruvie and Gilsanquar and the like
And I'm no just as bauld as aince lives."

Those that have successfully interpreted the lengthy work tell us that despite some comic moments, "A Drunk Man" is a serious poem on Scotland and the Scottish condition with complex references to Isadora Duncan, Dostoevsky, and Nietzsche. One critic compared MacDiarmid's style to James Joyce. I planned on dropping MacDiarmid's name at the first opportunity during my trek to demonstrate to any Scot who'll listen that I'm no American philistine but never got up the courage.

Rowardennan is a popular location with all types of hikers from walkers to ramblers and climbers to scramblers. Scotland is jammed with a variety of hiking and climbing organizations including the Ramblers' Association and the Scottish Mountaineering Association. There are even numerous walking festivals. The intensity of ascending Scotland's highest elevations got a huge jolt in 1891 when Sir Hugh Munro published a list of some 500 peaks over 3,000 feet. The Reverend A.E. Robertson announced in 1901 that he had climbed every mountain save one on Munro's list, thus kicking off a Munro-bagging frenzy, which has hardly dissipated. Sir Hugh died, never quite completed his list, with two Munro's to go.

The Scottish Mountaineering Club has since revised the official list of Munro's to 284. There's even a Web site that keeps track of all those who have completed the list. If that's not enough to keep you busy, there's the list of hills between 2,500 and 3,000 feet called Corbetts and the Grahams between 2,000 and 2,500. As you might expect, there are all kinds of unique records including Charlie Campbell who in 2000 conquered of all the Munro's in just over forty-eight days in one continuous frenzy of cycling, running, and swimming. (He swam over to the Isles of Skye and Mull.) Charlie might enjoy meeting Mark Obmascik. In 2006 Obmascik decided he wanted to climb all fifty-four of Colorado's 14,000-foot mountains known as the Fourteeners. No easy feat considering that more climbers have been killed attempting the Fourteeners than Mount Everest. Obmascik wrote about his midlife adventure in *Halfway to Heaven*.

The hike up Scotland's southern most Munro, 3,192-foot Ben Lomond, began just beyond Rowardennan. It was a seven-mile walk to the top and back. I was tempted but the West Highland Way beckoned, and it was a long way to Inverarman and Drovers Inn, my anticipated lodging that night. Drovers Inn first came to my attention via an article in National Geographic's *Adventure* magazine on the West Highland Way. The author's high praise for the place convinced me that it had to be my lodging for one night. *Lonely Planet* warned that the place shouldn't be missed. But first I had to get there.

The trail undulated through oaks, alder, and prickled yellow gorse and gained altitude where bluffs touched the Loch. There seemed to be some sort of highway to my right, but I never actually saw it, and the minimal traffic noise was a non-issue. The vista across the Loch and up the valley was impressive. The single thing that grabbed me most about Highlands was the scope of the mountains, the ruggedness of the topography. Northwest Scotland is not simply a land of rolling hills but of genuine mountains. True, the highest of them all, Ben Nevis, has an altitude of just 4,406 feet, but factor in its abrupt rise from near sea level, and you've got a real mountain.

Four hours beyond Rowardennan, the walking became difficult, and light rain began to fall. The Loch narrowed, and a crude sign painted on a rock said succinctly **CAVE**. This crevice in the rocks was billed as one of the hideouts of the legendary Rob Roy. There wasn't much to see, but it is apparently a significant tourist site for those who are curious about the life of the Scottish folk hero.

Rob Roy was a member of Clan MacGregor and spent much of his early life stealing, raiding, rustling, sword fighting, being incarcerated, and escaping. All this hard work and determination paid off, and he became head of the clan. He had a falling out with the evil Duke of Montrose, and his home was torched. Our hero fled to the mountains and lochs of the Highlands where he began a reprisal against the duke. The whole story of Rob Roy is more accurately laid out by Sir Walter Scott. The cave is so nondescript that I didn't waste a megapixel.

The light rain got heavier, and I dug into my pack for my rain pants. There was no alternative but to keep walking. I wondered what happened to my three Scottish hiking buddies. I began to get a bit anxious for human contact. Loch Lomond was behind me now. At the northern end of the Loch was a ferry dock for those wanting cross over to the Ardlui Hotel. There was no explanation as to how to summon the ferry. Besides, my destination was the Drovers Inn at Inverarman. The West Highland Way climbed up Cnap Mor, a minor hill, and descended through Ben Glas Burn.

There was a sign announcing Beinglas Farm with wigwams and camping. I glanced at the collection of rough wooden shacks and kept walking. They looked depressing. God help me if there was no room in the inn. Inverarman was really not much of a town. My guidebook said it had a post office and a grocery store, but they were well hidden. I was too tired, wet, and cold to look around. Fortunately Drovers Inn was easy to spot on the highway. It had been seven hours since I left Rowardennan, and I had walked fourteen miles.

The bar served as the reception desk at Drovers Inn, and there was one room remaining. It was not "en-suite." That meant that the room had no bathroom. The shared bathroom was down the hall and would probably be occupied in the morning when I needed it most. The use of the word "en-suite" in Great Britain struck me as odd. With all their much trumpeted language skills, you'd they'd come up with something better. William the Conqueror must have imposed the term on the Anglo-Saxons, and they just can't seem to shake it. Drovers Inn claimed to have provided food and rooms to weary travelers for three centuries, and from the look of it my room, it had been occupied every single night. I was too tired to care but motivated myself to head down to the bar. *Adventure* magazine's description of the place proved accurate. The pub was chock-full of enough old weapons, armor, stuffed animals, tartans, and nineteenth-century artwork to fill a small museum. It had character and characters.

"How did you find Drovers?" the heavyset, middle-aged, bearded man sitting next to me asked.

"My guidebook told me not to miss it."

"I'm Derrick Hamilton," he said extending his hand.

"Are you chasing your roots here in Scotland?"

"No, I'm Polish," I replied. "I always thought Hamilton was an English name until I started doing a little research for this trip and found out that the guy that stole the Stone of Scone was named Hamilton." He was impressed that I knew about the famous theft, which became a rallying point for Scottish nationalism.

"You're not related to that guy, are you?" I asked him.

"Maybe somehow," he said. "But I wish I could say that Ian Hamilton was my father."

Ian Hamilton was a member of the Scottish Nationalist Party and for many, a modern William Wallace. On Christmas Day 1950, Hamilton snuck into Westminster Abbey and, despite some significant miscalculations, managed to steal the massive rock that sat under the English throne, symbolizing the latter's domination over Scotland. Scottish kings had been traditionally crowned over the Stone of Scone, but English King Edward I seized the stone in 1206 and moved it to Westminster. The stone's absence from Scotland had been a major burr under Scotland's saddle ever since. Hamilton was charged with the theft but never prosecuted. He had made his point, much to the delight of those Scots who would like to see their independence restored. The whole story of Hamilton and the theft was portrayed in the 2008 film *Stone of Destiny.*

The British Parliament ultimately did bestow some level of quasi-independence on Scotland, and elections to a new Scottish parliament were held in 1999. Although the Scottish Parliament's authority was restricted primarily to domestic issues, that limited power may have been a bit too much for some to stomach. In 2009 the Scottish government's Justice Secretary Kenny MacAskill freed mass murderer, Abdelbaset Mohamed Ali Al-Megrahi, a Libyan. He had been convicted on 270 counts of murder for blowing up Pan Am Flight 103 over Lockerbie, Scotland, and given a life sentence. MacAskill's decision was rendered on grounds of compassion when doctors testified that the murderer was suffering from terminal prostate cancer. Two hundred forty-three passengers and sixteen crew members of the Boeing 747 were killed as a result of the explosion. Eleven residents of Lockerbie were killed when the wreckage from the plane fell on homes in the town. Al-Megrahi was the greatest mass murderer in the history of Great Britain. He was reported to be living in a villa in Libya following his release but was photographed on his deathbed in a near coma when Muammar al-Gaddafi was overthrown in the summer of 2011. Al-Megrahi died in 2012. (Scotland is scheduled to have a referendum on complete independence in 2014.)

"Who was Drover?" I asked Derrick.

"Drover's not a who," he told me. "Drovers were the fellows that moved the cattle from place to place. They drove them."

"In the States, we call them cowboys," I said.

From Drovers Inn at Inverarnan, the trail wound its way along the River Falloch toward Crianlarich and the West Highland Way's midpoint. That next day proved to be the most miserable day of my adventure. It began raining heavily early in the day and never quit. There was a youth hostel at Crianlarich, but the village was slightly off the track, so I foolishly decided to keep walking toward Tyndrum, despite the weather. At one point, the path took me through some private farmland. The rights of landowners versus walkers in modern Scotland is not without its conflicts and controversies, but the "Room to Roam" movement had a strong foothold in Scotland. Private landowners tolerated walkers' use of their land, without necessarily conceding that they actually had the right to trespass. In some locations, legal arrangements guaranteed access.

A dog barked as I walked through the farmyard, and I noticed that the owners had taken an entrepreneurial acceptance to The Way's route through their property by opening a tiny teahouse and pastry shop next to their home. I seized the opportunity to escape from the rain and took one of the four seats inside. The farm wife popped on over from her home a few yards away and soon I was enjoying hot tea and muffins. More important, I was out of the rain. Ultimately we ran out of small talk, and if I had ordered a third muffin, my hostess would have recognized that it was only to delay walking in the rain.

"Well, you'd better get going if you want to get to make it to Tyndrum by nightfall," she said politely. It was the only time in my life I had been thrown out of a tearoom.

I knocked at the first B&B I saw in Tyndrum. "I think we can fit you in," the owner told me. There were only two other people in the B&B that rainy night, and they were the owners. They had no problem fitting me in.

Serious mountain vistas highlighted the next day. A village with the intriguing name of the Bridge of Orchy was nothing more than a post office community with a church and railroad station. As I crossed the eighteenth-century bridge from which the town got its name, the western edge of Rannoch Moor appeared in the distance.

Guidebooks use a host of negative nouns and adjectives to describe Britain's largest swamp. "A wearier looking desert a man never saw," was Robert Louis Stevenson's description in *Kidnapped.* Others said it was a forbidding place of bog, lochs, and rock. From my vantage point along the West Highland Way, it had an Alaska-like appearance as distant mountains encompassed its vast emptiness. It seemed there just had to be some famous mention by Shakespeare to the swamp, but later when I Googled any reference by the bard to the famous moor, I came up empty. I did discover one literary reference to the big swamp. Wikipedia claimed that Rannoch Moor was the ancestral homeland of that penurious Scot Scrooge McDuck, thus proving that comic books can be great literature.

For those searching for a truly unique experience, there's a Scottish youth hostel located on Loch Ossian in the heart of Rannoch Moor. There's no road access and you have to walk from the Corrour train station. Wind and solar energy provide the electricity. Catch the train in Glasgow.

My plan was to do the nearly nineteen-mile walk from Tyndrum to the Kings House Hotel in a day, then leave the West Highland Way, and take the eleven-mile bus ride to Glencoe the next morning and look up Pete and Lynne in nearby Ballachulish. I used the phone at my B&B to make a reservation since I kept hearing that Kings House fills up early as it's the only place around. I've never walked that great a distance before but have learned that the challenge is not the muscle but the motivation. The Way gained altitude. The wind blew and a wonderful feeling of 'Where am I?' dominated my thoughts.

There were no other walkers in either direction for four hours. The track appeared to reach some sort of summit and from there was a view down into Glen Coe. My legs and feet began to experience genuine pain after seven or eight hours with three miles to go. Two Ibuprofen tablets brought some relief.

I was overtaken by a young couple. They were English. "We do this walk from Tyndrum to Kings House every year," the woman told me. "We were married in Tyndum seven years ago and walked to Kings House after the ceremony. It was our honeymoon. Now we do it every spring. This is our annual anniversary trek." You've got to love it.

We walked the rest of the way together. They were both physical therapists in Edinburgh, and I seized the opportunity to question them about the pain in my legs and feet.

"I think the body is simply not designed to walk more than seven or eight miles in a day," Gwen said.

Her partner, Martin, agreed. "It just doesn't matter what kind of shoes you're wearing or what kind of shape you're in. Even aboriginal bushman in the Kalahari get sore feet."

I figured some of the magic in their marriage was beginning to wear off when they insisted that I join them for dinner at the Kings House. She was a vegetarian, and the only thing on the menu that she'd consider ordering was pasta. "I've learned to accept it," Martin said. "But I don't get it. If God didn't want us to eat meat, he would have told Noah to load his ark with carrots, broccoli, and lettuce."

Glen Coe was one of the loveliest spots I saw in Scotland. The mountain scenery was breathtakingly beautiful, so it's a center for walkers, climbers, and those that just want to surround themselves with natural wildness. The youth hostel sat in the middle of it all, and it was just a short walk to the Clachaig Inn. The pub had an ice axe for a door handle and was a gathering place for all kinds of adventurers. I was the only person in my hostel's six-bunk dormitory. Life is good.

Glen Coe also is the site of one of the most tragic days in the history of Scotland—the Glen Coe Massacre. In January 1692 the English King William III ordered that the chiefs of all the Scottish clans sign an oath of allegiance to him. The chief of the MacDonalds, Maclain of the village of Glen Coe, rode to Fort William a few miles distant to sign the oath only to be told that he had to take the oath at Inveraray some sixty miles away. The mistake resulted in Maclain taking the oath past the deadline.

The king's secretary of state, John Dairymple, had a strong dislike for the MacDonalds of Glen Coe and viewed the failure of Maclain to sign the oath before the deadline as an opportunity to punish the clan. He ordered the MacDonalds to be slaughtered. "Cut off root and branch," he said and sent some 120 men, mostly Campbells, who had a long-standing feud with the MacDonalds, to do the job. The Campbells hung around Glen Coe almost two full weeks before they drew their swords against the MacDonalds. In fact the MacDonalds, honoring their code of hospitality, had allowed the Campbells to stay in their homes.

On the night of February 13, the Campbell men left their beds, announced their orders from Dairymple, and proceeded to shoot and stab their hosts. Maclain and thirty-seven other men, women, and children were executed. A few hundred fled to the snow-covered mountains where many more died from exposure. The soldiers opened sheep and cattle corrals, allowing the animals to escape, and burned the huts and homes of the MacDonalds.

Some of the MacDonalds had been alerted by the Campbells prior to the massacre and were saved, but even today the Campbell name is cursed throughout much of the Highlands. The MacDonalds that survived disappeared into cities or fishing villages. Some joined the army. Author William Faulkner wrote that some of the descendents of the Glen Coe MacDonalds turned up in America's deep South. A sign at the reception area of the Clachaig Inn kindles the animosity NO HAWKERS OR CAMPBELLS.

After two days in Glen Coe, I walked to Ballachulish. A fellow at the tourist information office knew Pete and Lynne Long and gave me a ride to their modest townhouse.

"They're gone for a few days," a neighbor told me.

I had not bothered to tell Pete and Lynne that I was coming. For some reason, I had decided that flying across the Atlantic and hiking from Glasgow to Ballachulish without warning them of my arrival would be fun. I left a note with the neighbor, saying that I was off to climb Ben Nevis near Fort William and would be staying at the Glen Nevis Youth Hostel.

It was a short bus ride to Fort William, the official end of the West Highland Trail, and I promised myself that after I'd conquered Ben Nevis, I'd finish The Way on foot. The Glen Nevis Hostel stood a few miles beyond Fort William at the foot of Britain's highest mountain—Ben Nevis (4,408 feet). Because of its preeminence, on most days there were usually plenty of hikers, ramblers, trekkers, climbers, and tourists struggling up the mountain.

On the morning of my attempt on Ben Nevis, the hostel's kitchen was full of early risers making their breakfast. I shared a stove with a tall, distinguished man. We had had a couple of beers together the night before and decided that misery loved company so we would do Ben Nevis together. His name was Frank Westcoat, and he told me he was employed at the London School of Economics. I was honored that an individual of his stature would want to share his day with me.

My Irish steel-cut oatmeal was simmering away, and Frank commented on my choice of breakfast.

"Ric, are you a porridge man?" he asked. His use of the word "porridge" struck me as something out of *David Copperfield*.

"What's so funny?" Frank asked.

"In all my life, it's just not a question I thought I would ever be asked," I responded. It reminded me that I was a long way from Wyoming.

Despite its relatively low altitude, Ben Nevis was a real mountain. The altitude of 4,408 feet is a bit misleading since the trail begins at an elevation of about 200 feet. Frank and I allowed a full day for our summit attempt. When the weather was good, there's a steady stream of hikers heading up the mountain. Frank and I saw all kinds that day. The prepared ones had trekking poles, gloves, rain pants, and climbing boots. The unprepared wore shorts and casual sneakers. The experienced erred on the side of caution. A few had ice axes and crampons since the top of Ben Nevis was only a couple of hundred feet below the permanent snow line. Rain, snow, and violent wind gusts were common. There are about five fatalities on the mountain annually. Although the trail was well marked, deaths occur when fog or a whiteout reduces visibility and a hiker walks off the edge. Exposure and hypothermia also took their share.

"Here we go," Frank announced as we began. "Up the highest mountain in Britain."

"The sad thing is that it's now the highest mountain in the British Empire," I teased.

"I never thought of that, but you're right. It all went downhill when we lost India, Pakistan, and the Himalayas."

"Say goodbye to, 'the sun never sets on the British Empire'," I said.

"Yeah, now it's more like the sun never sets on the British Commonwealth."

During the last hour of our climb, many descending hikers, who had passed us earlier, had turned around and were unsuccessful in summiting. Apparently they didn't want to face the wet and cold of the summit. Since it was April, we walked on snow for the final hour. It was windy, and there was a light rain as we neared the top. Visibility was very limited. There was a triangulation pillar near the summit. On clear days, using binoculars, you can see it for miles; it was useful for determining longitude and latitude. We congratulated ourselves by shaking hands. The climb up took us a little over four hours. I'd climbed higher peaks, but there was something about climbing the highest mountain in the British Empire that made it seem very special.

We headed for the Ben Nevis Pub after the three-hour descent. "You know, Frank, I never asked what you teach at the London School of Economics."

"Oh, I was a little misleading on that," he said. "I don't actually teach at the school. I'm in the maintenance department. But I like to use that line to impress women."

"Does it work?" I asked.

"It does when I tell them I'm a plumber."

"Wow! You're right. Anyone can teach economics, but plumbing's a real skill," I said.

There was a note for me at the hostel's reception desk. It was from Pete and Lynne, telling me they'd pick me up in the morning, and "We'll head up a few hills." I was pleased that they took the time to come find me and we'd spend some time together.

The next day proved to be the highlight of my trip to Scotland. We spent the day walking on high narrow ridges falling into deep green valleys connecting peaks with incomprehensible names like Sgorr Chalum, Mullach nan Coirean, Squrr a Mhaim, and Stob Ban.

"I can't pronounce them," Pete said. "Hardly anybody can."

The weather was perfect, and we had great looks at Ben Nevis and its rugged surroundings. I saw that the mountain had significant vertical relief with plenty of sheer faces to challenge the best rock climbers. At one point, Pete stopped suddenly and pointed to a distant mountainside. There, standing alone across the valley was a large red deer stag, a monarch of the Glen. We could see The West Highland Way winding its way through a valley to the south. Near the end of day, we talked about Munros, Corbetts, and Grahams. Lynne made me happy by telling me that we had climbed two Munro's today. Counting yesterday's Ben Nevis ascent, I'd bagged three Munro's. Only 281 to go!

I'd actually had enough hiking, but guilt forced me to bus back to the Kings House Hotel and complete the West Highland Way. It was just a two-day walk, twenty-three miles, to Fort William with an overnight in Kinlochleven. A couple of hours beyond Kings House, The Way passed Buachaille Etive Mor, which offered views of Glen Coe's mountains, and then it ascended the aptly named Devils Staircase. There was a rocky cairn at the top, marking The West Highland Way's highest point at almost 2,000 feet above the sea.

It was nearly all downhill to Kinlochleven and the Blackwater Hostel. My final day was highlighted with views of Ben Nevis and the ridges that I had walked with Pete and Lynne only two days before. The last few miles into Fort William was somewhat anticlimactic, compared to the excitement of ascending Ben Nevis and knocking of a couple of Munro's a few days earlier. Fort William itself was touristy and a bit of a downer but had an easy rail connection to the fishing town of Mallaig and the ferry to the Inner Hebrides' Isle of Skye.

Much of the romance of Skye's isolation was lost in 1995 with the opening of the controversial Skye Bridge connecting Kyle of Lochalsh on the mainland with Kyleakin on the island. Taking the ferry from Mallaig would restore some of that mystique, but a heavy sea had temporarily closed the ferry so I spent the night. Mallaig grabbed me. It was small, touristy, shabby, and busy; all in all, a genuine fishing port. There were lots of hefty fishing boats tied up along the waterfront. They were colorful but nonetheless serious working trawlers.

There was a rough-looking clapboard building at the end of the dock. It was operated by the local Mallaig fishing association and served as a gathering point for those that go down to the sea in ships. Its interior was plain and practical. There was a small kitchen with a basic menu of soups, stews, and teas. Plaques hanging on the wall memorialized local fishermen lost at sea. One commemorated a father and son whose trawler had disappeared a few years earlier. The fishing industry is universally recognized as the most dangerous of livelihoods. The plaques brought that fact home to me.

On another wall, a chalkboard had the day's weather report. A couple of its headings listed the distant waters where Mallaig's trawlers worked. There was a report for the "Outer Hebrides" and another for "Icelandic Waters." I ordered a mug of tea and watched out the window as fishing boats chugged across the harbor and loaded fresh ice. It baffled me that these trawlers still used ice to keep their catch cold rather than refrigeration powered by their diesel engines. I lacked the courage, however, to ask any of the fishermen around me about it.

As I wandered the waterfront, a woman in big rubber boots and a rubber apron was selling fresh fish. A sign proclaimed her occupation: FISHMONGER. The whole scene was charming but a bit medieval. I was not sure what the policy of Sheena's Backpacker's Lodge was when it came to frying fresh fish in the kitchen, but I couldn't resist. I made a deal with the fishmonger and headed back to Sheena's. My cod was too big for one, so I invited a couple of my bunkmates to get involved. Somebody had butter, another lemon. A bit of fresh parsley appeared.

"You just couldn't do this in the States," I explained. "You can't buy a fresh fish off the boat and cook it up in your hotel's kitchen." Three of us downed the fish with bottles of Hebridean Gold from the Isle of Skye Brewery.

> "Oats – A grain which in England is generally given
> to horses, but in Scotland supports the people."
>
> *Samuel Johnson*
> *1709-1784*

Skye has long been a tourist destination for the adventurous. Samuel Johnson, the compiler of the English language's first dictionary, visited the island with his biographer, James Boswell, in the summer of 1773 during the duo's three-month tour of Scotland. They spent almost half of the trip on the island. Each wrote a book detailing their experiences. Johnson's *Journey to the Western Isles of Scotland*, published in 1775, was a professorial description of what he saw and experienced. Boswell's *Journal of a Tour to the Hebrides*, published in 1785, was lighthearted and focused more on Johnson rather than Scotland itself.

Skye's topography is legendary, an island of rock and mountains with few trees surrounded by the Sea of the Hebrides and a body of water known simply as The Minch that separates the outer Hebrides from mainland Scotland. The weather can be notoriously wet and windy. Its most famous mountains are the Red and Black Cuillin. The mountains are never referred to in the plural.

"The Black Cuillin is visually the most impressive mountain range in the British Isles," my guidebook said without reservation. The traverse of the knife-edged, seven-mile main ridge of the Black Cuillin is a life goal for serious scramblers and climbers from all over Britain. The ridge is home to twelve of Scotland's 284 Munro's, including the Inaccessible Pinnacle. At 3,234 feet, it's the only Munro not climbed by the original Munro bagger, Reverend Robertson. Somewhere I recalled hearing that Edmund Hillary honed his climbing skills in the Cuillin. (Or was it George "Because it's there" Mallory?)

The tiny town of Sligachan was the jumping off spot for hikers heading into the Cuillin, and the manager of the hostel at Broadmoor told me that there's a bus to Sligachan every morning. The bus was not what I expected. It was a school bus filled with middle school kids.

"Is this the bus to Sligachan?" I asked the driver.

"Aye, it is," he said. He was the only adult besides me on the bus.

I was soon peppered with questions from the kids. "Where are you from?" and "Where are you going? were expected. But, "Is it true that lots of Americans carry guns so they don't get shot?" was a surprise.

It just made sense, of course, to allow the general public to use school buses to get around in rural areas. We would never be so creative in the States. I later learned that Scottish postal trucks serving isolated communities also accepted passengers for a small fee. Over the years, I've noticed half-empty school buses and post office trucks driving all across rural Wyoming, but accepting a passenger is unknown. It would be too rational.

I decided to tackle a mountain with the unpronounceable name of Bruach na Frithe. The trail to the top of the 3,142-foot Black Cuillin began just down the road from my bunkhouse at Sligachan. It was an ascent of some 2,900 feet and took me most of the day. There were low clouds hanging over the Isle of Skye at the summit, but the views of the ragged Black Cuillin and the softer Red Cuillin were expansive. Was this my third or fourth Munro? It might be easier if I could have remembered the names, but it was impossible to recall the name of some mountain that you are unable to pronounce.

I took the train from Mallaig to Fort William, then on to Glasgow. An American tourist was sitting across the aisle as we passed through Rannoch Moor. He was reading a book and never looked up. Not once. He just didn't seem to have any appreciation for the vista. His behavior upset me. I wondered what else he missed.

4

Camino de Santiago

Walking my way out of purgatory

Spain
485 miles

The way the medieval Roman Catholic Church saw it, a human soul had four very specific destinations once the spirit left the body of the deceased. A person who left this world with an unforgiven mortal sin on their soul was destined to burn in hell forever. Those whose souls were not stained by an unforgiven serious mortal sin or a less serious venial sin were immediately propelled to heaven. Good Catholics tried to fall into the latter category but few succeeded. One had to follow the prescripts of the church religiously and practice the seven sacraments. The sacrament of confession was the key to heaven because even if you transgressed, a good confession followed by genuine contrition could wipe your soul quasi-clean, although you might have to spend some time in purgatory.

Individuals who never had a chance to adopt Catholicism were placed in a separate category. They technically had done nothing wrong or right since they were not members of the church. Infants who had not yet been baptized, pagans, and heathens on distant lands like Pago Pago fell into this category. So did billions of Buddhists, Hindus, and Moslems. After all, it's not their fault that missionaries had not shown up and told them the joys of Christianity. All of these poor souls were sent to a nebulous place called limbo. Limbo was kind of a neutral hereafter, like a kid in a candy store whose mother refuses to buy her child a piece of chocolate.

Purgatory was as hot as hell, but not as bad as it sounds since there was a light at the end of the tunnel. One's time in purgatory was finite. You would get out eventually. Just how much time any given soul would spend in purgatory was dependent on how many venial and mortal sins you had accumulated. (They didn't dare even hope for a shot at purgatory if they had a mortal sin on their soul, which had not been absolved through confession.) According to the church, one could cut their time in purgatory by gaining indulgences for confessed sins by performing certain good works, like tending to the sick, sweeping the cathedral, making donations to the church or taking long walks to very holy places. These walks were called pilgrimages. The *Camino de Santiago*, The Way of St. James, was considered so important by the church that making the walk of hundreds of miles across northern Spain to the city of Santiago de Compostela would guarantee that your time in purgatory would be reduced significantly (assuming you qualified for purgatory only). What a deal! Catholicism is not unique in encouraging pilgrimages. Good Moslems are encouraged to make it to Mecca once before they die; Mormons are encouraged to visit Salt Lake City; and American college kids head to Panama City, Florida.

Modern Catholic trekkers don't even have to walk the entire way to get the "Get out of Purgatory" pass. The church has lowered the bar. Prove that you have walked at least a hundred kilometers along the Camino, and you can get the purgatory pass. Although there are numerous variations, including some that begin in northern Europe, a modern *peregrino* (pilgrim) usually begins at St. Jean Pied de Port in France or just a few k's away in Roncevalles, Spain, in the southwestern Pyrenees.

I started in Roncevalles. My plan was to walk the Camino along the southern slope of the Pyrenees through Pamplona and on to Logrono, a distance of just over ninety miles. From Logrono, I'd take the train across the flat *maseta* to Ponferrada and then walk the final 142 miles to Santiago de Compostela in the province of Galecia, Spain's rainy northwest corner. In order to be awarded the coveted purgatory pass known as the *Compostela,* the church requires a peregrino to complete the final hundred k's of the Camino (200 k's if you are bicycling). A piecemeal collection of starts and stops won't do.

I got my official credential *(credencial)* on-line through an organization known as the American Pilgrims on the Camino. It was a gray, six-inch by twenty-two-inch piece of cardboard folded accordion style with lots of blank space. As they walk the Camino, pilgrims ask to have their credentials stamped at the *albergue* or *refugio* where they are staying. If they get enough stamps (*sellos*) to prove they've walked the required k's, they can get their compostela, the official document issued by church functionaries that keeps them out of purgatory.

A word of warning: Don't let all this rigmarole and religion get in the way of why you are walking the Camino. It's damn fun! There are devout Catholics walking the Camino for religious reasons, but I didn't run across many. For Spaniards, it's kind of their Appalachian Trail. But trekkers come from all over the world to do the Camino. Everybody's there to soak up the sun, the red wine, the olives, the scenery, and the companionship. Don't let religion keep you from having the time of your life. It didn't stop this born-again pagan.

Technically the Camino is not a traditional backpack. You might carry a backpack filled with a lightweight sleeping bag, some cooking utensils, and a change of clothes. But leave your tent at home. There are lots of choices when it comes to sleeping accommodations. Most pilgrims stay in refugios or albergues along the Camino. These dormitory-style hostels are usually run by the local church or Camino organizations. Others are privately owned capitalistic enterprises. Of course there's nothing stopping you from staying in a hotel or even plush, government-sponsored, historic, upscale *paradores.* Camino purists usually choose the refugios where a bed can be had for as little as three euros or even a smaller donation. Most have common kitchens where you can prepare your own meal. All have hot showers, although cleanliness and privacy can be a variable.

In his *Iberia,* James Michener called the Camino, "The finest journey in Spain and one of the two or three best in the world." That's high praise but all things considered, Michener's critique is valid. There's just something special about walking in the Spanish countryside, passing through historic towns filled with medieval architecture, and gathering every evening at a table with new acquaintances from around the world, eating Spanish *aceitunas, queso, jamon, bacalao,* and *paella.* Two or three times during my trek, a jug of local red wine was placed on the table and refilled repeatedly. The refills never appeared on the bill. You didn't see that happen in *Sideways.*

Roncevalles is a full day's bus ride from Madrid, with a transfer in Pamploma. But don't rush to the bus without taking a couple days to savor Spain's capital city. (You might win a bar bet knowing that Madrid's altitude of some 2,000 feet makes it the highest capital city in Europe. You will definitely win a bar bet if you know that the highest point in Spain is not somewhere in the Pyrenees but on the Canary Islands.) Barcelona gets all the attention in the travel magazines, but Madrid has a special combination of sophistication and exuberance that's tough to top. I'm writing about the Camino de Santiago, but here's a list of places and experiences not to be missed:

(1) Plaza Mayor: Michener said Salamanca's Plaza Mayor is the finest plaza in Spain and one of the four best in the world. (His other three are Venice's St. Mark's, Mexico City's Zocalo, and the Registan in Uzbekistan.) Ignore Michener for a few minutes and take in the scene. It's touristy, yes, but the seventeenth-century cobble-stoned square encased by burgundy and sepia architecture is filled with ambiance and life. Take a seat at one of the outdoor cafés, order an over-priced glass of wine, and take it all in. You're in Spain!

(2) The Prado Museum: If you're going to visit only one art museum in your life, this is the one. You'll see more recognizable paintings here than anywhere else. Included are Goya's *Nude Maja,* and the *Third of May, 1808,* as well as El Greco's *Christ Carrying the Cross* and Velázquez's *Maids of Honor.*

(3) *Guernica:* This Picasso hanging in the museum Reina Sofia is the single most important piece of art in Spain. The masterpiece depicts the horrors of war as Nazi bombers, supporting Francisco Franco during the Spanish Civil War, obliterated the Basque town of Guernica, which was the first European city to be bombed from the air. Picasso refused to have the piece displayed in Spain until after Franco's death. The graphic painting is in black and white, and the image will sear your brain.

(4) *Plaza de Toros*: Never mind PETA. Attend a bullfight somewhere in Spain. Madrid is a good place to do it. Unless they come up with some sort of "Catch and Release" approach to bullfighting, the spectacle may soon disappear. (What's next? Rodeos?) It's already been banned in the autonomous province of Catalonia (Barcelona). The outcome is predictable, and even the Spaniards don't consider it a sport. Madrid's newspaper covers bullfighting in its "Arts" section. To complete your bullfighting experience, visit the Torre del Oro Bar Andalu on the Plaza Mayor. This watering hole is a

spectacle of bullfighting photos and world famous celebrities like Francisco Franco and Robert Kennedy. Another bar, La Taurina Cerveceria, near Puerta del Sol, is filled with historic photos of Hemingway, Ernesto "Che" Guevara, Francisco Franco, Ava Gardner, Orson Wells, and Salvador Dali at a plaza de toros. Get creative and take a photo of a photo and hang Ava and Ernie watching a bullfight on your wall at home.

(5) *Real Madrid:* Madrid's soccer team is a traditional European power, and, if you can get a ticket, the experience can be uplifting. Sure the score will probably be 0-0 or 1-1 when regulation time runs out with the result being determined by penalty kicks. Someday they'll figure out that the game would be more conclusive if they used two balls simultaneously, but meanwhile 50,000 screaming Maderenos can't be wrong. Spain won the World Cup in 2010, and it marked the first time that waving the Spanish flag provoked feelings of national unity rather than an opportunity for Basques or Catalonians to demonstrate for their independence.

(6) *Puerta del Sol:* This is Madrid's Times Square. All distances from Madrid are measured from here. It's hard to miss even if you want to avoid the place since it seems like all streets and metro lines begin and end here. The plaza is also a great place to have your pocket picked or your purse stolen. These artful dodgers are well organized and after grabbing your card usually sell it quickly to a Fagin-like specialist who will then attempt to acquire funds using your card. Did you write your Visa card's emergency cancellation phone number down somewhere else? If you get lucky and actually miss the Puerta del Sol, you might be better off.

(7) *The Royal Palace Armory.* Admittedly this is a guy thing, but the enormous collection of perfectly preserved armor is simply mind-blowing. Armored knights on horseback, crossbows, lances, maces, and swords make this a must-see stop. Getting a fully armored knight atop his horse must have been a challenge, and if he were ever knocked off, he had to be pretty helpless lying on the ground. "Get the can opener, Sancho." There's even a dog in armor. Don't miss El Cid's sword used for Moor mashing. Unlike England's Robin Hood,

whose authenticity is difficult to prove, El Cid was a real eleventh-century knight who spent his days attempting to throw the Moslems out of Spain during the *Reconquista.*

(8) *The Tapa Tour*: For me and most others, this will be the highlight of any visit to Madrid. Start late (around eight) and end hours later. Simply wander the narrow streets between Puerta del Sol and Plaza Mayor, eating and drinking. Don't worry, you're not driving. The number and variety of tiny bars serving tempting tapas is endless. Order a *cana* (small beer) or a *vino tinto* (red house wine), and they'll throw in a tapa. Thin slices of jamon (ham), queso (cheese) or *aceitunas* (olives) are common, but sooner or later you'll be served more unusual fare like *pulpo* (octopus), *boquerones* (anchovies), *pimento* (peppers) or *champinones* (mushrooms). There's even *oreja* (sautéed pigs' ears). Quit squirming. Don't be so provincial. You're not in Des Moines.

Far and away the most popular tapa is the thinly sliced jamon. There are various types, but the best is derived from black-hoofed pigs raised on acorns in western Spain. TV foodie Anthony Bourdain is so high on Spain's ham that he referred to it as "the single greatest Spanish product." You'll have to decide yourself, but apparently he's never seen Penelope Cruz.

If you're lucky, you'll stumble on a place serving bite-sized, deep-fried *bacalao* (cod). Spain has a deep love affair with cod. The Basques of northern Spain were among the first to harvest the species off the coast of Newfoundland and Labrador. The fish are dried and brought home where they were immersed in water and brought almost back to life to be prepared in a variety of ways. Bourdain be damned, the deep-fried bacalao croquettes are at the top of the tapa chain. Can't get enough of 'em? Head for Casa Labra Taberna. This restaurant just east of Puerta del Sol has been in the deep-fried cod business for generations. It's funky, crowded, and fun.

After a long, bus ride from Madrid, I transferred buses in Pamplona and caught the next one to Roncesvalles in the Pyrenees. A non-English-speaking Spaniard in the bus station helped me find the correct ticket agent.

"Peregrino?" he asked me.

"Si," I responded with a sense of pride that I was at last entering the realm of the Camino de Santiago.

Roncevalles was a small village at the base of the pass connecting it to the French village of St.-Jean-Pied-de-Port on the other side of the Pyrenees. The town is historically linked to the legendary French medieval epic, the *Song of Roland.* Roland was Charlemagne's nephew, and his exploits fighting the Moors in the eighth century in this part of Spain are extolled in the poem. He was killed near Roncevalles.

The town was dominated by the Colegiata de Roncevalles, a Gothic monastery with massive walls that served as the head office for those, like me, who are beginning their trek of the Camino here. It's even got an office with a sign, *OFICINA DEL PEREGRINO.* I got my first sello on my credencial in this office. I was officially off and walking. The church also housed the remains of someone the guidebook called Sancho the Strong. Sounds like you were more likely to have heard of him if you are one of his contemporaries.

The monastery also served as an official albergue, which consisted of a forty-bed dormitory and a dining hall. It was the only albergue that I ran into on the Camino that also had a cafeteria. There was some sort of stew and lots of bread. That evening, I attended an official church service for some thirty peregrinos that were beginning the Camino the next morning. I don't know if the service was in Latin or Spanish. I understood not a word of it but was taken aback when the priest began reading out our names and our country of origin. One at a time, each of the pilgrims walked to the front of the church and stood before the priest when their name was called. Nobody else stepped forward when he mumbled, "Peregrino Soomoolski, Estados Unidos," so I figured he meant me. He then gave his official blessing to our journey. Thus blessed, about twenty of my fellow pilgrims and I immediately headed down the street from the monastery to a bar where we got to know one another over beer and olives.

Walking along the Camino through the foothills of the Pyrenees that very first day had to be one of my most memorable trekking moments. The morning sun was caressing the meadows, and I saw patches of snow topping the surrounding peaks. The springtime melodies of nesting birds were interrupted by the soft sound of cowbells. Farther in the distance, I heard the monastery's church bell summon the faithful and probably a few that had been unfaithful. It all sounds a bit soapy, but gosh it was nice.

There were a couple dozen pilgrims who ate breakfast together and left the monastery that morning to begin their walk toward Galicia and the city of Santiago de Compostela. Their varied paces quickly caused them to scatter along the Camino in a loose line. Although I did hear English being spoken by some of pilgrims the evening before and at breakfast, there appeared to be no Americans among them that morning. There were Germans, Brits, Aussies, French, Argentinians, Canadians, and lots of unidentifiables. I fell in with two unidentifiables early that first morning. The young man and woman seemed to be speaking Czech or Romanian or some other eastern European language.

"Good morning," I said bravely, not expecting a reply in English.

"Good morning," the woman said.

"I've been trying to figure out your language, but I can't," I told them. "Are you guys Czech?"

"Czech! Where'd you get that from?" the woman replied with a critical laughing tone to her voice. "We're Portuguese. What are you? American?"

No wonder she laughed. Only an American would think the sound of a Romance language was Slavic.

"I'm sorry," I said. "It's just that I think I have never heard Portuguese before. And your English is very good."

"My mother is an English teacher in Portugal. She teaches at a college in Lisbon and spoke English around the house when I was growing up. She thought it was important for me to be familiar with your language."

Her male companion remained quiet. I assumed his English language skills were at the same level as my Portuguese.

"Not only didn't I recognize your language, I'm afraid I know only a little about your country. For instance, I'm not sure if you have a monarchy or a president or what."

"We have a president just like you. But we would never elect a guy like George Bush." she said without hesitating.

Her comment did not surprise me. During his presidency and the years that followed, I found that throughout my travels, it was rare to find anyone who had anything good to say about George W. Bush. I was about to remind her that Europeans were quick to be critical of the aggressive policies of the United States but were sure thankful when we stood up to Hitler. Then I recalled reading that Portugal, like Spain, although officially neutral during WWII, was sometimes suspected of being a bit too sympathetic with the Nazi cause. Time to change the subject.

"Most American school kids do learn about Vasco de Gama and his voyage around Africa to India," I said. "And Magellan. Wasn't he Portuguese, although he sailed for Spain?

"Wow! You know that? I'm impressed," she said.

"We know some things about European history," I told her. "Most Americans know that Brazil used to be a Portuguese colony. Too bad you let that get away. It's one of the world's fastest-growing economies."

"Yes," she said. "Many Portuguese have moved to Brazil. There's more opportunity there. Even the royal family of Portugal figured it out. In the early nineteenth century, the king declared that Portugal and Brazil were united under one ruler. The whole royal court moved over to Brazil when Napoleon invaded Portugal but stayed way long after Napoleon was thrown out."

"I never knew that," I answered. "Maybe that's what England's King George should have done instead of fighting the American colonists. The English royal family could have moved to New Jersey. Thanks for telling me about that. How do you say 'thank you' in Portuguese?"

"*Obrigado.*"

"Obrigado," I repeated, sending the word deep into my dictionary of foreign expressions in the far recesses of my mind where it would be quickly forgotten.

I left Roncesvalles on the horizon, and the Camino passed through the village of Burguete with its white farmhouses accented with red shutters. Some of the homes were decorated with scallop shells, the symbol of the Camino. Burguete's most famous resident was Ernest Hemingway who immortalized the town in *The Sun Also Rises.* It was here that the author caught trout in the small stream, the Rio Urrobi, running through town. He obviously liked the place. My *Walking the Camino de Santiago* informed me he wrote F. Scott Fitzgerald that "heaven would be a big bull ring with me holding two *barrera* seats and a trout stream outside that no one else was allowed to fish in." If the size of the stream was any indication,

Hemingway's Spanish trout couldn't have been very big. Perhaps, that's why he committed suicide in Idaho and is buried in that trout happy state.

The first reminder that I was now in the land of the Basques happened when I walked through the village of Lintzoain and noticed a *fronton,* the concrete, walled structure where the locals play the iconic Basque game of *pelota or jai-alai.* Mark Kurlansky, in his delightful *The Basque History of the World*, explained that *peolte* was a French word referring to the winding of string. Kurlansky pointed out that with the discovery of America, the Basques became the first people in Europe to use an actual ball made of rubber when the rubber plant was found in South America. The original game had numerous variations akin to handball but took a huge technological leap forward when a young farm worker with the memorable name of Gantxiki Harotcha decided to strap a long, scoop-shaped basket to one hand in order to propel the ball at faster speeds. According to Kurlansky, Gantxiki got the idea while scooping up potatoes in a basket. The game really took off when fans began placing wagers on the teams, especially in Miami and Las Vegas.

Kurlansky also credited the Basques with popularizing the ubiquitous beret. The hat is especially popular in Mediterranean countries, and you'd be hard pressed to find an old man in rural Portugal or Spain not wearing one. The French often refer to the hat as "*le beret Basque.*" According to Kurlansky, the beret is usually associated with the political left, a fact accentuated by Argentinean revolutionary, Che Guevara, who saw the headpiece as a symbol of the underdog fighting the establishment.

The Basques are credited with bringing a staple of the Spanish diet to the Iberian Peninsula. They sailed to the Grand Banks off Newfoundland in the fifteenth century to catch Atlantic cod. Their genius, according to Simon Winchester in his *Atlantic,* lay not only in the fact that they could make this long journey and return to the coast of Galicia, but they knew how to preserve the fish. Winchester explained:

> "They split open the fish, salted it liberally, and only then hung it out to dry: the resulting salt-fish survived for much longer than previously known by those salt-starved others (like the French) who knew only how to "wet-cure" their fish and then watched helplessly as it eventually turned green with age. The new technique allowed the Basques uniquely to make ever-longer sea journeys, even for many months, since they knew they always had supplies."

And only then comes the bacalao.

The Basques, according to one axiom, are like beautiful women. They have no history. More than any other characteristic, their language, *Euskara*, defines their culture. Linguists tell us that Euskara is the oldest-living European language, and its origins are unknown. Many Basques have long pushed to create some sort of quasi-independent state encompassing Basque lands on both sides of the Pyrenees. In fact, according to my *Walking the Camino de Santiago*, there are more Euskara speakers in France than in Spain due to Francisco Franco's incessant persecution of the Basques. Franco outlawed Euskara, and many of their cultural activities and publications were driven underground. The ETA, an organization seeking Basque independence, began resorting to violence and, like Ireland's IRA, gathered support but also repudiation from the very people whose cause it was championing. Today the Basque provinces have more independence than any other region in Spain.

The most famous Basque? Three can be nominated.

Michener would certainly include Ignatius Loyola. "He is my favorite Spanish saint," he said unequivocally. In the sixteenth century, Loyola founded the Society of Jesus or Jesuits who became the Pope's stalwart defenders of the Catholic faith against the Protestant Reformation. They became the first worldwide order of Catholic priests.

"If Martin Luther was the scourge of the Catholic Church, then St. Ignatius was the scourge of the Lutherans, and it was his movement in defense of Catholicism that helped to establish a balance in Europe," Michener wrote.

There are, of course, other Spanish saints like Dominic, "too bloodthirsty for my liking," wrote Michener, and Saint Teresa "too nebulous." The Jesuits became too secular and powerful and were thrown out of Spain and Europe's other Mediterranean Catholic countries by the pope in the mid-seventeenth century. They fled to Poland, Prussia, and Russia. In the early eighteenth, they were allowed to return to their old stomping grounds and, having learned their lesson, avoided temporal issues and focused on religion.

St. Ignatius Loyola's name is attached to four universities in the United States, including Loyola University of Chicago, which won the NCAA national men's basketball championship in 1963. Take that, Saint Teresa.

The most famous Basque you probably never heard of? It's got to be Juan Sebastian de Elcano. Your junior high social studies teacher told you that Ferdinand Magellan was the first to circumnavigate the globe. What he or she may or may not have mentioned was that Magellan was killed by natives in the Philippines and never made it back to Spain. Elcano, who ironically had been involved in a mutiny off the coast of South America against Magellan, became the commander of the expedition and successfully sailed the *Victoria* back to Spain, entering Seville's harbor on September 8, 1522. He had been at sea for more than three years. Four other Basques were among the surviving crew of eighteen. Laurence Bergreen's *Over the Edge of the World* detailed Elcano's reward. "Elcano's bonus included an annual pension of 500 ducats, a knighthood, and a coat of arms befitting the mariner who had sailed around the world. It depicted a castle, spices, two Malay kings, and a globe with the legend: *"Primus circumdedesti me"* (Thou who first circumnavigated me.)" Elcano also got a royal pardon for his role in the unsuccessful mutiny against Magellan. You can look it up.

Just before the Camino reached Pamplona, it passed through the suburb of Villava, home to Spain's cycling hero Miguel Indurain. This Basque won the Tour de France five consecutive years (1991–1995). And he did it drug free. Among Basques, his exploits are more celebrated than Elcano's. No list of famous Basques would be complete without Indurain.

The Camino entered Pamplona, passing through its medieval walls. The Roman emperor founded the old city, and its main cathedral was supposedly built on the site of the Roman capital. Cobbled, twisting streets quickly confused me, and I gave up attempting to follow the actual Camino and instead opted to walk through the city in a southwest direction and hope for the best. It was one of the few times that the Camino was not clearly marked with arrows or scallop shells. Most Americans associate the city with its famous "Running of the Bulls" held in conjunction with the annual San Fermín festival the first week in July, and I decided to find out where exactly the bulls ran.

"Fiesta San Fermín Toros aqui?" I asked a young man.

"Si," he responded.

That was good enough for me. I purchased a red handkerchief from one of the many souvenir shops lining the street and tied it around my neck like the young men who run with the bulls. I bought a local newspaper with the word PAMPLONA clearly printed at the top of the front page, and I was ready. I trusted my camera to a puzzled local teenage boy and hoped he wouldn't simply run off with it. He took my photo as I jogged down the street, looking fearfully over my shoulder and holding the newspaper in front of me, my finger pointing to the word PAMPLONA. The kid got it and laughed. I had run with the bulls in Pamplona. The fact that it was April and the bulls didn't show up wasn't my fault. It seemed funny at the time, and the photo wasn't too bad.

Spain has another famous festival that's not quite as well known as the Pamplona's bull running. It's the *La Tomatina Burñol.* Every summer in the small town of Burñol near Valencia, Spaniards pelt one another with surplus ripe tomatoes until their bodies and clothes run red. The festival participants also compete climbing a greased pole with a ham on top. It may not be as dangerous as bull running, but it's the perfect way to put purpose in one's empty life.

Still struggling to find my way out of Pamplona, I stumbled on to the grounds of a big university with serious buildings and extensive mowed lawns. Students were carrying books and laptops. It could have been any college in California. My guidebook said I could get another sello on my credencial here, but I was dubious that I'd actually find the correct place. Not to worry. The secretary in the first office I walked into took one look at my backpack and overall rustic appearance. "Peregrino?" she asked while simultaneously reaching into the top drawer of her desk for her Camino stamp without waiting for my reply. She also pointed me in the right direction to get me back on the Camino. There's a certain amount of satisfaction when things actually work out according to the guidebook.

A few days later, I had a brief conversation with a Canadian pilgrim and told him that the Camino got a little confusing as it passed through Pamplona.

"Yeah, I know what you mean. I took at cab," he explained.

"Isn't that cheating?" I said.

"It maybe cheating, but it's a lot less hassle. I just got a cab on one side of town and told the cabbie to take me to the Camino on the other side. It worked out fine. I'm going to do the same thing when I have to get through Burgos and Leon."

It was only few k's to the village of Cizur Menor just beyond Pamplona. The town was home to one of the more publicized albergues on the Camino. The place had a dormitory with thirty-five bunk beds and was on the grounds of the home of the "grande dame of village," according to the guidebook. The home had extensive gardens surrounding it and the dorm. The "grande dame" wasn't around, but an elderly man behind a desk at the door collected the five euro fee.

That evening, one of the pilgrims commented that Gwyneth Paltrow had stayed at this albergue when she did the Camino the previous summer. I was tempted to ask the old man at the door if it was true and if I could have her bunk, but discretion got the better of me for a change. Gwyneth's name did not appear in a search of the guestbook. I didn't sign it either and thus we bonded.

Actual fees for a bed at the albergues along the Camino ranged from a small donation to as much as ten euros. In Leon, a few days later, I walked up the top of the stairs to an albergue run by the local church. The door was guarded by a young nun (now that's an oxymoron). The stern-faced woman checked my credencial and pushed a cigar box toward me, containing a few coins. I dropped a five euro note into it as a wide smile crossed her face.

"You paid way too much," a scruffy British Camino walker chastised me later that evening. "They just expect a small donation. I paid one euro. You're going to spoil 'em."

So much for charity. He kind of put a damper on the concept of good Christians walking the Camino for spiritual reasons. Later that evening as a bunch of us sat around the albergue's kitchen table sipping local red wine from bottles without labels, the young nun appeared again and walked around the dorm, ringing a bell announcing that evening mass was about to be celebrated in the church. Only one pilgrim left the table to attend. It was the Brit. Go figure.

Historians differ on the precise details tracing the origin of the Camino de Santiago. All seem to agree that the story is a mixture of fable, faith, fact, and fabrication. It centers on the belief that the body of the Apostle St. James lays in the church in Santiago de Compostela. There are variations on exactly how it got there, however. According to Michener, it began with the beheading of St. James in 44 B.C. by order of King Herod in the Holy Land. He was the first of Jesus's followers to be martyred. Tradition says that prior to his death, but after Jesus's crucifixion, James went to Spain to spread the faith. There is not a grain of historical record, however, that he ever set a sandal in Iberia.

Regardless of the facts, a legend began to circulate in Europe that after his decapitation, his remains were disinterred and his head was intact and where it ought to be, despite his decapitation. James's body was taken onto a ship made of stone, manned by knights, and taken to Galicia. His body was buried in a Roman burial ground where it lay undiscovered for some eight hundred years. In about A.D. 812, a hermit, Pelayo, saw a bright star shining above a field. The bishop ordered the field excavated, and the body of St. James was found uncorrupted, despite the passage of eight centuries. The site of his burial became the most sacred spot in Spain, and St. James became a rallying symbol in Spain's attempt to rid the Iberian peninsula of the Moors.

Christian solders at the Battle of Clavijo in A.D. 844 reported that he led them into the fight while riding a white horse and yielding an enormous sword, killing thousands of Moors. James earned the title *Santiago Matamoros*, St. James the Moorslayer. It was under his banner that Christianity was victorious over the Moors and Spain was liberated. He became the patron saint of Spain.

Not many years ago, his likeness was sewn on the uniforms of Spanish soldiers when they helped liberate Iraq from Saddam Hussein under the banner of that other Moorslayer, George W. Bush. Recognizing that some Iraqis might be offended at the depiction of St. James the Moorslayer, an emblem of the Spanish uniforms was removed so that the soldiers would not appear to be prejudiced as they went about the business of killing those Moors who supported Saddam.

The exact meaning of the word *compostela* is open to serious conjecture. Michener said that the word "could have been derived from either the Spanish *Campo de la estrella* (in Latin, *Campus Stellatin* meaning Countryside where the Star Shone) or the Latin *Compost Terra* (from *compostum*, burying ground)." A Canadian pilgrim had incorrectly informed me that compostela was Spanish for constellation, and since the words look similar and stars were involved in the discovery of James's body, it made perfect sense to me. (Proof that you can't always trust Canadians.)

Many medieval pilgrims hung scallop shells around their necks when walking the Camino, and the shell symbol is usually used to identify the Camino's direction along with an appropriate arrow or two. The scallop shell is often painted on buildings and is used on the official directional posts throughout the trek.

Just how the shell became a symbol of the Camino is based on yet another legend. One source explained that when the stone boat containing

James's body arrived offshore, a pagan bridegroom riding a horse and headed to his wedding was swept into the sea upon seeing the strange boat and nearly drowned. Fortunately St. James intervened and the groom rose from the sea, his clothes covered in scallop shells. (You'd think the church would make him the patron saint of lifeguards.)

Another less glamorous version of the shell's identification with the pilgrimage says that pilgrims simply used the shells as ladles to scoop up drinking water as they walked under the hot Spanish sun.

By the ninth century, local churchmen began encouraging visits to St. James's burial site. Pilgrims were encouraged to touch the relics of the saint. Such behavior could result in indulgences and forgiveness of sins. It helped too that the pilgrims dropped a few coins along the way, and donations to the church grew because of the pilgrims. Pope Alexander III announced that Santiago de Compostela was officially a Holy City in 1189. He said that pilgrims who journeyed to the city during Holy Years (when the feast of St. James, July 25, falls on a Sunday) will never have to spend a minute in dreaded purgatory. Non-Holy Year pilgrims will see their purgatory time reduced by a full 50 percent. Wal-Mart and other retailers have picked up on this by using a variation of Pope Alexander's promotion in their "Day after Thanksgiving" sales by offering huge discounts to those who make the pilgrimage to their stores.

Making the pilgrimage to Santiago was one of three destinations where a good Christian could achieve extraordinary blessings. The other two were Rome, the city where Peter had formalized and organized the Catholic Church, and Jerusalem, the site of Christ's crucifixion. A huge church was built on the site of St. James's burial place in the twelfth century, and remains of that church can still be seen today in the existing cathedral.

An enterprising monk, Aymeric Picaud, even wrote a guidebook to the Camino entitled *Codex Calixtinus* in the twelfth century. The fact that few people could actually read may have affected sales. Thus the race was on, and, according to my guidebook, which was published much later, some half million pilgrims made the trek to Santiago in the eleventh and twelfth century. The successful re-conquest of Spain and the departure of the Moors back to Africa resulted in a drop in pilgrims, even though another guidebook written by Domenico Laffi, an Italian pilgrim, appeared in the seventeenth century.

By the twentieth century, only a trickle followed the Camino de Santiago until Pope John Paul II paid a visit to Santiago de Compostela in 1982. (He unabashedly arrived by plane.) His visit and the designation of the Camino as a World Heritage Site by UNESCO in 1993 increased interest in the Camino and the number of trekkers. The Spanish government spent big bucks in promoting the Camino in conjunction with the 1993 Holy Year, and the trek was revitalized. Today most walk for non-religious reasons, and Rick Steves says that 100,000 make the journey to Santiago every year. Over the centuries, Camino peregrinos have included St. Francis of Assisi, Dutch artist Jan van Eyck, Shirley MacLaine, who wrote a book about her Camino experience, and presumably Gwyneth.

It was at the albergue in Cizur Menor where I fell in with a group of pilgrims that would be my companions for the next six days. They were eclectic, fun, and outgoing. The group included a young Filipino-American woman from Boston. I never did figure out if she was an American citizen, a green-card domestic or a student. It seemed rude to ask. Most important, Telo spoke perfect Spanish. Life can be a lot easier when you have a traveling companion who speaks the local language. The problem was that

Telo was quite shy and refused to actually speak Spanish when her skill was most needed.

There was also a Canadian couple, Les and Christine, from Saskatchewan. Like most Canadians traveling abroad, they made it a point not to be mistaken as Americans. They had maple leaf emblems sewn on their backpacks and maple leaf pins on their caps. It's not that Canadians don't like Americans, but they know that some Europeans may not like Americans or at least American foreign policy. Conversely it's not often you'll see American backpackers identifying themselves with little red, white, and blue flags when traveling overseas.

There was also a French couple who spoke no English and communicated with us by looking us straight in the eyes and speaking French very slowly and highly enunciated. It didn't work, but at least they tried. Marie and Girard smoked Gauloise cigarettes as they walked. It was kind of refreshing in this health crazy era to see these iconoclasts.

Michael was an Irishman in his mid-thirties. He was an off-shore oil worker who said that he had been let go for bringing beer on to the rig. There was also a Brazilian who only spoke Portuguese and had an unpronounceable first name.

An Australian was the glue of the group. Suzy was in her early forties and mother of two young girls. Every morning, she would pull out her cell phone and call her daughters back in Brisbane while they were getting ready for bed.

"Don't forget to brush your teeth," she would tell them. "Did you have any homework? What did Daddy make you for dinner?"

The whole thing struck me a bit bizarre It was also a tribute to the power of the cell phone. Although she was on the other side of the world, Suzy was being a perfect perfunctory mom. To prepare for her Camino trek, she had actually taken a one-week course on walking. I don't know how she got around before taking the course. Fortunately I had learned to walk when I was just an infant without any formal training.

"A class on walking?" I asked her. "What did they teach you?"

"You should turn your socks inside out or exchange them from one foot to the other during the day when you're trekking. It's supposed to change the way your foot lies in your shoe just enough to make it more comfortable."

"I'll try it tomorrow," I said.

Leaving Cizur Menor behind, we walked in a loose group with the French couple, Marie and Girard, trailing behind smoking their Gauloises. It was a full seventeen k's to Puente la Reina, the day's destination. Michael told us that he was supposed to meet a fellow Irishman that evening in Puente la Reina, so we agreed to walk the full distance in a day. At a little over ten miles, it was one of my longest.

Passing through the village of Obanos, we saw storks nesting on a chimney. As a child, I recalled seeing pictures of the large birds but had never seen them in person. But there they were. The birds had red bills and black flight feathers. Technically called white storks, they spend the winters somewhere in Africa and then fly north to Europe in the spring to have their young, and to deliver someone else's babies.

Soon it started raining intensely and despite our commitment to make it to Puente la Reina, we began looking for an albergue or a cheap hotel. Michael said he'd keep walking. Serendipitously, just as we rounded a corner in the center of Obanos, we spotted several buses idling in front of what must have been the terminal. We climbed aboard the one headed to Puente la Reina. Nary a voice amongst us cried, "Foul." We were too tired and wet.

Certainly a short bus ride of a few miles wouldn't abrogate the indulgence we would earn by walking scores of miles along the Camino.

"What about those guys that do the Caminos on bicycles?" Les, the Canadian, said.

"They do the Camino on bicycles?" Christine asked. "I haven't seen any."

"Me neither, but my book says that people do it, and nobody says they're cheating. I think they have to do a lot more k's to qualify for their compostela," he said.

"They didn't even have bicycles back in the Middle Ages," Suzy interjected. "These Camino rules seem real flexible."

Les summed up the discussion. "It's kind of like playing golf alone. Only God and your conscience matter."

Puente la Reina is famous for its lovely six-arched bridge that crosses the Rio Arga. It was built in the eleventh century, specifically for pilgrims who had been forced to pay high prices to cross the river by money-gouging ferry operators. The town grew up around the bridge. As a light rain fell, our group of seven peregrinos walked across the beautiful structure, looking for the albergue. If any local citizens saw us getting off the bus, we hoped they wouldn't report us to the local priest for cheating.

The next day, we walked through olive groves and vineyards. We saw the lovely hill town of Cirauqui in the distance. (Its picturesque setting belies the origin of the town's name, which was derived from the Basque word for a "nest of vipers.") Much of northern rural Spain's charm lay in the fact that there were few homes between villages. It's pastoral. Unlike America, there was little urban sprawl and no junk cars, singular homes, and abandoned gas stations. As I walked the Camino, medieval walled towns were usually visible on the horizon. It's the way it ought to be.

The Camino entered the town through a thick gothic arch before winding up a narrow cobbled street and through a covered passageway. There, lying on a small shelf attached to the wall was a self-service sello. We lined up and stamped our credencials. Getting sellos on our credencials had become somewhat of an obsession, and each of us tried to get as many as we could. By this point in our trek, we had all figured out that there was no need to actually go to an albergue or some other church approved facility to acquire the stamps. We got them at restaurants, hotels, barbershops, cafes, and even bars. "Do you think bordellos have sellos?" Les asked.

Each sello was distinct, and the designs usually featured reproductions of scallops, swords, pilgrims, horses, angels or churches. Artisans creating cathedrals, sculptures, and stained glass windows may be a thing of the past, but in most Spanish towns there must be modern craftsmen meticulously creating intricate rubber stamps.

As we passed the town shops, and perhaps inspired by the vineyards and olive groves we had been walking through earlier, Suzy made a sudden announcement. "Picnic!" she proclaimed.

It seemed like a good idea, and we finished our time in Ciraugui, loading up on cheeses, wine, olives, ham, bread, and fruit. Shortly beyond town, we leaned our backs against the posts that supported grape vines and had lunch. It was all too perfect. An elderly woman walking along the Camino saw us and begged for a handout. We couldn't identify her language, and she probably wasn't a peregrino. It didn't matter. Her appearance added a touch of character to our lunch.

"There are only two families in the world,
the Haves and the Have-nots."

Miguel de Cervantes
1547-1616

After picnicking, we walked some time on a stone-paved road before Les, the Canadian, got out his guidebook and announced that we were on a 2,000-year-old road built by the Romans. The road seemed to be just a dirt farm track, but periodically the original Roman flat stones appeared in the dirt then disappeared before surfacing again.

We slept in Estella that night, surrounded by Romanesque monuments, churches, bridges, and the Palace of the Kings of Navarra. My guidebook told me it was a rare example of a Romanesque structure built for civic reasons rather than religious. And, according to James Michener, it was the only town in Spain where women were allowed to fight bulls. He did not elaborate. Michener loved Estella. "…if I were to live anywhere in Spain, I suppose it would have to be here."

Over the next few days, we passed through Villamayor de Monjardin, Los Arcos, Torres del Rio, and arrived in Viana. Viana's claim to fame was that the Italian scoundrel, Cesare Borgia, met his end here, fighting for the King of Navarra. We had trouble finding the guidebook's designated albergue and persuaded our reticent Spanish-speaking companion, Telo, to use her language skills to find us beds. She became the heroine of the day when she asked a local for help. He led us to a church where a priest guided us into a small dormitory with a fully equipped kitchen including dishware and silverware. It was perfect. We had the whole place to ourselves. Sometimes things just work out.

It didn't take Suzy long to assess the situation, and she began collecting ten euros from each of us before heading off to the town's largest grocery store. A couple of us cooked, a couple of us set the table, and the rest sipped wine. We made it a semi-formal dining occasion. We sat down together and ate together. Shoes were mandatory and hats were banned. We toasted, laughed, ate, and drank. The guy from Brazil made a lovely speech in Portuguese. Nobody, except him, understood a word of it, but we gave him a big round of applause anyway. Obrigado! The dinner party was one of the highlights of my Camino adventure.

It was just a six-mile walk the next day from Viana to Logroño where the albergue proved to be one of the tackiest I encountered along the Camino. Logroño was a busy place and the center of the region's wine production. It was also a railroad hub, and I decided it was time to catch a train across the center of Spain and pick up the Camino again somewhere to the west.

I had walked about ninety miles since leaving Roncesvalles ten days earlier. I changed trains in Burgos where my inability to understand fully Spanish numbers and read train schedules resulted in my waiting a full eight hours in the station before finally catching the train to Leon. The train passed through the heart of Spain's monotonous *maesta* between Burgos and Leon. The maesta, an expansive plain, was desolate. One wag described it as being "so flat you can see your dog run away for two days." I had made the decision to skip this lengthy and boring section of the Camino.

Leon held my attention for two nights. It was home to one of the most magnificent residences in Europe, the Hotel San Marcos, and one of the crown jewels in Spain's chain of government-sanctioned elite Paradors. I stayed at the municipal albergue where the old woman at the entrance stamped my credencial. She could have cared less that there was a huge void of sellos in my credencial between Logroño and Leon. (I have a hunch that, had I asked, the train's conductor would have stamped my credencial.)

Leon's glorious thirteenth-century Gothic cathedral was a world masterpiece. Walls of stained glass seemed to inexplicably support the soaring walls. Light danced through the interior in the afternoon sun. Do I exaggerate? Listen to Michener's description in his *Iberia*.

> "I have seen most of the fine sights of the world and know how exciting Ankor Wat can be at midnight with tiers of Cambodian dancers, or the Acropolis at dusk, or Borobudur in a jungle storm, but so far as sheer visual pleasure is concerned, I have seen nothing to excel Leon's cathedral at three in the morning, lighted from within, and I say this as a man who likes neither stained-glass windows nor Gothic."

Okay, Jim, that was nice, but it's still just a big church, and Leon's tapa bars were really great. Easter was on the calendar's horizon, and all of Spain was gearing up for its annual religious extravaganza, *Semana Santa* (Holy Week). Although most identify the annual multi-day event with the city of Sevilla, every city in the country has its tribute to Christ's crucifixion and subsequent revival featuring somber parades with participants dressed in macabre costumes, marching solemnly to slow methodical drumbeats and whining trumpets. Practice by the various organizations begins well before Holy Week, and Leon's preparation was well underway.

Each evening after the practice parades, the bars were crowded with penitents and pagans alike, downing wine, beer, and an assortment of tapas created by culinary artisans that would have Mario Batali and José Andrés begging for more. I couldn't get enough of the experience, although it was somewhat odd being in a crowded bar, knowing no one and with little hope of ever striking up a conversation with my schoolboy Spanish.

Soon after, I boarded a train for Ponferrada. The conductor woke me up as the train entered this hamlet. It was time to start walking again. I had some 140 miles to go before reaching Santiago de Compostela. Three days beyond Ponferrada, I approached O Cebreiro, knowing that this stage was the most physically challenging along the entire Camino. The village straddled a mountain pass at an elevation of 4,284 feet. The climb from the valley below was an ascent of more than 3,000 feet. Not overwhelming but attention getting.

The day before, two peregrinos told me that they were considering hiring a taxi for the climb. I chastised them for their lack of commitment to the true Camino spirit without mentioning that I had knocked off over 200 miles of Camino on the train. The hike up proved formidable, and for the first time, I was forced to pause occasionally to catch my breath. At one point, a taxi passed on the adjoining highway going my direction, and I thought I recognized the passengers as yesterday's companions.

I was now in northwestern Spain, Galicia, Spain's back closet, a region seldom visited by Americans and rarely by sun-seeking Brits and other northern Europeans who prefer the southern coasts. It rained a lot in Galicia. Even the people looked different. The *Gallegos* were stocky and had the demeanor of peasants. They worked their small farms and vegetable gardens, wearing rubber boots and heavy sweaters. The women wore aprons. Every farm seemed to have only one cow, and each farm had a small, oddly shaped granary known as *hórreo.* The granite storage bins were elevated on pillars to protect the grain from rodents. Side vents kept air circulating to prevent rain from ruining the crop. The whole contraption was covered by a gabled roof and a crucifix, which served as the last defense against an attack on the grain.

There was an aura of poverty, at least in the countryside. Galicia was one of the poorest regions in Spain. Celtic invaders a thousand years earlier had left their cultural imprint, and there was little Moorish influence. I had read that the national instrument of Galicia was a *gaita* but was taken aback when I actually saw a contingent of Galician soldiers playing the smaller version of the Scottish bagpipe in a Holy Week parade. Despite a degree in history, I did not realize that the Celts had settled beyond Ireland and

Scotland. Their traditional language, *gallego,* has no Celtic roots but an odd similarity to Portuguese, dominated by the use of the letter x. Francisco Franco, born in the Galician coastal city of Ferrol in 1892, was the son of a naval officer stationed at the city's naval base.

Just before my entry into O Cebrerio, the Camino began to be routinely marked with cement markers indicating the distance to Santiago de Compostela. The first indicated it was 153 k's to my destination. From then on, they appeared along the Camino every 500 meters. They are modern, but as the Camino neared Santiago, large medieval crosses, erected more than 800 years ago, still stood. Apparently they were meant to provide peregrinos yet another place to pray for their souls.

Beyond O Cebrerio, I overtook a man in his early forties, shuffling through a grove of chestnut trees. His modest pace and overall appearance made me think he was an accountant or some other desk-bound type. We greeted each other warmly in Spanish, but he quickly realized I was no Iberian and switched to English. His was pretty good. We began a warm conversation that lasted most of the day.

Jose Maria Luis was the most delightful personality I met during my trek across Spain. His professorial demeanor was overshadowed by the tenacity of his recent history. Born in the Canary Islands, his parents moved their family to Venezuela where he was raised. Jose Maria earned an engineering degree in Venezuela and became an entrepreneur. He and his partner began producing a machine part vital to the manufacture of household refrigerators. Their business prospered. In fact, it prospered too much.

"Hugo Chavez built his popularity by gaining the support of the poor people in Venezuela. He attacked anyone who was successful and appeared to be making money," Jose Maria told me. "Financially successful people were singled out and soon there were protesters in front of my home."

He explained that he had to fortify his home in Caracas with an iron fence because he and his wife feared things could turn violent.

"Ultimately I had to have my young daughter driven to school by an armed driver," he told me. "I began to realize that we would have to leave Venezuela."

He and his family considered immigrating to Canada and even went to British Columbia to look around. Ultimately they returned to their roots and settled in a subdivision of Madrid. Now he operated a small manufacturing plant and was back on the road to financial stability. His business was successful enough that he was able to take a couple of weeks off to walk the Camino de Santiago.

His story was fascinating and he earned my respect. We walked the rest of the Camino together all the way to Santiago, and his insights and the fact that he spoke Spanish enhanced my experience and opened a few doors for me. On one occasion, he managed to secure beds for us in an albergue when none were apparently available. We had walked a long distance and were both tired and sore. (Jose Maria frequently complained that his knees, legs, feet, or ankles were killing him but refused let the pain get the better of him and always kept moving.)

It was early evening when we reached the only albergue along a particularly rural section of the Camino. I had gone ahead because we were both fearful that the place might be filled. Sure enough, pilgrims had packed the place by the time I got there, and there were no vacant beds. Jose Maria shuffled in some time later, and I told him the bad news.

"Let me talk to the guy," he said. "You wait outside."

He reappeared a few minutes with a key in his hand. "Don't say anything to anyone, but we're staying in the room reserved for the handicapped," he said with a smile. The private room had two beds and its own bathroom. It helps to befriend a native when in a foreign country.

The next day, Jose Maria surprised me by interrupting our walk with a visit to a doctor to see about his sore knees, legs, feet, and ankles. I waited for him outside on the street.

"Well, what did the doctor say?" I asked him when he reappeared.

"Stop walking so much."

Jose Maria's wife's family was from Galicia, and he was quick to praise the merits of Spain's remote northwestern corner. There was no end to laudatory comments, especially the cuisine.

"The food in Galicia is the best in Spain," he told me. "Tomorrow we are passing through a town with a restaurant famous for one of Galicia's most popular dishes, and we'll stop there for a special lunch."

"What's the dish?" I asked.

"*Pulpa.*"

"What is it?"

"Octopus" he replied with a smile.

I'd eaten squid or calamari many times before, so the thought of dining on octopus was just one more culinary adventure. I had always been puzzled by people whose culinary tastes have never matured beyond those of an eleven year old and survived on beef, potatoes, white bread, and yellow cheese. A life without mussels and lamb is a life misspent. It's like looking at autumn's leaves in black and white.

Pulpa in Galicia was a specialty of Galician restaurants called "*pulperias.*" Ours was filled with old men smoking cigars and drinking Ribeiro wine in small ceramic cups. The murky white wine was poured from jugs rather than bottles. If you looked carefully, small, unidentifiable particles—perhaps grape skins or leaves left over from the wine-making process—could be seen floating in the wine. These remnants were presumably the reason for the cups rather than glasses.

Pulpa a la gallega is typically prepared by boiling the octopus in a copper pot. The tentacles are cut into small pieces, sprinkled with salt, garlic, paprika, and olive oil. The dish is served on a wooden platter and eaten with toothpicks. Jose Maria enjoyed the fact that I consumed the sea creature with enthusiasm. The most difficult part of the experience was walking out into the bright sun after having consumed lots of wine and pulpa and knowing that we still had ten k's to go before reaching the evening's albergue.

Our arrival in Santiago de Compostela was somewhat disappointing. After nearly three weeks of anticipation, I had formed an image that the famous Cathedral of Santiago would be visible from far away, sitting atop a hill, glowing in celestial light. I imagined the experience would be similar to Dorothy's when she and her friends first saw Emerald City bathed in effervescent green at the end of the yellow brick road on a distant hill. In fact, we had trouble finding the darned church, and after walking the city's uninteresting suburban sidewalks for a more than two hours, Jose Maria shared my frustration and finally asked for directions. Eventually we came around a corner, and there it stood.

The cathedral may not be the most beautiful in Spain, but it is massive and complex. The original cathedral was completed in 1211 A.D. with craftsmen throughout Europe, journeying to Santiago to work on the church. Much of the sculpting and design, including the magnificent portico, was done by Maestro Mateo, a native Spaniard whose name is associated with the cathedral almost as much St. James himself. Experts consider his work equal to Michelangelo's who apparently only had a better publicist. The building had undergone extensive renovations since then, but the interior remained essentially unchanged from the Middle Ages. Its size is difficult to comprehend until one actually walks around and through it. We walked up the steps together and knelt, and Jose Maria bowed his head in prayer. Outside, other peregrinos and tourists mingled and socialized. Semana Santa was in full swing, so the number of visitors to the cathedral was probably higher than usual. As in most European cities, mimes, jugglers, artists, and other entertainers vie for donations from the throngs gathered in the three separate squares that adjoined the cathedral.

"My wife is supposed to be around here somewhere," Jose Maria said. We found her sitting on the steps of one of the entrances of the cathedral. She appeared somewhat younger than her husband, and I was flattered when Jose Maria told her that my companionship and motivation helped him complete his journey. His wife had brought a basket of bacalao, and I was invited to share it with them. I thought that she was not aware that she should have made enough cod to share with a third person, so I begged off. It was time to say goodbye. Jose Maria and I hugged each other warmly, and I reluctantly drifted off through the crowd.

The next day, I returned to the cathedral to perform the traditions unofficially required of all who complete the Camino de Santiago. The first stipulates that a peregrino honor Maestro Mateo by tapping his head three times against the head of the statute of the genius in hopes that some of his genius will pass to you. Next I walked to the front of the cathedral and proceeded down a staircase to the crypt of St. James. There was a small line of pilgrims ahead of me, and slowly each of us took our turn touching the statue of St. James. Then I knelt before an encased solid silver reliquary containing the bones of Santiago. This was not a time for cynicism. I was engaged in a ritual performed by tens of thousands of pilgrims for over nine hundred years.

Finally I walked across the Plaza de Obradoiro, heading for the Oficina del Peregrino where I presented my credencial filled with sellos to an office volunteer. She asked for my American passport and carefully recorded my full name. After a brief wait, I was presented with my genuine compostela signifying my completion of the Camino de Santiago and granting me the indulgence shortening my time in purgatory by 50 percent. The document was a single sheet of paper completely in Latin. I was thrilled!

The next day was Easter Sunday. It was raining, and I had nothing else to do until my bus back to Madrid left the next day, so I decided to attend mass in the cathedral. I grew up with plenty of Roman Catholic ritual, but the experience of witnessing the celebration of mass on Catholicism's most holy day inside one of Christendom's most important churches was a super-sensory experience. The place was filled with tourists, pilgrims, and local Catholics. Even the bishop showed up. As shafts of light passed through the stained glass, organ and choir music permeated every niche and nave.

After communion, the celebration culminated when an exhibition was performed unique to the Cathedral of Santiago. Hanging from a massive pole carried by two men was an ornate iron censer called a *botafumeiro* or "smoke thrower." The device was about three feet high and weighed well over a hundred pounds. A thick hemp rope passing through a pulley far above at the cathedral's highest point was untied by eight red-robed men from one of the cathedral's pillars and attached to the device at the other end. A priest opened the contraption and ignited the incense inside the botafumeiro and started it swinging. The swinging intensified as the men pulled on the rope, increasing its height and arc like some sort of huge pendulum bisecting the transept of the church. Sweet-smelling smoke poured out of the thing as it passed just over our heads before reaching a height of some ninety feet. It was a great show. Michener said the botafumeiro experience may have originated in the Middle Ages as a way of counteracting the stench of pilgrims who often slept in the church. More likely, he said, it was begun as a bit of church show biz in an effort to enhance the uniqueness of the Cathedral de Santiago.

Whatever its origin, the whole extravaganza was a fitting exclamation point to my Camino experience.

5

Paine Circuit

Butch Cassidy and the Israeli girls

Patagonia
64 miles

Its very name has the sound of some distant place on the outer edges of the world. Lots of Americans have heard of Patagonia, but maybe some have it confused with the outdoor clothing and gear company of the same name. That's understandable because the California entrepreneur and outdoor adventurer, Yvon Chouinard, helped make the southern end of South America famous as one of the world's last best places by actually naming his company after this region of vast steppes, sweeping vistas, rushing streams, and lonely mountains.

Chouinard, a French Canadian born in Maine, first went to Patagonia in 1968, driving a Ford Econoline van. He pioneered a new climbing route up Patagonia's famous Mount Fitz Roy in Argentina not too far from the Chilean border. Chouinard was so taken with the rocky spire that he put it on the logo of his clothing company. His adventure has become a legendary road trip, recently retold using the original images taken on the trip in a documentary film released in 2010 entitled *180 Degrees South.* As he was in his business, Chouinard was ahead of his time.

Not too many North Americans went to Patagonia until the latter part of the last century. Some of that surge can be attributed to the popularity of Robert Redford's fly fishing movie, *A River Runs Through It*, released in 1992 and set in Montana. There had been a few well-heeled fly fishing enthusiasts who went to Patagonia in search of big trout for years, and they returned with stories of great trout fishing in the Carrileufu Valley and on the Corcovado River. The stage was set. Redford motivated thousands to jump into drift boats and float down the rivers of the American West, tossing out humpies and Chernobyl ants. They began spending serious money too. Winston rods and Orvis's Mirage reels run into the hundreds of dollars. No matter. They're fly fishing and intent on changing a relatively simple relaxing activity into a high-tech, expensive, and frustrating experience. Suddenly trout fishing in Montana wasn't good enough for many of them; they had to get down to Patagonia. Interestingly, Chouinard, once again on the cutting edge, became a proponent of *Tenkara,* a traditional Japanese fly fishing method, which takes fishing back to its Huck Finn roots by using long bamboo poles without any reels.

The Patagonia attraction for me was its mountains, not its fishing. It was the Patagonia Andes that had been in the back of my mind for a long time.

"You're going to have to go down there if you're serious about this great treks of the world thing," my wife told me before I had really considered going. The Paine Circuit, within Chile's Torres del Paine National Park, is on every single list of great treks. Over the years, I had met a couple of people who actually did the trek.

"It's incredible," one couple told me when I bumped into them while backpacking in the Wind River Range. "We did it last year and it's marvelous. Here's our e-mail address if you have any questions."

All my great treks seem to have begun with the purchase of the *Lonely Planet's* guide to the area under consideration. Their Patagonian guide was particularly inviting with its cover shot of the famous Cuernos del Paine mountains rising above Lago Pehoé in Parque Nacional Torres del Paine. The first time I saw the photo, I wasn't even sure what country they were in, but the title of the *Lonely Planet* guide across the top of the panoramic photo grabbed me—*Trekking in the Patagonian Andes*. It stayed in my mind, and over a three-year period, I would pick up the book and make notes on the inside covers. I purposely left it on the coffee table as motivation.

Names of people who had made the trek along with exotic sounding hostels like Portal del Sur and Los Inmigrantes began to fill up the flyleaves. I began familiarizing myself with the location of towns like Puerto Natales, Punta Arenas, El Calafaté, and El Chaltén. Some were in Chile and others in Argentina. Patagonia straddles both nations. Torres del Paine National Park is located in southern Patagonia near the end of the continent in Chile. It's a distinct geographical region famous for miserable weather, strong winds, and great mountains. According to *Lonely Planet*, the area had the most extensive glaciers outside of the earth's polar regions.

The exact meaning of Torres del Paine is unclear. *Torres* translates to 'tower' in Spanish, but the meaning of *Paine* is up for argument. Most authorities seem to think it's a variation of a native peoples' word meaning 'blue.' The names of its mountains are less well known to armchair adventurers but familiar to international climbers. By world standards, they are not high, but they rise dramatically from near sea level with all the vicissitudes of the extreme latitude and become formidable.

Patagonia's highest mountain, Mount San Lorenzo, has an altitude of just 12,155 feet, but like Britain's Ben Nevis, height is not the only measure of a mountain. Mt. Fitz Roy, for example, has an elevation of just over

11,000 feet, but more important, it jumps some 6,000 feet above the plain. Seeing it for the first time can take your breath away.

In January 2011 I received an e-mail from my trekking friend Morgan down in Australia. He apparently had taken our discussion of the world's great treks to heart when we were doing the West Coast Trail on Vancouver Island.

"I was considering the Camino de Santiago, but it sounds too social, and I want to do something a little more rugged. My dad and I are going to do the Paine Circuit. Want to join us?" he wrote.

I was flattered that he had contacted me and offered me the invitation. At sixty-eight, I wasn't getting any younger, and the thought of having someone else figure out all the logistics involved with the trek was tempting.

Another message arrived a few days later. "We are catching the 18:30 or 20:00 bus from Punta Arenas to Puerto Natales on arrival at Punta Arenas on March 7. We will stay the night in Puerto Natales and then catch an early morning bus to Torres del Paine. I think we can set off on the trek before midday."

Morgan obviously had done his homework, and I had to get out a newly purchased map of Chile to figure out his itinerary. Just where is Puerto Natales? How do I get there anyway? Over the years, I had accumulated quite a few frequent flyer miles and decided that maybe this was the time to cash them in. I was unfamiliar with the process and quickly discovered that there was quite a big difference in having the miles and actually getting a seat on a plane headed near your destination about the time you wanted to go.

Rule #1: When attempting to redeem your frequent flyer miles, be prepared to be flexible. (There are no other rules.) And I'll be damned that on my third phone call attempt, the nice woman for Delta Airlines told me that by using frequent flyer miles, they could get me from El Paso, Texas, to Buenos Aires, Argentina, and return via Santiago, Chile, then on to El Paso.

"You're on your own getting from Buenos Aires down to Patagonia," she told me. "You'll also probably have to buy another ticket to head north from down there back up to Santiago."

I hesitated. "Let me call you back," I said knowing that I hadn't yet officially discussed going on this adventure with my spouse.

"Sir, this is the third time you've called. If you're serious, you should have me book it. These seats won't be available tomorrow." She was right.

"Book it," I said, knowing that my wife was close by in the living room and listening.

"You're going then," she said when I hung up the phone. Like our dog, I had learned to focus on the tone of her voice rather than the words themselves, and her tone told me that I had her approval.

After a two-night layover in Buenos Aires, the plan was to fly to El Calafaté, Argentina, since there was no flight from Buenos Aires to Puerto Natales. From El Calafaté, I'd bus north to El Chaltén, Argentina, spend a couple of days day-hiking around Mount Fitz Roy, and then bus south to Puerto Natales, Chile.

I e-mailed Morgan. "I'll walk over from my hostel in Puerto Natales to yours on the evening of March 7."

It all sounded good, but the logistics of bus schedules and a border crossing were complicated. I put the odds of me actually showing up at Morgan's hostel on the appointed date at fifty-fifty. It would have been easier if I skipped Fitz Roy, but the famous mountain was only a day or so away from Puerto Natales.

The trip got off badly when a storm in Atlanta, Georgia, delayed my flight, causing me to miss my connection to Buenos Aires. There was only one flight a day to Buenos Aires, and I was on standby the next evening in Atlanta. The plane was almost taxiing down the runway when my name popped up on the stand-by screen. I was the last one aboard.

"What about my luggage?" I asked as the door closed. "How will they know I'm on this flight since I was standby?"

"They're putting it on now, sir," was the reply.

"Yeah, right."

My faithful, blue, GoLite backpack was on the luggage carousel in Buenos Aires when I arrived there nine hours later. How did they do that?

"A traveler has the right to relate and
embellish his adventures as he pleases,
and it is very impolite to refuse that deference
and applause they deserve."

Rudolf Erich Raspe
1737-1794

A few days later while day hiking around Fitz Roy, I met a Brit walking in my direction. Both of us were starving for an English conversation. After exchanging pleasantries, we kept talking while we leaned against a rock and enjoyed the vista. I told him about the problem I had getting out of Atlanta and into Buenos Aires. Travelers love to discuss the hassles of flying, involving lost luggage, missed connections, and cancelled flights. Each has a story to tell. His was one of the best.

"I got here a couple of days late because I missed a couple of connections in Toronto," he said.

"Two connections? In one airport? How's that possible?" I asked.

"Well, my flight out of there was delayed about three or four hours because there were some mechanical issues with the plane. So I went to the airport bar and had a couple of drinks. Maybe three. Maybe four. The bartender decided to cut me off, and I guess I became belligerent. The next thing I knew there's a cop there, and I'm under arrest. I had to spend the night in a Toronto city jail, go to court the next day, and pay a fine. Of course I had to buy a new ticket from Toronto to Patagonia. I don't think I'll mention anything about it to my wife. I'm sure glad to be here, though."

"At least you got a free room in Toronto," I added as I shook his hand and congratulated him for the great story.

Before I actually got out of the Buenos Aires airport, I had an unpleasant surprise. Just after departing the plane but before going through customs, signs started to pop up along the walkway warning travelers about some sort of *RECIPROSITY IMPUESTOS*. The sign had a Visa card logo on it. Soon enough, there was a turnstile and an Argentine official with a cash register and a Visa machine. Impuestos translated into tax. It was a flat fee to enter the country. The charge varied depending on one's citizenship. For Americans, it was $175; Canadians paid less. E.U. citizens even less.

The best my fellow travelers and I could figure out was that Argentinians entering the United States and some other foreign countries were being charged a fee, so they decided to tax some foreigners entering Argentina to get even. It was the only time in my travels I had encountered it. There was never mention of the entrance tax in any of the travel guides, Web sites, and articles I had read before heading to Patagonia. Surprise. Surprise. Do you think the fee we're charging Argentinians to enter the United States will reduce the deficit? No wonder so many Mexicans are trying to sneak in.

Buenos Aires was huge, intimidating, and, despite its name, polluted. Being cheap, I had booked a hostel based on price. One of the reasons it was cheap was because it was on a nasty street a few blocks from downtown.

I hid my money in my room and set out intent on seeing the famous Presidential Pink House *(La Casa Rosada)* where from a balcony Evita Peron rallied the crowds below in the *Plaza de Mayo* and Madonna sang *Don't Cry for Me Argentina* in the movie version of the Broadway play *Evita.* During the Falklands War in 1982, British military bands derided Argentinian enemy soldiers by playing the song with heavy notes of sarcasm.

"Did you see the film? What did you think of it?" I asked a distinguished gentleman.

"How would you react if we made a film about Eleanor Roosevelt with Madonna playing the lead role?" he responded abruptly. I backed off.

Modern Argentine politics have been unstable at best. The country had no less than twenty-four presidents between 1939 and 1983 but was dominated by Juan Perón and the Caudillo's second wife Eva. She died in 1952 but remains in the mainstream of the nation's collective conscience. Like Vladimir Lenin and Trigger, she was embalmed, but the location of her body was unknown for over a decade until it showed up in a crypt in Italy. Juan had her body shipped back to Argentina and affectionately kept it on display in his living room, apparently with his third wife Isabel's approval. Thankfully she was finally laid to rest in Buenos Aires's upscale Recoleta Cemetery, one of the mandatory stopping points on any tour of the city.

Despite the Perónists' thug-like approach to politics and suppression of personal freedoms, there's no lack of love for the couple. You can't buy a postcard of Francisco Franco today in Madrid. But in Buenos Aires, every kiosk has cards with portraits of Juan Perón and Evita. He died in 1974, and the nation was ruled by an ultra-right-wing junta, which tortured and executed thousands of Argentine liberals, union leaders, and students during the heinous Dirty War. The internal struggle was marked by numerous clandestine atrocities including the drugging of opposition members who were then thrown out of airplanes to their deaths. In Argentina, these execution rides are referred to as *Los Vuelos de la muerte*—The Flights of Death.

The Mothers of the Plaza de Mayo still gather every Thursday, demanding to know the whereabouts of their missing relatives and seeking justice for the perpetrators. There were about a hundred women on hand for the weekly protest when I happened by chance to be there on a Thursday. They were raucous but non-confrontational. Some sat on the street while others paraded with poster board placards. One guy was playing a trumpet and another beating a drum. A couple of food vendors circulated among the gathering, pushing their carts. If you did not know the protestors' history, you could have misinterpreted the event as simply a strike by retail sales clerks.

But just beyond the demonstration, close enough to intervene quickly if necessary, were armed soldiers, water cannons mounted on armored vehicles, and agitated guard dogs. They brought a sense of sobriety to the scene. Want more? The 1985 Argentinian film, *The Official Story*, detailed the story of a couple who adopted a child and discovered that the child's parents were among those who disappeared during the Dirty War. It was the first Latin American film to be honored with an academy award for Best Foreign Language Film.

My visit to the Paris of South America lasted just two nights and one full day. I was glad to be flying south.

"I've gone to Patagonia."

Bruce Chatwin
1940-1989

Bruce Chatwin left Buenos Aires by bus at the age of thirty-four, heading south. It was 1974. Chatwin, an Englishman, had quit his job at Sotheby's auctioneering house where he specialized in impressionist art. He enrolled at Edinburgh University to study archaeology but lacked the scholarly instinct. He then took a job writing for the *Sunday Times* and was sent to New York to conduct research for a story on the Guggenheim family. A month later, he sent a telegram to his editor, announcing that he was tired of New York and was now in South America where he intended to write a book. Published in 1977, *In Patagonia* became an instant classic in league with the likes of travel writers, Paul Theroux and Jack Kerouac. The book ostensibly traces Chatwin's search for a cave near Puerto Natales where a distant relative had found the remains of an extinct giant sloth in the nineteenth century. Chatwin's tale laced his adventures with stories of Welsh immigrants, communist revolutionaries, vivid descriptions, and lost legends like Butch Cassidy and a Frenchman claiming to be the king of Patagonia.

Like numerous backpackers before me, I had a paperback copy of *In Patagonia* with me. In an attempt to give a false impression that I was a cosmopolitan traveler, I made certain to stick it on the outside of my pack in such a way that the title was always visible.

El Calafaté, Argentina, was a refreshing surprise after the hassle and grit of Buenos Aires. The town was small and touristy with most buildings, especially along the main street, appearing to have been built in the last twenty years. It served as the jumping off spot into Los Glaciares National Park including nearby Moreno Glacier. Every hotel and hostel offered tours to the glacier where one can stand on a boardwalk along the glacier's tongue and watch as it calves huge ice chunks. The more adventurous can don crampons and hike on the glacier. Moreno Glacier is nineteen miles long.

It's also only a four-hour bus ride from El Calafaté to the northern section of the park and the Mount Fitz Roy massif.

I had limited time and since the Torres del Paine trek was still my principle priority, I opted to skip the Moreno Glacier and head for Fitz Roy. After spending the night in a hostel where I shared a four-bunk dorm room with a couple of German newlyweds (apparently honeymoons aren't what they used to be), I boarded a bus for the little town of El Chaltén and Fitz Roy. The ride itself was a highlight of my entire trip. We scooted across the Patagonian plain on a newly paved road. It was my first real look at the Patagonian steppes. It was a near cloudless day, and the views were endless.

Although the vistas were similar to my home state of Wyoming, with mountains rising on the edge of vast plains, there was a difference. Most striking was the purity of the landscape. Wyoming's outback is frequently marred by dirt roads. They're used for gas and oil exploration, hunting, and ranching. And there are fences. Barbed wire fences parallel nearly every inch of the Cowboy State's paved highways.

That was not the case, at least in this part of Patagonia. With the exception of a rare *estancia*, there were no roads, no buildings, no gas rigs, no fences. Instead of the ubiquitous antelope, there were the strange-looking guanacos. These long-necked members of the camel family are related to alpacas and llamas. They were frequently visible, grazing in small groups. After a couple of hours, the understanding bus driver pulled over so that we could all scramble out and enjoy the moment. There in the distance was the Fitz Roy massif. It was impeccable.

The village of El Chaltén was created in 1985 to lay claim to the area by Argentina, which was in a border dispute with Chile. The argument was settled, and tourism is now the main reason for the town's existence. Despite El Chaltén's touristy demeanor, the place was a hiker's nirvana with numerous low-priced hostels, a couple of small grocery stores, and even a brew pub—all under the shadow of Fitz Roy. A sign on the edge of town reminded me of why I came: THE TREKKING CAPITAL OF ARGENTINA. Rough dirt roads crisscross the town and, best of all, I could simply roll out of my bunk in the morning, walk out the hostel door, and begin hiking. Trekkers need only walk a couple of k's before spectacular views have them filling their cameras' memory card.

That evening over beer, I fell into a discussion with a fellow American. Although a flatlander from Iowa, David had seen many of the world's great mountains, and we compared the vista we had seen today with some of them.

"Of course, what's unique about Fitz Roy is the way it shoots up abruptly from the valley. There are not many mountains that are comparable," he offered.

We agreed that Switzerland's Matterhorn, Canada's Assiniboine, and Wyoming's Tetons all fell into the "abruptly rising" category. I tried to add Colorado's Maroon Bells to the list, but David argued that they lacked the classic apex necessary for inclusion.

"It's a very subjective list," I added. "How about another beer?"

Mount Fitz Roy was named in honor the captain of the *HMS Beagle*, the ship, which in 1834 sailed through the tip of South America, carrying the evolutionary Charles Darwin to the Galapagos. Despite the onset of modern rock climbing technology, reaching Fitz Roy's summit is still considered a significant achievement. A French expedition first reached the mountain's top in 1952.

The Fitz Roy massif's other crown jewel is Cerro Torre. Although some 800 feet lower than its neighbor, the granite shaft erupts 4,000 vertical feet from the glacier below and was long considered unclimbable. But in 1959 the Italian Cesare Maestri and his climbing partners Australian Toni Egger and fellow Italian Cesarino Fava claimed to have made the first ascent via the north ridge. The news was hailed by mountaineers worldwide as a monumental achievement. Egger fell on the descent, but Maestri became an instant climbing legend—if only in Italy.

Over the years, however, skepticism grew as subsequent climbers using various routes could find no trace of the bolts and hardware Maestri claimed to have used in the ascent. Suspicious climbers also said that the approach to the top did not match Maestri's description. (An Italian team made the first documented ascent of Cerro Torre in 1974.) Maestri's claim was mired in controversy until 2005 when three other Italians, Rolando Garibotti, Alessandro Beltranni, and Ermanno Salvaterra, reached the summit via Maestri's supposed exact route but never found a trace of metal in the rock authenticating Maestri's claim. Despite the lack of evidence documenting his successful ascent of Cerro Torre, Maestri has remained steadfast regarding his alleged triumph, refusing to recant his version of his 1959 climb.

In 1970 Maestri managed to compound the disrespect that other climbers held of him by using an air compressor to imbed hundreds of bolts into Cerro Torre's southeast ridge in another attempt to reach the summit. He left the air compressor dangling from the headwall and never completed the climb.

The next day, David and I hiked to within a mile of the base of Fitz Roy. It was only about a three-hour walk from our hostel. The relentless Patagonian wind blew my hat off as I was taking my umpteenth photo of the mountain. David and I searched for the hat among the scrubby beech trees and thorny caliphate, to no avail.

"You know what they call the wind here?" David asked me. "It's called 'The Broom of God.' It sweeps everything clean."

I turned my head for one last look at Fitz Roy as the bus left El Chaltén for El Calafate. There, I caught another bus headed south for Puerto Natales. It took six hours including the border crossing where we left Argentina and entered Chile. The checkpoint was a bleak, desolate, and windy station complete with a few Chilean soldiers and customs inspectors. The inspection was not perfunctory. The Chilean customs officials took their job seriously. There were only about ten of us on the bus, all tourists. Apparently Argentinians don't travel to Chile.

We were required to get off the bus and pass through customs with our bags and backpacks. The process was made considerably more complicated when a young Swede, with whom I had been chatting earlier, mistakenly told the young customs agent that he had some salt and pepper in his pack. The officer's response was immediate. He reacted as if the spices were a heinous violation of regulations and told everyone to empty their bags completely. He confiscated a variety of innocuous items from most of us including matches, dehydrated soup, dry milk, chocolate bars, cigarettes, aspirin, and my propane canister. One older German was particularly upset when his prescription medicine was confiscated. Everyone was sympathetic with the guy, but no amount of pleading could change the inspector's decision. The whole process took almost two hours. At least I didn't have to pay another Reciprocity Impasto.

The bus ride resumed, and I had my first look at Chile. It was dusk when suddenly I noticed a large, ostrich-looking creature running across the Pampa. It was a lesser rhea. The funny-looking bird spread its wings as it ran away in a zigzag pattern. My bird book said that the zigzagging was characteristic of the bird, although it didn't explain why they ran in such an unusual pattern. Maybe to escape some natural enemy that can't zigzag.

Puerto Natales, in Chile's extreme south, proved to be an interesting town of about 20,000 isolated souls with the distinct feel of a port city. From there ships can weave their way through a complex archipelago and reach the open waters of the Pacific or head southeast to the Strait of Magellan and the Atlantic. Most of the buildings in the business district were made of corrugated metal giving the place a unique character. As I walked the streets, I had the feeling that I might bump into Ernest Shackleton any second. I loved it.

There was no problem finding Morgan's hostel. He and his father, Ralph, were sitting in the lobby, waiting for me. "You're late," Morgan said with a smile as if I had only come from across town rather than across three quarters of a hemisphere. We shook hands warmly and chuckled at the fact that we had actually pulled this reunion off. Considering the logistics, it was an accomplishment. Later that evening over dinner, we discussed which of us had traveled the greatest distance to get there. I don't remember our conclusion on the subject, but I do remember the dinner.

For whatever reason, I had not associated Chile with seafood, but that was pure ignorance. Pencil-thin Chile has 2,600 miles of coast, and nowhere in the nation is there a location more than 250 miles from the Pacific. It's a seafood lover's nirvana. That evening, for less than US$6, I had an aquarium of chowder filled with an assortment of fresh fish and shellfish so abundant I could have walked across it. We started the meal with a selection of appetizers including oysters, squid, and some sort of sea urchin. It was a lesson learned and during the rest of my time in Chile, I ate seafood at every single opportunity. I was never disappointed.

The next morning, after a stop at a grocery, the three of us boarded a bus for the 116-kilometer ride to the *Guardería Laguna Armarga*, one of the main entrance points to Torres del Paine and the beginning of the trek. Morgan had done all the planning for the actual adventure, and it was a relief to actually start what *Lonely Planet* called, "Truly one of the world's great treks."

After more than a week of chasing planes and buses, and searching for hostels and ATMs in strange cities, it was wonderful not to have to worry about those logistics. The plan was to walk the sixty-two-mile circuit in nine days in a counterclockwise direction, camping eight nights. We'd gain altitude each of the first five days before finally crossing John Garner Pass at 4,000 feet with views of the Great Grey Glacier. Although camping was unrestricted throughout the park, all the trekkers we encountered stayed each night at developed sites like Campamiento Los Perros, Refugio Dickson, and Campamiento Italiano. Those sites had refugios and small, dormitory-style accommodations with a few beds and basic kitchen facilities. Reservations had to be made well in advance. Meals could be purchased at some of the refugios, and a couple had a sprinkling of groceries for sale. Like most trekkers on the circuit, we tented every night.

Torres del Paine is an isolated land of mountains, enormous azure lakes, and great glaciers. At four miles wide and ten miles long, the Great Grey Glacier is the largest in the park. The park's glaciers help make up the Southern Patagonian Ice field—only the ice fields of Antarctica and Greenland are larger. The Paine Massif rises some 9,000 feet from the surrounding grasslands to Cerro Paine Grande's 10,000-foot elevation. The mountain is the highest in the park and is topped with a unique ice mushroom formation found in few other places in the world. The signature peaks of the park, which routinely adorn the covers of adventure and travel magazines, are the jagged Cuernos (horns) del Paine and the three Torres del Paine towers after which the park is named. It was overcast the day we arrived, and we saw none of these gems although a fellow trekker assured us he had seen the towers the evening before and they were spectacular.

"I guess I'll have to take your word for it," I said.

The first day's walk was miserable. Early into the day, the three of us ended up standing under a tree for two hours waiting for the rain to quit. It refused to stop, and eventually we surrendered to the elements and marched on quietly encumbered by rain pants, all-weather jackets, and backpack rain covers.

Breaking a long period of silence, Ralph tried to make light of the situation. "We're having fun already," he said to me. "I was hoping we'd get to experience the real Patagonia."

Six hours later, we arrived at our destination, a bleak campground with a couple of picnic tables and an outhouse. There was also some sort of ranger station, but the building was locked. We stood under the eaves of the building in an attempt to get out of the rain. We each had the same 'What have we gotten ourselves into?' look on our faces. It was still raining, and although there was plenty of daylight remaining, we put up our tents, ate, and prepared for bed.

It was almost dark when two diminutive young women popped out of the trees and started putting up their tent on the far side of the campground. Each girl, weighing not more than a hundred pounds, carried a very large pack. We took turns trying to guess their language. Ralph and I were certain they were some sort of Scandinavians, but Morgan suggested that they might be Dutch or Czech. The next morning was depressingly overcast. The Scandinavian-Dutch-Czechs were still in their tent as we began walking up the valley of the Rio Paine along an undulating trail.

Early on, I heard a repeated "prrr-prrr-prrr" sound accompanied by a double knocking and stopped to find the noise was coming from the scraggly beech trees along the trail. There was no problem spotting three, large, black birds with pointed, red heads and large bills enthusiastically chopping at the tree trunks. They were male Magellanic woodpeckers, over a foot long, quite tame, and not fazed by my presence. They let me get very close, and I took numerous wonderful photos of the birds.

Obviously they were named for Ferdinand Magellan, but subsequent reading about the birds did not reveal whether the Portuguese sailor was the first European to actually see the species and took credit for their discovery by naming it after himself. Probably not. Magellan had more important things to discover in 1520 when he sailed through the strait at the tip of South America only about a hundred miles south of where I was standing. Magellan may not have named the woodpecker, but the king of Spain made certain the explorer's name would be forever attached to the discovery of the waterway connecting the Atlantic and the Pacific.

It was Magellan, of course, who came up with the term, Patagonia. There are a couple versions to the word's origin. The dominant theory is that summed up by Laurence Bergreen in his story of Magellan's circumnavigation of the earth, *Over the Edge of the World.*

> "Eventually, Magellan gave the Indians a name—*Pathagoni*, a neologism suggesting the Spanish word *patacones,* or dogs with great paws, by which he meant to call attention to their big feet, made even larger by the rough-hewn boots they wore. So, these were the Bigfoot Indians, according to Magellan, who later gave the name to whole region, known ever since as Patagonia."

Bruce Chatwin's theory as to the word's origin is creative and complex enough to confuse the most dedicated etymologist. He credited an unknown Greek sailor, who was with Magellan, with using a Greek word to describe the local Indians. When spoken, the word sounds like our Patagonia. According to Chatwin, Antonio Pigafetta, the Venetian who sailed with Magellan and wrote a journal of the voyage, may have coined the word Patagonia upon hearing the Greek use the word. Chatwin argued that Pigafetta described the Indians as "roaring like bulls" at the sight of Magellan's ship and that the Greek sailor on board used the Greek word, which means 'a roaring' or 'gnashing of teeth.' Chatwin admitted that he could find no record of a Greek sailor on Magellan's ship, but that didn't stop him from arguing that the word Patagonia had Greek roots. He said an Argentinian professor told Chatwin that Magellan may have had a copy of a Spanish fantasy entitled the *Primaleon of Greece* on board, which included a half man/half monster called the "Grand Patagon." Whew!

The second day's walk was just over eleven miles to the refugio and campground at Lake Dickson. By now, we realized that unlike many other long treks we would seldom overtake or be overtaken by other walkers. The lateness of the season—March and the beginning of the austral autumn—was also an obvious factor contributing to the lack of hikers. There seemed to be very few people actually doing the complete Torres del Paine circuit. Although there had been scores of people at the trek's principal trailhead at Guarderia Laguna Amarga, we soon figured out that many simply made the twenty-four-mile round-trip walk up to the iconic granite towers, staying overnight at the refugio near the towers or the campground. Others preferred to do what has become known as "The W," with views of the snout of the Grey Glacier, the wonders of the French Valley (Valley del Francés), and then the towers. The forty-seven-mile route is similar to the shape of the letter "W" and is usually done in four or five days.

"We've decided that we are doing the complete circuit," Morgan had told me when I first showed up in Puerto Natales, crushing any hopes I had of getting off a little easier by simply doing "The W." When we did finish the trek, I always pointed out triumphantly to anyone who asked, "I did the complete circuit, not just 'The W.'"

The trail followed the Río Paine, made milky blue by the glaciers above slowly grinding away at the rock, creating a fine dust, which saturated the water. A couple of hours of climbing brought us to a saddle and a panorama of jagged peaks forming the border between Chile and Argentina. Rather than being picturesque, the grey day, wind, and chill created a sensation of isolation.

"Where exactly are we?" I asked Morgan. We got out the map and attempted to pinpoint our location.

"We're somewhere around here," Morgan said not all that reassuringly.

Ralph tended to be the most taciturn of the three of us during the day but was capable of interjecting wonderful bits of useful information when needed. "Did you know that all the eels of the world migrate to the Sargasso Sea once a year?" he announced at one point during that afternoon in an effort to stimulate discussion and break the monotony of the walk.

"Get out of here," I said, not letting a second elapse without rebutting his factoid. "What about the ones in the Great Lakes between Canada and the U.S.? They'd have to squirm their way through the locks of the St. Lawrence Seaway to make it to the Atlantic Ocean."

"I think it's just the eels in the oceans," Ralph said, back-peddling only slightly.

"Where the hell is the Sargasso Sea anyway?" Morgan interjected.

"How would I know? I'm not an eel. Probably somewhere in the Atlantic," Ralph answered. "But the eels know. They head there every year."

Aided by that stimulating discussion, the seven hours from our first night's camp at Puesto Serón to Refugio Lago Dickson passed by with glacial speed. Late that afternoon, we summited a ridge and the lake came into view. We were tired and relieved to finally see the day's destination. We saw a huge field of ice clinging to a mountain just above the lake where it calved into the milky blue water. It was a scene I had never seen before. There were a few ice chunks floating on the lake's surface. It took us more than an hour, walking the undulating trail before we finally saw a building next to the lake in the distance with the red, white, and blue Chilean flag waving from a pole. Refugio Lago Dickson and its adjoining campsite were relatively upscale. The lodge itself had a small dining room and some bunks. It even had a tiny grocery store with mostly potato chips, pop, beer, and candy bars.

"It's got hot showers we can use," Morgan reported after a brief inspection of the facilities. "And flush toilets."

"How much is the beer?" I asked, revealing my priorities.

There were a few picnic tables scattered throughout the campground, which was located beneath a stand of trees that provided a little extra protection from the periodic rain showers. There were some horses in a corral and four tents at the far end of the campground. The tents were a bright orange and identical. It took us a few days to figure out that the refugios and campgrounds throughout Torres del Paine are all contracted out by the park to private companies and that the tents were sleeping quarters for the employees. They charged us about five bucks to camp.

The bunks were for paying guests, although at this refugio, just one couple was staying in the lodge. The two Californians appeared to want to distance themselves from backpacking trash like us. They had arrived on horseback two days earlier and said they were "just hanging out."

It baffled me for quite some time as to how the concessionaires were able to bring supplies like food to the refugio. We also saw propane canisters used for cooking and providing the hot water for showers next to the refugio, but the canisters were far too big for even horses to carry. Ralph got out his map and solved the mystery.

"They haul the stuff in by boat," he said. "There's a road way up at the end of the lake, maybe thirty miles away. That's how they do it." Other than at the circuit's two trailheads, we would discover that only one other refugio, Refugio Grey, had the ability to bring in supplies by boat.

It took a leap of faith to take a shower. The thing was nothing more than a three-sided closet exposed to the elements with swinging doors for privacy. You shared the shower with the hot water tank and a pipe ran from the tank outside along the ground, where it took in water from an uphill stream. It was all pretty basic, but it worked. Morgan tested the shower and despite having to stand naked and exposed to the 45-degree outside temperature while undressing, toweling off, and dressing, he reported that the experience was sobering but cleansing. Ralph and I avoided confronting the shower for an hour or so but finally caved.

At dusk the two mysterious women who had shown up late the night before arrived. They still carried really big packs, which were larger than any of ours, on their slight body frames.

"You guys made it," I said wondering if I would get a reply in English, Czech or Scandinavian.

"Yes, it was a terribly long day. We're glad to get here," one replied in almost perfect English with a slight accent while simultaneously throwing her pack to the ground as if it were some sort of enemy. They immediately set to work putting up their tent and preparing dinner.

"We tried to figure out your nationality when we heard you talking last night. You guys weren't speaking English. We thought you might be Swedish or Czech? Did we guess right?" I asked.

"We're Israeli," the two said in unison.

"Sorry, we're not very good linguists," I replied.

I had seen Israelis backpacking in other rugged places before. There had been a large group of them on New Zealand's Routeburn Trek. They had all just been discharged from the Israeli army and were using their new freedom to see the world. It was almost a rite of passage. "You've paid you dues, now go have some fun," was the message from their elders.

It seemed that the traditional getaways and activities done by American college kids, like backpacking across Europe, were too mundane for these Israeli army veterans. They wanted bigger challenges. I had also walked with a group of young Israeli army veterans on the Annapurna Circuit in Nepal. Now here were these two women. Sure enough, they told me that they had served as lieutenants in the army.

The two women also represented another backpacking trend. More and more young women seem to be taking to the hills. That's something that you would not have seen a couple of decades ago. Female backpackers, without the accompanying males, are a common sight in the Rocky Mountains of the United States. I had been blown away when I saw a young Ukrainian woman wearing pink sneakers doing the Annapurna Circuit alone. Times were changing. Although we never walked together, the two Israeli women showed up each evening for the rest of the circuit. They were high spirited and tough.

Once again, the women were still in their tent when we began our third day, which would end at Campamiento Los Perros at the base of the dreaded John Garner Pass. It was only about six miles to the next camp, and we stopped frequently to rest, talk, and seek a bit of shelter under trees from the incessant, light rain. The temperature began to drop.

We looked back at views of Lago Dickson and the snout of the ice field dropping into the lake. We climbed above a river valley with the enchanting name of Rio de los Perros (River of the Dogs) and then crossed a second stream with the equally charming name of Rio Cabeza del Indio (Indian Head River) via a log bridge. It was here that we encountered our first trekkers doing the circuit in the opposite clockwise direction. They were a middle-aged, olive-skinned couple. I figured they were Chileans.

"We crossed the pass the day before yesterday in a snowstorm," the woman told us. "It was scary."

We all used the chance meeting as an excuse to drop our packs and chat. They told us that we were the first trekkers they had come across on the trail in three days, although there were a few people at Campamiento Los Perros last night. We exchanged nationalities, and when they told us they were from Turkey, I was somewhat taken aback.

It had taken me only a couple of great treks to realize that the world was getting smaller and that serious backpacking in exotic places wasn't restricted to Americans, Germans, and Canadians. But running into a couple of Turks in the Patagonian Andes was somewhat surprising. They were well dressed and equipped, and I figured they must be high income earners, but I did not have the nerve to ask them their occupations. We hung out for almost an hour eating lunch together. They told us they were doing treks all over the world.

"Last year, we climbed Kilimanjaro, and we're thinking of doing the Sierras in California or something in Canada if we survive this," the man said.

Morgan mentioned the West Coast Trail on Vancouver Island, and they said that they had read about it and that it was on their list. We parted heading in different directions.

"I'll be darned. Turkey," Morgan said. "That's kind of surprising."

A wet snow was falling by the time we arrived at Campamiento Los Perros where a curl of smoke was coming out of a primitive shelter. The structure was no more than a few vertical log posts connected together by a few horizontal logs covered on top by plastic with more logs on top to keep the wind from blowing the plastic away. The walls were made of canvas tied in place, and there was a crude door. There were a couple of rickety tables made of rough lumber, and a wood-burning stove. It was heaven.

Inside, a motley group consisted of three Chilean pseudo-trekkers and a couple of Chilean *vaqueros* who had hauled the three dudes up to this point on horseback. As my son would say, "Some people have too much money." The vaqueros kept the fire going, and by the time everyone had fired up their small propane stoves for dinner, the place became cozy and comfortable. Everyone seemed to have some sort of whiskey or other fortifier, so life was good. It had been snowing, and there about three inches were already on the ground. Morgan was especially excited to see the snow.

"I've seen this only a couple of times in my life," he said. Morgan was from Perth in west Australia, a place that has a Mediterranean climate and seldom has temperatures below freezing. I was not enthused about the snow. Tomorrow's John Garner Pass at over 4,000 feet was the high point of the trek. If there were three inches here, there was bound to be much more on top. But for now, I sipped my whiskey and enjoyed the ambiance of the smoke-filled hut. The Israeli women arrived on schedule that evening and joined in the camaraderie.

While eating dinner, one of the vaqueros noticed that the large plastic mug I was eating out of had the letters NOLS prominently displayed on it. In broken English he told me that he was familiar with the National Outdoor Leadership School and wondered if I had taken one of their courses.

"No," I said. "NOLS is based in Wyoming, and I am from Wyoming." He then told me that an NOLS group had done the Torres del Paine Circuit last year, and he supplied them by horseback. It didn't surprise me that NOLS had been here. The organization had come a long way from its modest beginnings forty years ago in Wyoming's Wind River Mountains and now offered to the young and the restless wilderness adventures anywhere in the world. It was nice to have something in common, coincidental and trivial as it was, with a Chilean cowboy sitting across from me in a smoky hut deep in the Patagonia Andes.

"Who was John Garner?" I asked him. He shrugged his soldiers. I then asked him what we might expect tomorrow going over John Garner Pass especially since it was snowing.

"Don't worry," he laughed "It's a piece of cake."

Although the morning was dreary and windy, the snow had stopped, and we headed up toward the pass. My *Lonely Planet* guidebook said we had to ascend 2,200 feet from our camp to the top of the pass. Not overwhelming but significant.

"Because that's where the money is."

Willie Sutton
1901-1980
(alleged reply when asked why he robbed banks)

My new vaquero friend may not have known anything about John Garner, but Bruce Chatwin included Garner as an interesting sidebar to the tale of Butch Cassidy and the Sundance Kid in his *In Patagonia.* Most are familiar with the story of the two robbers who were the worst thing to happen to banking until sub-prime mortgages. Chatwin and most historians agree that Butch (Robert Parker) and Sundance (Harry Longabaugh) along with Sundance's main squeeze Etta Place ended up in Patagonia in the early years of the last century and that Butch and Sundance may or may not have died in a shootout in Bolivia. However, according to Chatwin, Etta had complained of a grumbling appendix while in Patagonia and wanted to return to Denver for an operation.

"There is another possibility," Chatwin wrote. "…that appendix was a euphemism for baby and that the father was a young Englishman, John Garner, who was ranching in Patagonia for his health."

Maybe as we climbed John Garner Pass, we'd find some clues supporting Chatwin's supposition like the couple's initials scratched on a rock encircled by a heart. We climbed through the exposed terrain to the top of the pass. The weather was gnarly but not so serious that we considered turning back. Painted vertical stakes guided us through the rocks and the spitting snow, and within a couple of hours after leaving camp, we found ourselves looking down on the Great Grey Glacier.

The view was one of the principal reasons for doing the complete circuit rather than the abbreviated "W." It was not disappointing. A river of ice filled the valley some 2,000 feet below. It appeared to be a couple of miles wide and simply disappeared into the northern horizon. One guidebook said it was twelve miles long. For the first time, we had a conception of the scope of the Patagonia Ice Field. Abutting the glacier were uninviting mountains that looked especially forlorn because of the grayness of the day. The scene was one of intimidating isolation and an unexplored glaciated wilderness.

"Do you think anyone has ever been over on those mountains?" Ralph asked me, raising his voice to the wind. It was the right question.

We had been warned that the 2,500-foot descent to Lago Grey, and the next camp was steep, muddy, arduous, and could be dangerous. The warnings were valid. For the next two hours, we hung on to trees and bushes as we slipped down the muddy trail. In the real tricky spots, there were railings installed by park authorities, and even some tall, iron ladders. It was one of the more challenging portions of the entire circuit.

The steepness of the descent was the main reason all the guidebooks recommended doing the circuit in a counterclockwise direction. We made our way over rock-strewn gullies caused by small avalanches, fallen logs, boulder fields, and fast-moving streams. For the last couple of hours, we walked alongside the tongue of Grey Glacier and saw the blueness of the ice for the first time. Bypassing an older primitive campground, we kept walking and camped at Campamiento Paso that night. It was not until the next day that we actually reached the glacier's end and began to see the massive ice floes, which had calved off the glacier's 300-foot high snout and were floating in the northern end of Lago Grey. When we finally camped at Refugio Grey on our fifth night, Morgan managed to get some ice from a small ice floe near shore, and we celebrated our accomplishment by using it to chill the whiskey in our cups.

Refugio Grey is the overnight destination for those doing the "W" from the park's other main trailhead at Refugio Pehoé and wanting to see at least the snout of the Grey Glacier. It's a "full service" facility with a few bunk beds, a restaurant, and hot showers. There were six or seven tents when we arrived in the early afternoon. We were now only eleven k's from the trailhead at Lago Pehoé. We felt like we were almost back in civilization, especially when we noticed a boat passing through the ice floes on Lago Grey, carrying provisions to the refugio. The three of us were inspired at the sight of the boat unloading its cargo, and Ralph summarized our common thoughts succinctly. "Let's drink some beer," he said.

We were well into our second can of Austral Lager, brewed in Puerto Natales with a picture of the Cuernos del Paine Mountains on the label, when the Israeli women showed up right on schedule.

"We were worried about you guys," Morgan said.

"We spent last night at the old campground," they explained. "We were just too tired to go any farther. Yesterday crossing the pass was the hardest day of our trip."

"It couldn't be that bad," I said. "You guys are veterans of one of the toughest and most respected fighting forces in the world—the Israeli Army. How does this trek compare to your basic training experience?"

"It's much more difficult, especially with the cold and rain. And we're carrying way too much weight. If those early Zionists had put Israel in Patagonia instead of Palestine, it would have gone under in a week. We're desert flatlanders."

Morgan and I agreed that the Torres del Paine Circuit was more exhausting than the West Coast Trail on Vancouver Island, which we had done together. Looking back, I would also consider it more difficult than the much longer Annapurna Circuit. A porter carried most of my stuff on the Annapurna Circuit, and I spent every night in a bed with a roof over it. I never cooked meals either. They were prepared for me.

Before setting off, I wandered through the campground, looking at tent brands. The Israelis told us they had rented their tents in Punta Arenas for about $10 a day. We had seen a number of tents like theirs and it made sense. Why hassle a tent for your entire trip when you need it only for the nights you're actually trekking? They told us that you could rent most anything in Punta Arenas including sleeping bags and even backpacks. We saw many tents with the same brand as theirs at various camps, so it must have been a common procedure for many trekkers.

Most of the other tents were recognizable brands—Marmot, Sierra Designs, and North Face were common. On this morning, one tent, however, caught my eye. It was a Hilleberg, the Holy Grail of lightweight backpacking shelters. They're made in Sweden and can cost as much as $750. I had never actually seen one before. The owners were having breakfast, and I complimented them on their choice of tent. They were Dutch.

"We wouldn't buy another one," the young woman told me. "One of the poles broke the first time we used it last year. When I contacted the company, they refused to replace it for free and of course it cost us like $50 for a new one." Not a very good testimonial.

We started walking along the length of Lago Grey, heading for Refugio Lago Pehoé. It should have been an easy downhill seven-mile walk, but Morgan started developing knee problems. I realized how significant his knee problem was when I found myself in the lead most of the time. That rarely happened. I was the slow one. At one point, I put my pack down and waited almost half an hour before he and Ralph appeared. As they approached, I could see that Morgan was actually walking backward down the steep sections of the trail. He was in pain.

"Maybe I bit off more than I could chew," he said with a cheery Aussie demeanor. The thought of having to get Morgan carried out to safety went through my mind, but he kept slowly truckin' along. During our entire trek, we had not seen a single park ranger of any sort, although there seemed to be full-time employees at the refugios. An injured hiker apparently had to depend on his comrades if he got in trouble. During our trek along Vancouver Island's coast, I had developed some semi-serious foot problems. Morgan had slowed his pace considerably in order to give me moral support as I crippled along.

This time, Ralph stuck by Morgan, and he eventually straggled into Refugio Lago Pehoé. The refugio was the main trailhead for doing the "W" and trekkers took the bus from Puerto Natales to Refugio Pudeto, got ferried across Lago Pehoé, and began their hike. From this point on, we frequently ran into hikers, and they were usually a welcome diversion to the sometime monotony of the trek's longer stretches. Refugio Pehoé had nearly every amenity. Hot showers, cold beer, a restaurant, and bunks. There was even an enormous Buckminster Fuller-type shelter with electricity, sinks, tables and chairs, and facilities for preparing meals. Not having to worry about our meal being interrupted by rain was especially welcome. The place was full of trekkers, and it was fun to bounce around the room, striking up conversations with half the world. Unswerving in our commitment to tent the entire circuit, we did not even bother to check for any vacancies in the hostel but headed for the campground.

The next morning, Morgan insisted his knee had improved, and we marched on to the next campground nine miles away along the base of the famous Cuernos peaks. At times, the hiking seemed endless as the track undulated over the hills along Lago Skottsberg and then the ten-mile-long Lago Nordenskjold. The vista was pure Patagonia. The view across the lake was uninterrupted by a single manmade object. Beyond the lake was an expanse of pristine steppe ending in distant mountains capped with snow and ice.

There was another major highlight of the trek along the way. We stopped for lunch at the mouth of Valle del Francés (The French Valley) and witnessed one of nature's premier mountain shows. At first, we thought we were hearing the sound of thunder as a loud rumbling repeatedly echoed down the valley. But what we were listening to was the sound of avalanches coming off Cerro Paine Grande, the park's highest mountain. We stood with necks arched, watching the spectacle. High above, we could see the burst of snow explode on the mountain well before the sound reached us below. I stood mesmerized. The experience was a first for me, and I had to force myself to get on trekking.

Later that afternoon, we saw three Andean condors making lazy circles high in the sky. The lack of perspective against the sky made the actual size of the birds, with their eight-foot wingspans, difficult to appreciate. We had no trouble appreciating the moment, however.

Our last night camping was at Campamiento Chileno near the base of the actual Torres del Paine towers. That afternoon, Ralph and I walked partway up the trail above the campground along Ascencio Valley for a better look at the park's namesake shafts of granite. "This is one of the most scenic sights in the world," one of the park brochures said, stating the obvious.

The campground adjoined a refugio, and we went inside to fire up our stoves, using the same tables on which the paying guests were eating. We knew we were pushing our luck and, sure enough, one of the staff politely but firmly told us that although we could eat inside, we had to cook outside. Fair enough. The place was packed with guests and tenters who had hiked up from our starting point eight days earlier at Refugio Laguna Amarga. There were a few who were beginning the complete circuit and some like us who had just completed it. A kind of international revelry broke out as everyone realized we were at a very special place, and it was unlikely that many would ever be here again.

There was plenty of beer and wine to lubricate the celebration, and a group of four Danes broke into song. Improbably Morgan and I joined in the singing, although "Copenhagen"' was the only Danish word we knew.

Ralph, Morgan, and I parted ways after busing back to Puerto Natales. We said our farewells over bowls of seafood chowder at the same restaurant where we had eaten the evening before our adventure began. They were headed north to Argentina's Parque Nacional Los Glaciares and Mount Fitz Roy where I had been earlier. I was catching the morning bus to Punta Arenas, Chile, before flying home.

"Well, we pulled off another one, Ric," Morgan said. "What's next?"

"You know, I've been thinking about the GR20 in Corsica."

"Let me know, but I don't speak any French."

"Me neither," I said. "My second language is Danish."

▲△▲

Punta Arenas proved more interesting than expected, and I immediately wished I had more than an afternoon to explore this city, which was almost as far south as it gets in the western hemisphere. For $40, one could take a tour of the nearby penguin colony. I'd never seen a penguin in the wild. Indigenous women were selling crafts and hand-knit alpaca sweaters on the city's main square, the Plaza de Armas. A memorial to Ferdinand Magellan stood in the plaza and reminded me that the body of water I could see just down the street was the famous strait named in honor of the earth's first circumnavigator. Magellan passed by here in 1520 on his way to gaining immortality in every junior high school geography book. I walked by a small restaurant appropriately named THE BEAGLE CAFÉ. In 1833, Captain Fitz Roy sailed the *HMS Beagle* through these waters with his famous passenger, Charles Darwin. Had he known them, Darwin could have used the two Israeli women as proof for his theory of natural selection and the survival of the fittest.

As I watched the waves of the Strait of Magellan chop against Punta Arenas's embarcadero, I couldn't help but wonder what time of the year the eels started heading back to the Sargasso Sea.

Lake McKellar Hut
1 hr
McKellar Saddle
1 hr 30 min
Upper Caples Hut
5 - 7 hr
Lake Howden Hut
1 hr

6

New Zealand

Captain Cook and the Lord of the Rings

Caples, Greenstone, Kepler, & Routeburn Tracks 86 miles

My arrival at Auckland's international airport and through the typical customs procedures was interrupted by unfamiliar questions. Carrying a backpack quickly identified me as a trekker.

"Are your boots new?" An official asked.

"No," I responded, puzzled by the question.

"You'll have to take them off and have them cleaned," he told me. "Do you have a tent? Is it used?"

"Yes, I've had it for a couple of years."

"I'll have to have that too. We need to clean it."

Apparently New Zealand had come full circle in its attitude toward the introduction of foreign species into the islands. Before the arrival of Europeans, New Zealand's flora and fauna were unique. Being separated from other land masses, the islands developed a solitary ecosystem with scores of undiscovered species. Birds occupied a particularly singular dominant position in the animal chain. Having no natural enemies (the bat being the only mammal), they wandered through the flora with little to fear, and some species, like the kiwi and the moa, lost their ability to fly through evolution. Humans arriving on the islands unfortunately interrupted this peculiar balance because they imported a variety of mammals hostile to birds. The Maori showed up around A.D. 900, carrying dogs and rats in their canoes and quickly hunted the moa into extinction. But the real environmental damage was done by the Europeans, who carried in their ships so many mammals alien to New Zealand that Noah would have taken notes. Native species of fauna were decimated by frogs, dogs, possums, goats, pigs, and horses. Endemic plant life was also challenged as the arriving British insisted creating a "new" England and introduced pine, bushy gorse, and all kinds of fruits and berries. New Zealand's ecology was irreparably damaged.

Now, in an effort to make up for past sins, the government of New Zealand has declared war on all foreign species, even tiny insects, seeds, and mole spores that may have been hiding in my tent and boots. My boots and tent were sprayed with some sort of insecticide. The procedure took about thirty minutes and another fifteen to properly shove my tent back into its stuff bag and restore order to my backpack.

"If I had known you guys were going to do this, I would have brought my laundry," I said sarcastically. The foreign species prevention officer responded with an intimidating glare. (I restrained from asking him if there was any plan to send the most intrusive invasive species—white people—back to Europe and handing the country back to the Maori.) I trotted off quickly in order to avoid recrimination caused by my loose tongue and to catch my connecting flight to Queenstown on the South Island.

New Zealand is not the only nation in a quandary over the introduction of non-native plants and animals. The United States has a very subjective policy when it comes to the introduction of foreign species. U. S. Department of Agriculture inspectors examine luggage of arriving tourists at international airports for illicit cheeses, sausages, hams, and fruits that might contain harmful bacteria and molds. For decades, immigration policies favored Anglo-Saxons and northwestern Europeans over Africans, Orientals, and Caribbeans. Miles of fencing have been constructed to prevent the illegal entry of Mexicans into the United States.

Certain foreign species, however, are encouraged. There would be an enormous outcry from American hunters and fishermen if environmental authorities announced that efforts were being made to eliminate the German brown trout or the Chinese ring-necked pheasant. And few of us are opposed to lining the streets of eastern cities with the Dutch elm or having a Scotch pine in our living room at Christmas. And then there's always the question of Brussels sprouts.

Despite my cynicism, one rarely hears anything negative about New Zealand's neo-conservatives criticizing the hallmark plank of the country's foreign policy, which prohibits nuclear powered vessels, like submarines, from entering its waters. That policy, adopted in 1984, is a burr under the saddle of its staunchest allies like Britain, France, and the United States who would like to use New Zealand's ports to supply and repair its nuclear-powered aircraft carriers and submarines. Others might criticize the country for its subjugation of the native Maori in the nineteenth century. And although New Zealand does not engage in commercial whaling, eco-greens have criticized the government for not taking a tougher stand against Japan, Norway, and Iceland that hunt whales in the nearby international waters.

But for most, New Zealand has a warm and fuzzy image, and tourism has become a mainstay of its economy.

In recent years, the South Island, and especially Queenstown, has become the adventure capital of the world, and thrill seekers head there to challenge the forces of gravity with jet boats, mountain bikes, whitewater rafts, sails, surfboards, skis, and bungee cords. In 1986 New Zealand's A.J. Hackett brought bungee jumping to international prominence when he attached a glorified rubber band to his leg and jumped from the Eiffel Tower. River sledging has also gained in popularity, but if you don't know what it is by now, you're probably too old to learn.

Fortunately plain old-fashioned hiking is still an accepted recreational activity, and trekkers come from across the world to hike the Southern Alps. Not particularly high but rising precipitously from sea level, the range extends the entire length of the South Island and includes the country's highest peak, Mount Cook (12,313 feet). New Zealand's hikers refer to themselves as trampers. Tramping took hold in the late nineteenth century, and construction of the nation's most famous hiking trail—the Milford Track—occurred in 1888. The thirty-three-mile walk through Fiordland National Park passes across alpine meadows, rainforests, and stunning waterfalls. It begins at Lake Te Anau, then winds up the Clinton River, and crosses Mackinnon Pass before following the Arthur River to Milford Sound. Like Canada's West Coast Trail, it's promoted as "The Finest Walk in the World." Its fame has resulted in it becoming crowded, expensive, and highly regulated. The fact that all hikers are required to walk in the same direction, from Lake Te Anau to Milford, helps bring some sense of isolation to the trek. Transportation is available by boat and bus to and from the trailheads, and hut fees can total $300. *Lonely Planet's Tramping in New Zealand* doesn't mince words in stating its opinion of the Milford. "If regulations, high cost, and lack of wilderness outweigh outstanding scenic value, skip this track."

The resort city of Queenstown sits on the shores of Lake Wakatipu with mountain vistas nearly everywhere. I didn't like it. It was a cross between Aspen, Colorado, and a sterilized New Orleans. It was hectic, touristy, upscale, and almost crass. If rural New Zealand charm is what you're after, you won't find it in Queenstown. It had the demeanor of an adventure theme park, and of course that's exactly the image the chamber of commerce wants. Sadly as more and more travelers journey to find rustic getaways, they find more and more Queenstowns. There are some places out there, but it takes a bit of looking. Avoid Fort William, Scotland, and head for Glen Coe or Mallaig. There's lots of shopping in Victoria, B.C., but Port Renfrew is more to my liking. El Calafate, Argentina, is nice, but El Chalten is better. Great getaway towns need rough edges. Yuppie Missoula and Bozeman are not really what Montana is supposed to be all about. Jackson should have been expunged from the map of Wyoming long ago and relocated in California. For me, the final nail in the coffin occurred when the iconic Jackson Drug on the town square closed some years ago, and an upscale shop specializing in Asian rugs took its place. "Hey, honey, while we're here in Wyoming, let's pick up an Oriental rug."

Walking the tourist area of Queenstown, I was approached by a young woman who handed me a menu. She was promoting a restaurant. "We've got a happy hour tonight," she said politely. Restaurants in Jackson Hole and Aspen, still in the Dark Ages, just slip a menu under the windshield wiper of your vehicle.

I had the foresight to book a hostel reservation in Queenstown before I left the United States. It was a wise decision. Lodging in most N.Z. resort towns can be expensive and difficult to get during the summer tourist season. The Black Sheep Backpackers Hostel was crowded, and a bit dirty, but the price was right.

The only thing older than me in the place was the furniture. The majority of the inhabitants were college kids. From the nature of the advertisements on the hostel's bulletin board, the main attraction seemed to be heart-stopping activities like para-gliding and bungee jumping. About ten kids were sitting around the small bar and on the porch, drinking beer as their flip flops dangled from their toes.

I struck up a conversation with an American couple from Illinois. "I'm taking a semester off from school," the shaggy-haired guy said. "This is supposed to be my senior year, but I liked it down here, so I decided to stay longer." The two said they were "attending" Western Illinois University. (The fact that it was March, and that they are about as far away from the state of Illinois as they can get, and were admittedly in no hurry to return to their studies at WIU didn't stop them from using the word "attending.")

"Aren't your athletic teams called the Leathernecks?" I said trying to relate to them.

"How would you possibly know that?" the surprised coed answered. "Did you go there?"

"No. I've just spent most of my adult life filling my brain with useless information."

"Tomorrow I'm doing the jump from Kawarau Bridge," the young man told me. "We went up there today and I booked it." He explained that the 140-foot bungee leap was one of the more popular jumps. The Kawarau jump was not the highest in the Queenstown area. The Pipeline over Skippers Canyon provided a 334-foot bounce, and something called the Nevis Highwire offered a 440-foot free fall toward the river bottom below before the bungee kicked in and saved the jumper from death. These jumps were not cheap, running anywhere from $125 to $200. The two didn't ask me why I had come to New Zealand. I was relieved. Trekking suddenly seemed so twentieth century, and my appreciation for intentionally jumping off structures was confined to Billie Joe McAllister and the Tallahatchie Bridge.

His girlfriend was not in any rush to return to college either. "I'm thinking about getting some sort of job down here," she told me. "Maybe next year, I'll go back to school." I had run into these short-term American expatriate students all across the globe. They had all kinds of reasons for not being in class, from sabbaticals to work-study programs. You'll find American college kids in Siena and Florence, in Paris and Lyon, and even India. Granada, Spain, seemed to be a particular popular destination. When my wife Rosemary and I were there a few years ago, there were scores of American college women claiming to be in some sort of foreign studies program. When I teased a few about their reason for being in Spain, they all testified that they were there studying Spanish. Judging by the frequency with which we saw them in Granada's bars, the bistro had replaced the college classroom. Parental love is unconditional.

Exhausted from my flight halfway around the world, I headed for my dorm room. There were seven other bunks in the room, and, despite the fact it is nearly 10:00 p.m., they were all empty. When I awoke in the morning, every bed was occupied. I had slept hard and never heard any of them arrive. What could they have been doing so late? Studying English as a foreign language?

That morning while I strolled around town, I stumbled upon a small cemetery. It was a mellow place hiding in a corner of busy Queenstown. Two headstones caught my eye. They were the resting places of a couple of Brits who were members of an expedition involved in the early twentieth-century frenzy to explore Antarctica and reach the South Pole, a race won by Norway's Roald Amundsen in 1911. Their graves jerked me into a realization of just how far south on the globe I had traveled. The South Island had been a jumping-off spot for some of those early Antarctic expeditions.

Trekkers headed for New Zealand are usually advised to have a reservation for some of the more popular tracks before arriving, although a couple of Web site chat room users had said that solo trekkers can get the necessary permits if they were flexible. I arrived in New Zealand with no set trekking schedule and not a single permit or trekking reservation. My first stop the next morning at the Department of Conservation (DOC) office in Queenstown validated my decision. I had targeted the Routeburn, Kepler, Caples, Greenstone, and Milford Tracks as my preferred destinations. The Routeburn, Milford, and Kepler Tracks were classified as "Great Walks" by the DOC, and permits to hike them were supposed to be notoriously difficult to get. Hiking these "Great Walks" was on the bucket list of every serious trekker. Mine was a shotgun approach. I'd take whatever permit the DOC offered. I already knew that, except for the Milford Track where camping is not allowed, it's not so hard to get permits to simply hike the track, but securing tickets to sleep in the huts along the track can be tough. You can camp with your tent, but because of the frequency and tenacity of the rain, sleeping in the huts is the way to go. During my treks, I saw only a handful of tenters, and because of the rain, some of them erected their tents on the porch under the extended protective roof of the huts.

"We had a cancellation for the day after tomorrow for the Kepler Track. You'll need reservations at three different huts along the track, and I can make them for you now," the woman at the DOC desk told me. It was easy. Life is good.

I give her $50 for the three hut reservations, and a couple hours later, I was on a bus headed through rural New Zealand to a town called Te Anau on the edge of Fiordland National Park. Te Anau is the jumping off spot for the Kepler Track.

"Some weasel took the cork out of my lunch."

W.C. Fields
1880-1946

The two-hour bus ride to Te Anau was the first opportunity I had to see rural New Zealand. As expected, it was pastoral and green. There were millions of domestic sheep.

I have long wondered exactly who eats all the mutton that's raised in this world. Someone in New Zealand told me that Muslims like mutton. It certainly isn't the Americans.

I thought I was seeing things the first time I saw them, but looking out the window, I spotted large, fenced areas enclosing red deer. They were big creatures resembling the elk found in the American Rocky Mountains. The fenced herds seemed to number in the hundreds. Red deer were introduced into New Zealand from Europe for sport in the mid-1800s and, like the possum, soon became a nuisance as they competed with sheep and cattle for grazing forage. By the twentieth century, the government had declared an all-out war on the red deer in an attempt to reduce their numbers. Today they're raised on farms, and the venison is exported. There's a liberal hunting quota too. I never saw one in the wild, however.

A young couple, John Hohl and Dawn Wilburn from Michigan, were sitting across from me on the bus. They told me they came down to do some trekking, but their primary interest was fishing for big trout. Rainbow and brown trout are yet another introduced species and, like Patagonia, lots of Americans head south to catch them rather than staying home all winter, tying flies and waiting for the ice to go off our streams and lakes. I had brought along my rod, and, although fly fishing was not the primary motivation for my trip, I was planning on at least trying it.

The bus stopped in front of something called the Te Anau Holiday Park. We saw some tents on the grass behind the main building. "Let's go for it," John said "This looks as good as anywhere." The three of us piled off the bus with our gear. Across the street was an enormous sheet of water. Lake Te Anau stretched for forty miles and was the second largest lake in the country. It abutted Fiordland National Park, and the famous peaks of the southern Alps rose abruptly from the far shoreline. The Holiday Park was a gem. Although it offered a full range of accommodations including private rooms and dorms with bunks, the tent sites proved to be a real deal. We were able to pitch our tents for about $10 a night. Included was the use of a hot shower, a communal kitchen, and a dining room. Te Anau's Holiday Park became my trekking base and I took full advantage of its amenities. The grocery store was just down the street, and I cooked my food in the kitchen. There was even a television lounge. I learned, however, that in New Zealand, it seemed there was only one TV program worth watching. Its national rugby team, the All Blacks, dominated the tube. When they were not playing, the TV stations run reruns of their matches, followed by reruns of the reruns.

I had waffled about taking my tent during the planning stage of my trip. The consensus in the guidebooks and on the Web was that a tent was not needed because trekkers stayed in the huts when they are hiking. That was true. I never stayed in my tent on any of my New Zealand treks but rather in the huts. But, except for the two bookend nights in Queenstown at each end of my trekking adventure, I stayed in my tent every night that I was in this or that town between treks. Not only were the more sophisticated accommodations like motels, hotels, and B&Bs expensive, they were tough to book. Every morning in Te Anau, I witnessed tourists and trekkers lined up at pay phones or using their cell phones desperately trying to find a place to sleep that night or the next. Bringing my tent was the smartest thing I did, although it felt a bit odd leaving it in one of the Holiday Park's storage lockers when I actually went off to trek.

It was raining that first afternoon in Te Anau, but it didn't stop John from remembering why he came to New Zealand. "Let's go fishing," he announced not twenty minutes after we'd set up our tents.

"Where?"

"I don't know, but where there's a big lake, there's rivers. Someone at the store where we buy our licenses will tell us," he said with all the authority of a man that had fished strange places before.

A couple of hours later, after walking a hefty distance out of town through the rain, John, Dawn, and I were casting flies on the water. The river was swollen from the rains, and I waded through knee-deep overflow just to get to the riverbank. John and Dawn, more serious than I about fishing, were wearing waders. It was getting dark. It was cold. The water was far too turbulent. It was raining hard and it was miserable. No matter, we were fly fishing in New Zealand. We weren't just talking about it.

After about an hour, John faced the reality of the weather and made an announcement. "Let's go drink some beer." John was a wise man. The Moose Bar and Café provided welcome relief from the cold and rain. Dawn and I slid on to our bar stools as John headed for the bathroom. The place was not particularly interesting. The only thing that distinguished the bar from any tavern in the United States were the names of the beers. SPEIGHT'S and STEINLAGER seemed to dominate the signage, and after a bit of hands-on research, I figured these brands were the Budweisers and Millers of New Zealand. Later research revealed that just like home, there were lots of local craft beers, like Monteith's and Emerson's that were more to my liking. They were hoppy and full of character.

"What's with the name Moose Bar?" I asked our bartender. He told us that a number of years ago, moose from Canada were transplanted to Fiordland National Park. "It didn't work. The DOC said that people kept shooting them, but I think there was something about the vegetation that wasn't suitable for them. We decided not to change the name of the bar. It gives it character."

Turned out there was more to the story of Fiordland's moose. Ten moose from Saskatchewan were introduced on to the South Island in 1910. The last authenticated sighting was in 1952 in the Dusky Sound area of the park. But like Sasquatch and the Yeti, sightings continued to be reported. Ken Tustin, a wildlife scientist, spent almost forty years trying to document the continued presence of moose. In 2001 DNA testing verified that a hair sample found by Tustin, hanging from a tree was from a moose. More recently, a fuzzy video of an apparent moose taken by Tustin raised further speculation of the creature's existence. New Zealand university students even produced a documentary on the mysterious moose of South Island. The film was scheduled to be shown in December 2011 in Dunedin at two Moose Bars. (Where else?)

John returned and announced that he has been doing some important research. "I watched which way the water was spinning when it went down the sink drain," he said.

"I forgot about that. Good job. What'd you decide?" I asked.

"Well, it went down counterclockwise, just like in Michigan," he reported.

"That's disappointing. All this way for nothing. I thought they were supposed to drain in opposite directions. I also read somewhere that cyclones rotate in opposite directions in the northern and southern hemispheres," I said.

Dawn interrupted us. "Cyclones are only in the southern hemisphere. I think they're called tornadoes in the northern hemisphere."

"What's the difference between hurricanes and typhoons? This is getting serious. We need another beer," I said. John mumbled something to Dawn about hair whorls. I wanted to know more.

John knew more. "Well, from what I read, the direction of the whorl of hair on the back of our heads is determined by the hemisphere in which our ancestors lived over hundreds of generations. If you studied the hair whorls on the heads of babies in the northern hemisphere their whorl would rotate in the opposite direction of a baby's in the southern hemisphere."

"You mean the bartender's whorl is different than mine?" I said.

"No, it takes countless generations for the effect to kick in," John explained with a straight face. "The bartender's ancestors were probably from Britain. We need to find a Maori and check out the back of his head."

"We'll do that first thing in the morning. Let's have another beer," I responded.

Dawn brought the beer-enhanced conversation to a welcome close but couldn't quite let go. "What about horse racing? I think in Australia and New Zealand they race counter-clockwise, and back home we race clockwise. Does that have anything to do with this?" she quipped.

The next morning, the three of us were at the DOC office bright and early. I already had my hut reservations for the Kepler Track and was interested in seeing what else was available. It was still raining.

"Oh, there are lots of permits available," the park person explained. "It's raining here and snowing up in the mountains. We're encouraging people not do the Kepler Track for a couple of days until the weather clears. We've closed the Milford Track due to the extreme mud. Lots of people have cancelled everything."

John and Dawn were not fazed by the report. Like me, they'd come too far to let a little rain dampen their enthusiasm. They went ahead and bought the necessary permits for the Kepler. I seized the opportunity provided by the bad weather and got reservations for huts along the Caples and Routeburn Tracks for next week. I was a happy guy. Despite all the rumors about the difficulty of securing hut reservations, I now had reservations for three of the most storied New Zealand tracks. Two of them, the Routeburn and Kepler, were officially classified as "Great Walks." Maybe the weather would clear.

Later that morning, we jumped on the shuttle bus to the Kepler Track trailhead. We were excited. We would have been more excited if it wasn't raining. The Kepler was a four-day loop of twenty-eight miles that began and ended just outside of Te Anau. It was only a nine-mile tramp to that day's destination, the Mt. Luxmoore Hut. We walked along the edge of Lake Te Anau and passed a beech tree forest. Exotic ferns bordered the track, and we soon crossed a swing bridge. The bridge over the small stream reminded me that I wasn't in Kansas anymore. There must be swing bridges in the national parks and wilderness areas of the Rocky Mountains, but I couldn't recall any. Swing bridges proved to be common along the South Island's tracks. Some are suspended unnervingly high over the river and made you pray the builders knew what they were doing. There was a signpost at a beach, and we began a steep climb. After a couple of hours, we broke out of our bushy surroundings. Our *Lonely Planet Tramping in New Zealand* promised a sweeping panorama of the lake below and the mountains of Fiordland National Park. It didn't happen. Much of the vista was shrouded in mist and low-level clouds.

Occasionally a trekker, smarter than us, passed in the opposite direction, heading down. "I got up this morning at the Luxmoore Hut and tried to keep going over the saddle, but it was snowing. I'm going back," one guy told us." We were not easily intimidated and donned our rain pants, rain jackets, and pack covers. Much of the South Island is famous for its torrential rain, but it wasn't actually supposed to happen when I showed up. After all, I'd come a long way, and the trip cost a lot of money. Besides, according to the government of New Zealand, this is, "One of the World's Great Walks." Did they factor in the climate when they made that pronouncement?

We finally saw the hut straddling a ridge in the distance. We had gained nearly the 3,000-foot elevation since leaving the lake. The hut, with Mt. Luxmoore visible through the low clouds just beyond, was a welcome sight. The term "hut" was misleading. Like all the huts on the Kepler, Caples, and Routeburn Tracks, it is big. This one had fifty bunk beds. There was a large dining area, a kitchen equipped with propane stoves, and flush toilets. There was also a warden at every hut who checked to see that you had a permit, sometimes gave a short talk in the evening, and made certain that you were out and gone by 10:00 a.m. The cost of a bunk in a hut can vary depending on the season but can be as high as $40 a night. We hunkered down for the night with an eclectic bunch of fellow trekkers from around the world. All were frustrated with the weather.

Our hopes for clear weather in the morning were not realized. It was windy, and there was a steady drizzle along with some snow flurries. John and Dawn decided to head back down, retracing yesterday's steps. It was twelve miles of exposed high-level trekking to the Iris Burn Hut, and I decided to go for it. I didn't go far before a ranger appeared out of the low clouds that were hugging the trail and told me that they'd closed the track until the weather cleared. Reluctantly, I turned and headed back for Te Ainu. It was a long and lonely slog but at least it was mostly downhill.

The next morning, the weather seemed to be improving. John and Dawn said they were going to hang out and do some fishing. I was not giving up on the Kepler and headed for the DOC office to get new hut permits. "Because of the weather, more people have been coming out of the mountains than going in," the guy behind the desk told me. "There's lots of vacancies." He patiently re-permitted my entire itinerary including the Routeburn and Caples Tracks. He also explained that I could even walk the Greenstone Track after the Caples. Hut reservations were not necessary on the Greenstone because it was not within the boundaries of a national park but rather in some sort of protected natural area. I placed all my trust in the DOC and signed up. I even got credit for my two unused hut permits on the Kepler. New Zealand's DOC people were very accommodating.

My plan was to walk the Kepler Track in four days, staying at the Moturau Hut, Iris Burn Hut, and finally the Mt. Luxmoore again. Early on, I fell in with an Australian. Michael Rolfe was from Brisbane and upbeat despite the events leading up to this trek.

"My girlfriend and I were packing for this trip when she lays it on me," Michael told me. "We were actually putting stuff in our backpacks when she announced that not only is she not tramping the Routeburn, she's not tramping down the aisle with me either. We were supposed to be married this summer."

"Tramping down the aisle can sometimes be pretty dangerous," I responded in an effort to inject a bit of humor into the situation as we continued to walk across the bluff overlooking the Waiau River.

"Are you still going to get married?" I asked

"Oh, sure," he said with surprising confidence. "I just don't know to whom."

The rain had finally stopped and my trek around the Kepler Track was all I expected of New Zealand. A boardwalk got us across the Amoeboid Mire. Swing bridges carried us over cascading streams, and endless switchbacks took us to new heights. Nearly clear weather provided us with views of Lake Te Anau's South Fiord and the Darran Mountains where Edmund Hillary trained for Everest. At one point on the approach to Iris Burn Hut, we walked along a boardwalk suspended along the side of steep precipice. There was water everywhere. Distant lakes, fast-flowing rivers, lush greenery, and mountain panoramas dominated the three days. It was a grand adventure. I felt a sense of accomplishment. I had knocked off one of New Zealand's "Great Walks."

I killed a day exploring Te Anau. The town appeared to be a destination for British pensioners, and scores of them were walking along the shores of Lake Te Anau. Some of them were holding hands. Shops selling clothing made from New Zealand wool seem to dominate the tourist area. The prices were steep, but the multitude of Japanese tourists didn't seem to mind as they emerged from the stores, loaded with woolen sweaters.

I stumbled upon a lawn-bowling match and took a seat to watch the action. The game seemed to be some sort of variation on Italian bocce ball, but rather than being played on dirt, the battle was waged on a manicured lawn. I could feel the tension. The players on both teams were clothed totally in white including their shoes. Their apparel reminded me of something the staff members at a psychiatric hospital might wear. The atmosphere was very staid, and the only sound was the rapping of colliding balls followed by a mumbled murmur of satisfaction or dismay from the combatants. New Zealand can be very polite. I left before I fell asleep.

It was Saturday, and there was a bake sale at one of the Anglican churches. Still in a celebratory mood from my completion of the Kepler, I bought a large chocolate cake. It was a big hit with my fellow trekkers that evening at the Holiday Park campground.

"The face of the country bears a very rugged
aspect being full of high craggy hills."

Captain James Cook
1728-1779
(describing South Island's Fiordland coast in 1770)

The first European to arrive in New Zealand was the Dutchman, Abel Tasman, who showed up in 1642, only to have three of his crew murdered by natives on his only landing attempt probably because they refused to have their boots fumigated. He got the hint and sailed away. Tasman's greatest legacy may be in naming of the islands 'Zeeland' after a province in the Netherlands. It was the Englishman Captain James Cook who literally put the archipelago, consisting of two main islands and a few smaller ones, on the world map. Cook was arguably Britain's greatest sailor. Between 1768 and 1780, he circumnavigated the world three times, stopping and exploring New Zealand on each trip. Cook was the first guy to figure out that New Zealand consisted of two main islands and therefore not connected to an anticipated but not-yet-discovered southern continent. He sailed completely around South Island in 1770 in the HMS Endeavour. He left his permanent mark on the islands by naming countless geographic features including the Banks Peninsula, Dusky Sound, Endeavour Inlet, and Queen Charlotte Sound. Cook refused to sail into narrow Doubtful Sound because he was 'doubtful' that once inside the narrow fiord, there would be sufficient wind to blow him back out to the ocean. The significance of his explorations was saluted by NASA when it named the space shuttle after his ship. Cook, who bumped into all kinds of Polynesians on his adventures, from Tahitians to Hawaiians, pointed out that the Maori of New Zealand were the first to use colored inks for their tattoos. Today's rockers owe them a debt of gratitude. Like Magellan, he ended up being murdered by natives on a faraway beach. His 'round the world adventures came to an abrupt end in Hawaii in 1779 when he was stabbed in the back by a native using a dagger. The chiefs honored Cook's bravery by eating his heart.

In making my hut reservations the second time for the Routeburn and Caples Tracks at the DOC office in Te Anau, I discovered that I had not paid enough attention to the specifics of the logistics. The Routeburn, the Caples, and the less-publicized Greenstone Tracks were all connected, but in order to access my Routeburn trailhead, I would have to bus back through Queenstown to the village of Glenorchy on the east side of the Humboldt Mountains divide. From there, I could knock off all three tracks.

Glenorchy was a tiny place tucked along the northern end of Lake Wakatipu about thirty miles north of Queenstown. The picturesque town had a population of less than a thousand with just enough rough edges to make me feel that I had stumbled on some place a bit off the beaten path. It's rural and bucolic. It may have been off the beaten path, but it was the hub for trekkers aiming to walk some of New Zealand's most famous tracks. Besides the Routeburn, Caples and Greenstone, it also was the principal access point for the Rees-Dart Track, which some guidebooks said was the toughest of the four. Thrill seekers can also book a two-hour jet boat ride up the Dart River. Backpacker Express Bus Company provided efficient and economical shuttles to the trailheads. I put my tent up at the Glenorchy Holiday Park. The place didn't have the same level of amenities as its namesake in Te Anau, but it worked for me.

With a day to kill before heading for the Routeburn, I wandered the town. For the discriminating shopper, there was a funny little shop selling an assortment of wallets, gloves, and clothing made from possum fur and leather. The bush tail possum was introduced into the islands with the hope of establishing a trade in possum fur products, but the creature had no natural enemies. It didn't take authorities long to realize that messing with Mother Nature was a huge mistake. The possum decimated the eggs and the young of New Zealand's flightless bird species. In addition, they have been linked to a strain of tuberculosis that can be transmitted to cattle. Possum are nocturnal. I never saw one in the wild, but I did see a photograph documenting the extent of the problem—a leafless tree had more than twenty of the adult marsupials clinging to the branches and five or six have young clinging to their mothers' backs. Cheap cardboard possum traps were available in stores everywhere. New Zealand had declared war on the possum, but it was bit too late.

That evening, I decided to prepare for the Routeburn Track by heading for the bar at the Glenorchy Hotel. One wall was covered with black and white photographs taken during the filming of Peter Jackson's *Lord of the Rings*. Jackson, a Kiwi, filmed the trilogy in 1999 and 2000 all over New Zealand including Kahurangi National Park in the northwest of South Island, in Fiordland National Park near Te Anau, and here. Jackson filmed the trilogy in sixteen months. Middle Earth's Lothlorien Woods, where Boromir, the Captain of the White Tower, was fatally wounded, sat just beyond Glenorchy. A bar patron saw me studying the photos and couldn't help himself.

"That's me in the back with the sword," he said.

"You mean you were actually in the film?"

"Sure a bunch of us from around here were extras. We all made a few dollars. It was great fun.

"Wow, you're famous." I said. "You hung out with Frodo and the Hobbits."

"I don't know if I'm famous, but it was the best job I ever had. Too bad it didn't last. I'm back to paintin' houses."

The Backpacker Express shuttle bus took me to the Routeburn Track trailhead the next morning. It was about an hour ride. The track began with a four-mile ascent through a beach forest of twisted trees. The lush green surroundings reminded me of the Hoh River Trail in Washington's Olympic National Park. The entire Routeburn Track is just twenty-eight miles long, climaxing in a climb over the 4,000-foot Harris Saddle, the backbone of the Humboldt Mountains. Like me, most trekkers broke the tramp into three nights by staying at huts at Routeburn Falls, Lake Mackenzie, and finally Lake Howden. On that first day, I crossed swing bridges and looked down on sapphire blue pools of the Routeburn River. The thick flora was dominated by rainforest ferns. Jade green mosses border the trail. There was a hobbit behind every tree.

It was only about four hours from the trailhead to the Routeburn Falls Hut. It was raining again, and the place was packed and full of activity. I stretched out on my bunk and struck up a conversation with a genuine Kiwi from Wellington who was about my age. Ken did this trek before but had come back for more. I told him that I was trying to do all of the world's top treks. He told me exactly what I wanted to hear since I wouldn't be doing the Milford Track.

"This is my third time. It's too bad it's gotten so crowded." He said. "Twenty years ago, it wasn't this way. The Routeburn has actually made the cut above the better publicized Milford. I've done that one too but it's so often foggy. This one's better. It should be in the top ten hikes 'round the world."

Two Australian trekkers showed up very late that evening after most of us were in our bunks. Their arrival created a minor fracas. Apparently the two did not have permits and attempted to sneak into the hut since it was raining hard, and they didn't have a tent. The two had barely rolled out their bags on the floor near me when the hut warden arrived and told them they must get out. Harsh words were exchanged before the two moved outside on to the porch floor.

"Aussies can be like that," Ken said. "They're sometimes a bit arrogant. I think it has something to do with the fact that the whole damn place was once a penal colony. Ya know why Christ wasn't born in Australia?" he asked me. "Because there's no way he'd have found three wise men and a virgin."

The next morning, Ken and I began to climb out of the trees and head for the Harris Saddle. It was on the dividing line between two of New Zealand's national park crown jewels—Mt. Aspiring National Park on the Routeburn side and Fiordland National Park on the west. It was the crux of the Routeburn Track's biscuit. After about an hour, the trail entered an area of sub-alpine expanses and world class views. Lichens bordered the track as it edged along Lake Harris just below the saddle. Strange reddish-green birds with a cat-like cry whined in the distance. Ken recognized them instantly as alpine parrots called keas.

"They're cheeky bastards, and smart too," he explained. "They tear up the rubber around your car's windshield as they try to pick off dead bugs. They can be a real nuisance at trailhead car parks and ski areas. They nest on the ground in the roots of trees, but normally they don't have to worry about possums eating their eggs because possum don't get up to this altitude."

Later in the day, I saw a kea on a rock with mountains on the horizon behind the bird. It was weird to see a parrot almost above tree line. I made a note to put the bird on my life list.

From the saddle's Conical Hill, we looked down on the Hollyford Valley. Ken told me that on clear days it was possible to see the Tasman Sea and waves breaking on Martins Bay from where we were standing. I wasn't certain where the Tasman Sea was located on the globe, much less Martins Bay, but the view was mind blowing. I was glad I came.

According to *Backpacker* magazine, "The first half of this section of the Routeburn is arguably New Zealand's single most spectacular day of hiking." Who was I to disagree?

We lunched on the steps of an emergency shelter on the saddle. The track then began a sharp descent down into the valley, using wooden steps across the nearly vertical Hollyford Face. We switchbacked our way through silver beech trees. For the first time in my backpacking life, I passed guided trekkers with porters carrying their clients' packs. It was a little upsetting, and I couldn't decide if the trekkers were too lazy, too rich or just smart. I vowed that I'll never pay someone to carry my pack, a vow I later would break in Nepal.

A couple of hours from Harris Saddle, we got our first glimpse of Lake Mackenzie. We could see the hut on the far shore. We had walked about seven miles, went up about a thousand feet, and dropped down another 800 feet. It was a good day. That evening in the dining area of the Mackenzie Hut, we chatted aimlessly.

"So what do you think of New Zealand?" Ken asked me.

"Well, that's not fair because I've seen only one corner of South Island and just the tourist places at that," I said. "But it's awfully white."

"White? You mean British?"

"Not that so much. It's just so American. There are lots of things about it that make me think I'm still in the States. If you guys started driving on the right-hand side of the road, it'd be tough to tell the difference. Don't be offended, but it's kind of like Iowa with big mountains and lots of rivers and ocean. Restaurants serve burgers and fries, you call your currency 'dollars,' and many Kiwis have little or no accent. I saw a few Maori in the airport in Auckland, but down here the only non-whites I've seen are Japanese tourists. Wait till the Mexicans find out about this place. That'll change things. "

Surprisingly Ken laughed and didn't take offense. "If you think that's the case here, you should go to Australia. They're really searching for an identity over there. Do you know the difference between a cup of yogurt and Australia?" he asked.

"No."

"Well, after enough time, the yogurt will develop a culture of its own."

"We knocked the bastard off."

Edmund Hillary
1919- 2008
(upon summiting Mount Everest)

New Zealand does have plenty of over-achievers in whom the country takes great pride. Edmund Hillary was a Kiwi. The son of a beekeeper almost went through life following in his father's footsteps until the lure of the mountains made him hang up his hives. There are plenty of Kiwi actors too. Russell Crowe is a Kiwi, so is the model Rachel Hunter. And of course there's Xena the Warrior Princess, Lucy Lawless. Some years ago, a poll was taken in New Zealand, asking Kiwis to list their most respected countrymen. Hillary finished in third place behind two people whose names most non-Kiwis would not recognize. Suffragette Katherine Sheppard placed second. Sheppard was the force behind New Zealand becoming the first nation to grant the franchise to women. It happened in 1893. She became an international advocate for women's suffrage. The most respected Kiwi of them all? That honor went to physicist Ernest Rutherford, who split the atom in 1917. He was honored by being buried alongside Isaac Newton in Westminster Abbey.

For trekkers, the most famous New Zealand residents are the sandflies. The flying devils can devour an ounce of your flesh before the pain reaches your brain. Their bite can leave a trench a quarter of an inch deep. Only fools wear shorts when trekking Fiordland in sandfly season. Even Captain Cook was impressed by the sandflies, calling them, "...mischievous animals that cause a swelling not possible to refrain from scratching."

It's a short five miles from the Lake McKenzie Hut to the Howden Hut. The sky was almost cloudless and the track was level. We crossed tributaries of Roaring Creek using a swing bridge and then started ascending before we entered a clearing known as The Orchard. Ken explained that the small trees were not really fruit trees but a species native to New Zealand called ribbon wood.

"People mostly associate New Zealand with our unique birds," Ken told me, "but we've got plenty of plants and trees that aren't found anywhere else."

"Walking around Queenstown, I had gone into a sports clothing store and noticed that some sort of plant is frequently used in association with your All Blacks rugby team. What's up with that?" I asked.

"Yeah, funny you'd notice. That's the leaf of the silver tree fern. It's one of our national symbols, and it's used by the All Blacks. It's part of the team's logo. The fern is sometimes called a *ponga*."

"What about the kiwi bird?" I asked. "Any chance of seeing one?"

"Probably not," Ken told me. "They're pretty secretive and mostly nocturnal. Probably your only chance of seeing one in the wild is on Stewart Island off the south coast. There are five or six different species. You can see them in captivity in numerous zoo-type places."

My trekking partner was an encyclopedia of Kiwi trivia, so I decided to push him to the edge.

"Ken, I know this is kind of silly, but what about Kiwi shoe polish? It's the most common brand in the States, and I was surprised to see some in a store in Te Anau. What's it got to do with New Zealand?" I asked.

"You know I actually looked that up once. The guy that invented the stuff back before the first World War was actually Australian. He married a girl from here and named the polish in honor of her."

"Wow, Ken. You know a lot of stuff!"

"Maybe I got too much time on my hands."

We passed through several forest clearings caused by avalanches, and the openings provided us with the chance to take in distant alpine vistas. I took photos of Earland Falls as it tumbled 250 feet down the mountainside. The whole package was breathtaking. We reached Howden Hut early in afternoon. Numerous trekkers were sitting on the porch, enjoying the sunshine. Ken and I said goodbye. He was going to keep walking another hour to The Divide trailhead at the highway to Te Anau. A shuttle bus would take get him into town.

"I've got to get back to Wellington and see if I'm still married and have a job," he said as he tramped down the track.

Three tracks—the Routeburn, the Caples, and the Greenstone—all met near the Howden Hut. My plan was to hike the sixteen miles along the Caples Track from the Howden Hut to the wharf on Lake Wakatipu. I already had the ticket for the jet boat ride back to Glenorchy in my pocket. I'd shower and re-supply in Glenorchy, then head back across the lake, and walk the twenty-two-mile Greenstone Track back to The Divide trailhead.

My destination the next morning was the Upper Caples Hut some nine miles away. It was raining. The junction of the Greenstone Track and the Caples was not far beyond the Howden Hut and was clearly marked. I took a left and switchbacked up the McKeller Saddle. It was a 1,500-foot climb and a boggy descent. Intermittent boardwalks helped protect me from the slop. This was the headwaters of the Caples River, which flowed downhill from here before finally flowing into Lake Wakatipu.

Two or three small groups of trekkers passed me, going in the opposite direction. Two Americans from Ohio asked me about the trail. "One foot at a time," was about the only advice I could give them. Like me, they were college basketball junkies and asked if I knew any results from the NCAA Tournament that was being played on the other side of the planet. Of course, I knew nothing.

"It was just starting when we left home," one said. "Sure the track is tough, but not knowing how my Buckeyes are doing is a real inconvenience."

Since it's not an official "Great Walk," the Caples had less trekking pressure. The scenery was not quite on a par with the Routeburn, but the relative solitude made up for the lack of dynamic vistas. The trail improved as it descended the saddle and passed through a forest of huge red and silver beech trees with twisted branches. It was almost spooky. There were more hobbits hiding in the bush.

I'd been walking for six hours, and, despite my protective rain gear, I was getting soaked by the intermittent downpours. Bunks in the huts along the Caples cannot be reserved and were taken on a first-come basis, so I was worried that there wouldn't be any room in the inn. Sure enough, the Upper Caples Hut was almost full. Compared to those along the more glamorous Kepler and Routeburn, the hut was Spartan. There were just twelve beds, and the hut was heated by a coal stove. The coal had been brought in by helicopter. The place was jammed because a group of eight Germans, who arrived yesterday, decided to spend an extra night at the hut.

"Is it okay to do that?" I asked the warden when he showed up the next morning to collect the $10 fee.

"Things here aren't has highly regulated here as on Routeburn Track or the Kepler Track. We're not in either Mt. Aspiring or Fiordland National Park," he explained.

I got the idea that these areas were some sort of protected conservation areas similar to wilderness areas in the states, which often abutted national parks but are not subject to all the regulations regarding camping. Later that evening, a group of six Israelis showed up. Larger groups apparently end up walking the Caples and Greenstone because they don't have to hassle the reservation system. There was no room inside, so they erected their tents on the porch where they talked into the wee hours. It was just over ten miles from the Upper Caples Hut to the Greenstone Wharf on the shores of Lake Wakatipu. I was the first one out the door that morning and tramped quickly along the edge of a dramatic gorge and through tussak grasslands. Across the Caples River, I saw a large structure that looked like an old sheep station. Apparently grazing was allowed in the area prior to it gaining protection.

What appeared to be a mother and daughter were waiting at the dock when I showed up. They were British and had come across the lake from Glenorchy for the day. They knew the boat schedule, and sure enough, it showed up about an hour later. It was my first jet boat ride, and I didn't particularly like it. The obnoxious ride across the lake brought an abrupt end to my five-day wilderness experience. Glenorchy was a welcome respite, however. I treated myself to a room at the Glenorchy Hotel, showered, and purchased groceries for my trek up the Greenstone Valley beginning tomorrow. I was a glutton for punishment.

That evening's stroll took me past a small monument commemorating Kiwi soldiers who lost their lives during World War I on the Gallipoli Peninsula in Turkey. Some 8,500 Australians and 3,000 New Zealanders died in the 1915-1916 battle. The event is commemorated annually in both countries. It is considered a defining moment in their history and the birth of a national consciousness for both nations. The landings and attack on the entrenched Turkish troops also resulted in the deaths of 44,000 French and British troops and accomplished nothing militarily. The failed invasion was Winston Churchill's idea, and he was subsequently demoted from his position as the First Lord of the Admiralty. The 1981 film, *Gallipoli*, starring Mel Gibson, did an outstanding job depicting the horrors of the battle as seen through the eyes of naïve Australian soldiers.

It was a twenty-two-mile walk from the Greenstone dock up the Greenstone Valley to the car park at The Divide alongside the highway that leads back to Te Anau. My walk up the Greenstone proved to be another highlight of my South Island trekking adventure. There was a tranquil aura about the walk, which wound its way along the river and passed through stands of southern and silver beech trees. The track went across open tussock-covered flats, and there were frequent views of the river's deep pools as it twisted through the valley. The real attraction for me was that the valley was not some hyped-up spot with lines of trekkers in a regulated national park. It was pure New Zealand wilderness, and I was the only one around. But not for long.

The tranquility was suddenly aborted by the sound of a small helicopter. Its chop-chop-chop grated on me. The machine landed on an exposed flat on a bench above the river. Three men emerged. Their presence was explained by the fact that two of them were carrying fly rods. I watched as the two men with rods stopped walking before reaching the Greenstone River. The third was carrying some sort of a milk-crate-looking box and walked to the river's edge where he stood on top of the box and began carefully inspecting the river for trout. He was obviously the fishing guide, and he moved up and down the river's edge, each time standing on the box. After about fifteen minutes of examining the river's pools, the guide motioned and one of the other two men moved to the river bank and cast his fly on the water. There was a splash as the trout made its move. The rod bent and then straightened. The ban on conversation was over. I clearly hear the fisherman's "Ah, shit!" reaction. He missed it. All three huddled and discussed the experience. I took the opportunity to show myself and approached them. The two fishermen were Canadians, and the helicopter/fishing guide was a Kiwi.

"What's up with the milk crate?" I asked.

"The Greenstone River is famous for large brown trout," the guide explained. "The one we just missed was probably four or five pounds. You don't want to alert them by just casting about hoping to get lucky. We don't drop a fly on the water until we actually see a fish."

They climbed back into the helicopter and disappeared over a ridge. I felt really stupid because my fly rod was sitting in a storage locker in Te Anau.

The Mid Greenstone Hut was another Spartan affair with just twelve bunks. There was a more upscale cabin for the warden just behind it. I had the whole hut to myself and was a most happy trekker. Despite the earlier helicopter interruption, there was a pleasant feeling of remoteness. I lay in my bunk, watching the beech trees move in the wind through the window, but the stillness was suddenly interrupted by the high-pitched chattering of female voices. Their language was unrecognizable. The hut door opened and three Japanese women entered. They nodded and gave me an incomprehensible greeting. We introduced ourselves. Asuka, Hoshi, and Michiko were somewhere between fourteen and fifty years old. I couldn't even begin to guess. Their knowledge of English was zero. The only Japanese word I knew was sushi, although I once watched a film version of the *Mikado.* It was as if they dropped in from space. They were fun, constantly laughing, and talking. Maybe they were talking about me. I hoped they were saying something nice.

Hoshi reached into her pack and pulled out a piece of inflatable red plastic, which she transformed into a ball by using her breath. Outside they used their trekking poles as goals and began playing a very short-handed game of soccer along the banks of the Greenstone River. The scene had a certain charm to it. Hoshi, Michiko, and Asuka were kicking and laughing when the warden came down from his cabin on the hill to collect our hut tickets. Peter was a young guy about thirty and spent his days walking between the two huts in the Greenstone Valley, collecting fees and making certain everybody's doing okay.

"*Doumo*," he said to the three women as they handed him their tickets.

"You speak Japanese?" I asked him.

"No. 'Doumo' is the only word I know. There are quite a few Japanese trekkers that come through here, and I figured I should learn how to say thank you."

The women got back to their soccer scrimmage and enticed Peter and me to join them. The scrimmage quickly evolved into a contest with Peter and me competing against the women. It was Orientals vs. Occidentals, but Pearl Harbor and Hiroshima had nothing to do with it. The Japanese squad took a quick 3-0 lead, but the contest came to an abrupt end. Hoshi knocked the ball between our trekking poles, and the ball caromed off a rock and bounced into the river. Peter and I watched as Asuka, Hoshi, and Michiko ran laughing along the riverbanks and attempted to retrieve it. But the women could not outpace the swiftly flowing Greenstone. The ball floated around a bend in the river and disappeared.

That evening, I walked through the bush to the next large clearing and enjoyed the scene as dusk took hold. The quiet was occasionally interrupted by the song of a hidden bird. Despite the open meadow and the approach of darkness, I had accepted the fact that no large mammals would show themselves. In the American West, such a place would lend itself to the expectation of seeing an elk, deer, moose or, if you're lucky, a bear. Although Peter had told me there were feral red deer in the Greenstone Valley. I didn't see any large mammals. That's how it is in New Zealand, and considering the country's struggle with imported species, it's for the best.

I went back to the hut and saw Peter and the women staring at the sky. Peter was trying to point out the Southern Cross. The constellation can be seen only in the southern hemisphere. Its four principal stars were clearly visible to me overhead.

The Japanese women were apparently focused on the stars overhead, but the language barrier prevented a positive confirmation that they understood what Peter was trying to show them. He jogged up the hill to his hut and returned with his backpack. Sure enough, there was a flag sewn on the pack. I had forgotten that the Southern Cross was depicted on the Kiwi flag. Peter pointed to his flag and then to the constellation above. The girls got it. They smiled and indicated their understanding. "Doumo, doumo," Asuka, Hoshi, and Michiko said to Peter.

It was a long thirteen-mile walk from Mid Greenstone Hut, past Lake McKellar and over the Greenstone Saddle to the car park at The Divide. I did it in a long day and arrived at the trailhead car park late in the afternoon. There was a group of about twenty trekkers waiting for the shuttle bus back to Te Anau, which wasn't due for another hour.

"Hasn't anyone tried hitching?" I asked the gathering. There were only some mumbled replies. Intent on demonstrating my American initiative, I crossed the highway and prepared to stick out my thumb when the next car approached, only to hear laughter from the group across the road.

"Te Anau's the other direction. You're on the wrong side of the road," a male voice called out from the crowd. I was baffled. 'That guy's really confused,' I thought to myself. I heard the sound of a vehicle approaching and warmed up my thumb. There was problem, of course. It was headed in the proper direction but was across the road in the other lane. I suddenly realized why I was the subject of some snickering from my fellow trekkers standing across the highway. The voice called out again, "Hey, Yank, we drive on the left side down here."

Tiġ Ċóilí
Drink
INNESS
good for

7

The Dingle Way

Saint Brendan sails to Florida

Ireland
110 miles

Exactly why the nuns of St. John de LaSalle Elementary School were so obsessed with St. Patrick remains a mystery to me. The real St. John de LaSalle was French, and we kids were mostly of Italian and Polish extraction. No matter, the days leading up to March 17, the anniversary of his death, were always filled with anticipation and preparation. The black-and-white-robed nuns would lead us in the singing of traditional Irish melodies like *Galway Bay* and *Danny Boy*. It was fun because, unlike a lot of Christmas carols, there were no super religious songs. (I distinctly remember Sister Mary Mean, the nun from hell, actually making us tear out *Oh, Little Town of Bethlehem* from our Christmas carol booklets because it was allegedly written by the evil Martin Luther.)

The Irish songs were mostly lighthearted and silly. Who did put the overalls in Mrs. Murphy's Chowder? My favorite was *Clancy Lowered the Boom*. Who can forget the legendary refrain?

"Oh that Clancy,
Oh that Clancy.
Whenever he got his Irish up
Clancy lowered the boom!
Boom, boom, boom, boom."

And with that, despite the fact that most of our grandparents spoke Italian or Polish, we all became little Irishmen and women—at least on March 17. That cultural baptism is not something one walks away from even in the face of the aging process. If you were raised in America's northeast, there's forever a warm spot in your heart for Ireland and the Irish, and you tip your glass to the Auld Sod each St. Paddy's day. Most Americans raised west of the Mississippi don't get it, and it's their loss.

We could tell we were flying to Ireland from New York by scanning the passengers. Some were tourists, like Rosemary and me, but lots were real Irish from Ireland. There was nothing hip about their apparel. Many were wearing frumpy coats and sweaters. Their slacks were made of gabardine or some other mysterious synthetic material. We noticed that the luggage they stowed in the overhead compartments was not luggage at all, but Wal-Mart shopping bags. It was a short flight from Ireland to New York and relatively inexpensive. Our Irish flying companions had come over to America, not to see a Broadway play or get their face on the *Today* show. They'd gone shopping and probably stayed with relatives while they were visiting. After all, some thirty-five million Americans claim to have Irish roots, so there are lots of beds for relatives on both sides of the pond.

There were some Irish soccer players on the flight too. Many of them were drunk. Apparently they had had a game in New York City that same day because they were still wearing their shorts and team jerseys. Why should they shower? They'd be home in a few hours. You don't get that same atmosphere on your flight if you're heading to Paris. We were heading to extreme southwestern Ireland to walk the Dingle Peninsula.

We landed at Europe's westernmost airport—Shannon (if you don't count Iceland). The logic of Shannon's location on Ireland's west coast was based on the fact that it is the shortest flying distance between Ireland and New York. That was a serious consideration back in the early days of flying when prop-driven planes barely had enough range to cover the distance across the Atlantic.

The airport proved to be a pleasant place. It was small. More like the one you'd expect if you landed in Wichita or Great Falls. We simply grabbed our backpacks and headed out front to catch a bus. The only problem was my backpack failed to appear. We couldn't help but wonder why both our backpacks started the trip together nearly joined at the hip but one disappeared.

"It'll be here on the next flight for sure," the young Irishman at the lost luggage counter assured me with an obvious lilt in his speech. "Would you be wanting to have us send it ahead to your hotel or would waiting for it to arrive on the next flight be easier for you? It'll be there this evenin' for certain if sendin' is what ya want."

"How come this guy puts his verbs in the wrong place?" I whispered to Rosemary.

"It's that James Joyce stream of consciousness way of speaking," she explained.

Without even asking for my input, she gave the fellow the address of our B&B in Tralee.

"It will be there this evening," the lost baggage man assured us.

In an attempt to make the flight over as comfortable as possible, I wore my Crocs rather than my hiking sneakers. They were on my feet as we climbed on the bus. "I hope I'm not the first person to walk the entire Dingle Way wearing Crocs," I told Rosemary.

"Ah, sure you can be wearing my departed husband's things until your backpack arrives," the nice lady at the B&B said. She opened a closet filled with a man's clothing and told me to help myself when we headed out later in the day.

"What did she mean by 'departed'? I asked Rosemary when we're alone in our room. "Has he gone on a trip or is he dead?"

"Maybe they just got divorced, and he forgot to pack some of his things," Rosemary said.

"Divorce? Do they have divorce in Ireland? I know they don't allow abortions. The women go to Britain for abortions. It doesn't eliminate them; it just makes it more inconvenient and expensive. Surely they don't allow divorce."

Rosemary had had enough of my diatribe and collapsed onto the bed. We were both exhausted from the trip and needed sleep. Not ten minutes passed before there was a knock on our door.

"Tis hot water bottles I've brought you," our B&B hostess said. "You'll need them to warm up the bed." We were a bit dumbfounded. I hadn't seen a hot water bottle since I was ten and had chicken pox. We accepted them graciously and shoved them into the bottom of our bed. After our nap, we showered. The shower itself is worthy of comment. Ireland could have the smallest shower stalls on Earth. Does the *Guinness World Records* have this category? It should. They were so tiny that when I dropped my bar of soap I had no alternative but to step outside the shower and then reach down to retrieve it. You can't turn around in most Irish shower stalls, much less bend down. They're like vertical caskets.

We walked the streets of Tralee to check it out and looked for the beginning of the trail out to the Dingle Peninsula. I was wearing the "departed" husband's twill topcoat and a checkered newsboy flat cap. I almost looked like a local as long as no one noticed my Crocs. It seemed disrespectful to try on his shoes. Tralee, the capital of County Kerry, struck me as rather undistinguished.

"Isn't there a song called *The Rose of Tralee*?" I asked Rosemary.

"Maybe, but I think it's the name of a big rose festival they hold here. I think I saw a poster promoting it," she replied.

"No, that's in Portland, Oregon. They hold a big rose festival there every year."

"No, the big rose festival is in Pasadena. You know The Rose Parade, the Rose Bowl on New Year's," countered Rosemary.

A lack of facts should never be an impediment to discussion.

There was nothing very remarkable about the stores along the city's main drag. We stumbled into a bookstore. It was a dark and somber place. Wooden ladders on rollers provided access to books on the highest shelves. There was only one clerk. An elderly man, he wore a suit and tie and looked out from beneath a green plastic visor on his head. He had a scholarly look about him, the perfect guy to ask a question that had been troubling me for years. "I'm going to ask him something," I told Rosemary, who rolled her eyes and disappeared into a back corner of the shop.

"Excuse me, but I've been wondering if there's any truth to the story of the Black Irish? Do you have an opinion the subject?" I asked.

"For sure I have an opinion, but whether it's factual or not is yet another matter," he answered. "What have ya heard?"

"What I understand is that following the defeat of the Spanish Armada, a big storm came up and some of the ships were sunk or crashed on Ireland's beaches. The ships were full of virile, young men. One thing led to another and there was considerable consorting between the Spaniards and the Irish girls. Nine months later, some olive-skinned babies started showing up. Is there any truth to that?" I asked.

"Your version of the story is what everyone says, but there's no real documentation as to its accuracy," he replied.

"What about names like Costello and Ireland's first president, Eamon de Valera?" I asked. "They sure sound Spanish."

"Well, I can't explain Costello, but Eamon de Valera's father was Cuban. He was born in New York," he patiently explained. "But I guess the bottom line on the whole subject of the Black Irish is that it might have some substance."

Rosemary rescued the man from more of my questions by grabbing me by the arm and tugging me toward the door. "One of the reasons we came to Ireland is to get to the bottom of some of these things that I've been wondering about for a long time," I told her.

We made another stop. If you're interested in Ireland's modern history, you can't walk by the Sinn Féin office. Rosemary had made certain I was aware of Ireland's violent modern history before we left. She had made me watch *In the Name of the Father* with Daniel Day Lewis and *Michael Collins* starring Liam Neeson.

The first film relates the true story of the false arrest and conviction by the British of four Irish individuals for the 1974 IRA bombing of a pub in England. Four British soldiers and a civilian were killed. The other film tells the story of an IRA leader who led the fight against British rule between 1919 and 1921. Michael Collins ultimately hammered out a peace treaty creating a quasi-independent Ireland but allowing the six northern counties (Ulster) to remain under British rule. The treaty also required members of

Ireland's parliament to swear allegiance to the British crown. Collins was labeled a traitor to the republic and was ambushed and killed by IRA hardliners who were especially angry over the oath of allegiance provision in Collins's treaty. Both films are recommended for those wanting a deeper understanding of Ireland's troubled modern history.

The Sinn Féin office was a two-story affair. The stairs that led up to the second level were blocked with a rope and a PRIVATE sign. I couldn't help wondering if that's where the local Irish Republican Army (IRA) members plot to recapture Ireland's six northern counties that make up Ulster, thus uniting all of the island under the flag of the republic. The IRA is outlawed in Ireland, but its political wing, Sinn Féin, is not.

The explanation for this arrangement has always been confusing to me. Maybe it's kind of like the Ku Klux Klan. It's not illegal to voice racist opinions, but it's illegal to actual implement racist actions. The IRA, however, doesn't wear white sheets with pointed hoods. We perused the downstairs, which is mostly filled with literature, brochures, and bumper stickers, promoting the IRA—Whoops!—the Sinn Féin cause. There was a memorial to a few Sinn Féin martyrs. Their photos were framed in black. It was a somber place.

Rosemary was pretty knowledgeable on the whole IRA/Sinn Féin thing and pointed to a photo of Bobby Sands on the wall. She refreshed my memory. "He's they guy that was jailed by the British and went on a hunger strike and died in jail. The deal was that the British classified him as a common prisoner, like a thief or a killer, and he demanded to be treated as a political prisoner. So he protested his status by starving himself to death."

"Well, if he was an IRA member that was involved in blowing up people, doesn't that make him a common killer?" I asked her.

Rosemary glared back. I backed off. Rosemary was a closet IRA sympathizer.

A young man working in the office overheard our discussion and offered to answer any questions. Rosemary looked askance as I opened my mouth. "Which way do we go in the morning to walk the Dingle Way?" I asked. Rosemary was relieved.

The whole world is in a state o' chassis!

Sean O'Casey
1880-1964

As promised, my backpack was at the B&B when we returned that evening. The next morning, we began walking. Our plan was to do The Dingle Way in seven or eight days. The Dingle Way is not a wilderness hike but rather a walk through the Irish countryside punctuated by picturesque villages and neighborhood pubs. We would stay at B&Bs. The Way is a loop around the Dingle Peninsula, beginning and ending in Tralee. The tip of the peninsula is the most westerly point in Europe. Two of the days of our theoretical itinerary looked a bit long, totaling almost eighteen miles each. Of course, there are no rules, and the goal was to enjoy the adventure, so we figured we'd make adjustments depending on our progress or lack of it.

Although there were baggage services that could transport our luggage ahead each day, we decided not to use that option. That gave us plenty flexibility in the event our pace was slower or even faster than planned. The obvious disadvantage was that we must carry all of our belongings with us for the entire trip. That proved not to be as big a burden as one might expect. Since we were staying at B&Bs, we needed no tent, sleeping bags or cooking stuff. We abandoned any sense of fashion and kept our clothing needs to a minimum. Admittedly we did grow tired of wearing many of the same things daily.

Also, Ireland is not the heart of Africa or the back side of the moon, so we washed socks and other unmentionables at launderettes along the way. We did not made a single advance reservation at a B&B. It was bit of a gamble, but we've been assured that since it was May and early in the tourist season, we shouldn't have a problem. That proved to be the case. We never had a problem finding a room for the night and, more importantly, a pub for the evening.

Our target on that first day was the village of Camp, some eleven miles away. The Way began just beyond the Ashe Memorial Hall in Tralee. The large stone building was named after Thomas Ashe who became Ireland's first hunger striker and died in 1917 for the Irish independence movement. The structure housed the Kerry County Museum, but we were anxious get walking so with apologies to Mr. Ashe's legacy, we skipped it.

A signpost marked the start of the Dingle Way and it pointed our way west. The sign was in both conventional English and indiscernible traditional Irish. The Republic of Ireland is officially bilingual, and many of the road signs were printed in both languages. There's a serious effort to preserve the traditional Irish language in the country. Instruction in Irish is required in schools there, but the jury's still out on whether the effort is successful.

The Dingle Peninsula is one of the strongest bastions of the Irish language, and we frequently overheard conversations in traditional Irish, especially among the elderly. "I'm not sure if they need to bother with preserving Irish," Rosemary commented at one point. "When they mix their brogue and lilt with normal English, it already sounds like a second language to me."

Only a couple miles out, the trail followed a canal where the big, white Blennerville windmill dominated the scene. The guidebook said it's the largest working windmill in the British Isles. The four-bladed contraption was originally built about 1800, but it lay derelict for over a century until the Tralee locals restored it in the 1980s. We walked on by and crossed the Curraheen and the Derryquay Rivers. We used a stile to cross over our first fence. The Slieve Mountains accented the skyline to the south. The view was pleasant but not particularly picturesque. Some guidebooks recommended skipping this part of The Dingle and begin walking further on in Camp or even Annascaul. We didn't care. We were happy. We were not just talking about it; we were walking the Dingle Way.

Camp village overlooked Tralee Bay and served as a junction point for those who were walking the Dingle in a clockwise or counterclockwise direction. In the morning, we'd follow the clock. Camp was a memorable stop. For the first time in my old life, I tasted a Guinness Extra Stout on draught in an Irish pub. The moment was iconic. To be sure, there are plenty of other things to experience while visiting Ireland. Some may choose to purchase Waterford crystal; others may want to walk Dublin's streets in Leonard Bloom's shoes as he did in James Joyce's incomprehensible "Ulysses." For the unimaginative, there's the Blarney Stone. But for deep thinkers, a glass of Guinness in an Irish village pub is right up there with one's first sexual experience. And like that first sexual experience, it was somewhat disappointing and failed to live up to the anticipatory hype.

Those first experiences didn't keep me from ultimately enjoying both, however. A pint of Guinness is creamy and rich with a chocolate taste. As one wag described it, "It's a meal in a glass, but for some it's an acquired taste." And who was I to argue with the world's best marketing slogan—"Drink Guinness. It's Good for You"?

There's a standard ritual associated with the pouring of a glass of Ireland's famous brew, and that ceremony did not vary from pub to pub. "The Pour" is a traditional two-step process that involves holding the pint glass at a forty-five-degree angle and filling the glass three quarters full. The bartender then waited as long as three full minutes for the glass to settle before topping it off with another pull, this time with the glass held perpendicular to the tap. Excess foam was then removed by passing a table knife across the top of the pint. (Experienced drinkers order two pints simultaneously to cut down on the waiting time.) Now drink your Guinness. It's good for you.

The next day's walk toward Annascaul began along an old hedge-line road over the western edge of some hills officially called the Slieve Mish Mountains. We climbed over an 850-foot pass that led to the south side of the upper reaches of the Emlagh River Valley and the south side of the Dingle Peninsula. Just beyond the Emlagh River bridge, we got our first good views of Dingle Bay and the famous Inch Strand that edged along the bay. The strand or beach had a place in movie-making history. It was on this beach and further down the coast at Slea Head that director David Lean filmed many of the scenes in his 1970 melodrama *Ryan's Daughter*. The story was set in 1914 in the backwaters of World War I amidst Ireland's modern-day struggle for independence. The film told the tale of a young provincial Irish girl, Rosy Ryan (Sarah Miles), who married a dull school teacher (Robert Mitchum) but became involved with a troubled British officer (Christopher Jones). The whole thing was bit sappy, but the panoramic scenes of the Irish coast and countryside will have you calling Are Linus well before Rosy gets her due when her clothes are torn apart and hair cut short by the outraged local villagers. *Ryan's Daughter* won two academy awards and is must viewing for anyone doing the Dingle Way.

"So that's the beach that Sarah Miles and Robert Mitchum walked along," I mentioned to Rosemary.

"Yes, but she would have rather been with that British officer. That's why the townspeople were so outraged. It was bad enough that she had a tryst or two on the beach, but doing it with an English soldier really was just too much," she explained.

"Oh, I think I missed that point. Maybe I'll have to watch it again when we get back," I said.

We walked the last two miles to Annascaul in a driving rain. My umbrella and all of our rain gear were eventually overwhelmed by the weather. We got soaked and were miserable. As we entered the village, I spotted a sturdy two-story building painted a bright blue. My spirits soared. I had been anticipating this moment ever since we began planning our trip.

"It's Tom Crean's South Pole Inn. There's even a penguin on the side of the building!" I announced. Although I had educated Rosemary on the life of Tom Crean, she was primarily interested in just getting out of the rain. The pub was small and heated by a free-standing coal stove. There were four or five other walkers, equally as soaked as we were, huddled near the stove. There was a burlap bag of coal next to the stove that was labeled PRODUCT OF POLAND. So much for the legendary Irish peat.

We ordered a Guinness and warmed up before I began wandering around the pub, looking for Tom Crean memorabilia. Sure enough, there on a wall was a collection of old black and white photographs of men dressed in parkas and mittens surrounded by Antarctic snow and ice.

Tom Crean was born near Annascaul in 1877. He served with Sir Robert Falcon Scott on two expeditions to the Antarctic. He was also a member of Earnest Shackleton's famous 1914 expedition to the Antarctic, which resulted in their ship, ENDURANCE, being crushed by the pack ice. Many are familiar with story. The men ultimately sailed three lifeboats across 350 miles of frigid ocean landing on remote Elephant Island. While most of the crew remained there, Shackleton, Crean, and four others sailed another 800 miles to South Georgia Island.

Shackleton, Crean, and Frank Worsley then trekked over the mountainous spine of the island to the safety of a Norwegian whaling station. All of the twenty-two crewmen left behind on Elephant Island were subsequently rescued, and not a single man who was on the ENDURANCE perished. The entire adventure is legendary, as is Crean. If you haven't read Alfred Lansing's *Endurance, Shackleton's Incredible Voyage*, or any of the other accounts of the adventure get after it.

Crean served in World War I, then returned to Annascaul and opened the South Pole Inn. He died in 1938. For a long-suffering romantic and adventure history nut like me, Tom Crean's pub was just plain wonderful.

We had a nap and shower at the Old Anchor Inn B&B. Like many Irish B&Bs, the Old Anchor prided itself on having something called a "drying room." (Be forewarned that when making travel plans, you can expect lots of wet weather in any region where accommodations include a drying room.) Thankfully guests do not have to be completely dry before going up to their rooms, but courtesy demands that they separate themselves from their wet jackets, parkas, boots, and umbrellas beforehand.

Any couple renting a room should not take the experience for granted in traditional Ireland. In his delightful book, *McCarthy's Bar*, Peter McCarthy reminded us that times have changed:

> "Twenty years ago it used to be a problem getting a room for two in Ireland. Stern-eyed ladies would give you the once-

> over. Immorality was suspected; and if you claim to be married, where were the children then? Sorry no sinners."

We returned to Tom Crean's for a dinner of Guinness, fish, chips, and Guinness that evening. Van Morrison music played in the background. We ate at the bar and found ourselves sitting next to a despondent young man from Germany. He was in his early twenties and seemed distraught. From what we could figure out from his rough English, he began the Dingle a couple of days earlier and got into a big fight with his hiking partner. The two split up.

"I do not have anywhere to sleep anymore," Werner told us in pretty good English. "My girlfriend had our tent. I couldn't leave her without a place to sleep." Now I'm nowhere to sleep every night." Werner told us that last night he slept in a covered bus stop and nearly froze. Rosemary and I admired his chivalry for leaving the tent with the woman that dumped him.

We actually hadn't realized that the Dingle could be walked using a tent instead of staying at B&Bs or hostels, but Werner told us that in Ireland it's usually okay to camp on private land if you ask or you can just put your tent up in the trees somewhere. Rosemary was glad I hadn't known this for fear that I might have suggested it for our trip. In that case, I'd probably be Dingling solo.

"Werner, why don't you stay in the hotels or B&Bs?" I asked him.

"I cannot spend the money because I don't have any. I am a student," he told us while simultaneously ordering another Smithwick's Irish Red Ale for himself.

"Where are you going to sleep tonight?" I asked.

"I have no idea," he answered. "I went to the hostel, but they want too much money, and I can't go home because my airline ticket isn't good until next week."

"I don't know whether to believe this guy or not," I whispered to Rosemary.

Often the cynic, she too was suspect. "I think he's getting ready to hit us up for a handout," she said. "If he's a student, what's he doing walking the Dingle? It seems like here in Europe anyone under the age of thirty-five calls themselves a student even if they haven't been to class in the last decade." We finished our Guinness and abandoned Werner to his fate. There was no guilt.

"If the rich are unhappy, it's their own fault."

Vladimir Lenin (attributed)
1870-1924

We left Annascaul in the morning, heading for Dingle about twelve miles down the track. It was still raining but not too hard, so we were optimistic about the weather. An elderly man was walking in our direction while urging five or six cows down the trail with a stick. He was wearing the standard flat checkered cap and calf-high gumboots.

"Good morning to you," I said.

"And a good day to the both of you," he replied. "'Tis a soft morning."

"Yes, it is," I answered as Rosemary and I kept our eyes down in an effort to avoid the fresh manure left by his herd. We were to hear the greeting, "Tis a soft morning," a couple more times along the Dingle. It seemed to be the standard salutation when there was a gentle rain.

The Dingle Way undulated across minor roads, passing through farmland. It edged along hillsides. After a steady climb, we descended to Minard Castle, which sat on a small bluff overlooking Dingle Bay. We had been looking forward to the castle, but the fortress proved to be a disappointment. Our guidebook hyped the castle, but it was no more than a small tower that has fallen into complete ruin. The book said it was destroyed in the seventeenth century by forces under the command of that dastardly Protestant Oliver Cromwell.

Beyond the castle, the track headed inland, passing through the hamlet of Lispole before crossing over the unpronounceable Owenalodrig River. We walked for over four hours, and the soft morning deteriorated into a hard rainy afternoon. We were getting soaked again. The Dingle Way paralleled the main highway into the town of Dingle. We saw vehicles and buses, and abandoned the track and headed for the N86. A woman was standing on her porch, watching the traffic, so we approached her.

"Is there a bus along here into Dingletown?" I asked.

"Of course," she replied. "It should be along in about twenty minutes. Sit and look up the road. When you see it coming, walk out and wave him down. Would you like a cup of tea while you're waitin'?"

Rosemary and I sat on her porch, sipping our tea and watching for the bus. "Is this a great country or what?" I commented.

"'Tis a great country for sure," Rosemary said, using her best Irish lilt. "But isn't taking the bus kind of cheating? Aren't we supposed to be *walking* the Dingle Way?"

I was up to the challenge. "According to the rules, you're allowed to use public transportation two times as long as the rain is moderate to heavy," I answered. Rosemary didn't question the rules. She embraced them. She was wet enough.

Dingle is the tourist capital of the peninsula. It's a harbor town with fishing boats, colorful houses, and shops. Some of the shops are totally committed to the tourists. They specialized in stuffed leprechauns, green beaded rosaries, and pillows in the shape of shamrocks. There's also the mandatory fishhook sweater store. During our time in Ireland, the only person I saw wearing one of these was an overweight tourist from Chicago who had added a ketchup blotch to accent the whiteness of the wool.

Dingle seemed to have enough pubs to serve all of Ireland simultaneously. One source set the number at fifty. Pretty good for a town with a population of around 1,500. There was no attempt to upgrade the bars with phony names like the Fishing Fleet Inn or Tam O' Shanter's Pot 'O Gold. They're named after their owner. There was Paudie's, Ashe's, Moriarty's, Murphy's, Geaney's, Mrs. Brenner's, Dick Mack's, and, of course, O'Flaherty's. I resolved to try every one.

We headed for Dick Mack's that evening. *McCarthy's Bar* described the place as Dingletown's most famous combination shoe repair store and pub. They put the shoes away in the evening to make room for the drinkers. Outside on the street, there were stars set in the pavement that paid tribute to the pub's famous customers including Julia Roberts and Robert Mitchum.

Inside, a Kerryman (That's what the locals called themselves.) began explaining to us that Dingle may not actually be "Dingle" anymore. He told us that Dingle became the subject of a controversy in 2005 when Ireland's Office of Cultural Affairs announced that the road signage referring to the town as Dingle had to be replaced by the Irish language version *An Daingean.*

"Most of us were upset about it. We figured that tourists like you wouldn't find the place." He said there was a big vote, and the locals supported keeping the English version. "But the government said the vote didn't count, 'cause we didn't have the right to decide such matters. By Jeezus, it's the government tellin' us what language to use."

A pint later, he told us that the County Kerry officials then pushed to officially have a bilingual policy, but road signs would only be in Irish. "So some of us got tired of the whole thing, and someone just grabbed a bucket of paint and started paintin' o'er the signs and puttin' the Dingle. What a feckin' mess the whole thing is."

While walking a couple days later, Rosemary and I did notice a road sign that had been altered with the name DINGLE painted over the original sign. It looked pretty professional. The anti-Irish language road sign vandals had used a stencil, but it was crooked.

An Daingean (or is it Dingle?) was a center for Irish music, and most pubs seemed to have a band each night. Despite our advancing age and the lateness of the setting sun at this northern latitude, we pushed ourselves to stay up until the dancing and banging started. We were not disappointed. The atmosphere was charged with gaiety, music, dancing, and laughing. The Irish refer to these kinds of doings as a "crack" or craic, not to be confused with the illegal drug. The band consisted of a fiddle, a tin whistle, a guitar, pipes, and a small goatskin drum. A young, tattooed woman with a ring through one eyebrow sang in traditional Irish, but no one tried to paint her over. An old man from the states even danced with his wife. The couple was in the midst of walking the Dingle and had just enough energy left that evening to get the job done.

In the morning, while checking out of our B&B, we had a minor hassle over the price of our room.

"We stayed here because Rick Steves mentioned it in his guidebook," I told Mary the proprietor. "He wrote that you'll give us a discount if we tell you we saw your place in his book."

"To be sure," Mary said, "But you should have said so in the first place when you checked in. It's too late now."

"But if I had told you first, you could have simply raised the price to cover the discount," I said.

"Now, I wouldn't be doing that, now. Would I?" she said with a smile.

It had become our routine to stop by a grocery store each morning and purchase lunch items to eat along the Dingle Way in the improbable event a pub was not handy. The grocery store was modern and clean and could be mistaken for one in a small town in the States, with one exception. It was not heated.

As far as I could tell, public buildings in this part of Ireland had no central heating. It was true of the pubs, the B&Bs, and the shops, although some B&Bs did have a small electric heater in the rooms. Residents and employees in public facilities relied on sweaters and jackets to compensate for any chilliness. Despite the fact that Ireland is located farther north than Newfoundland, they can get away with no central heating, thanks to the Gulf Stream, which provides a mild but wet climate. We spotted lots of trees, shrubs, and flowering fuchsia that seemed almost tropical and out of place considering the latitude. There were even palm trees in Dingle, although they're not native.

A wild dolphin showed up in Dingle Harbor in 1983 and must have found the water temperature to his liking. The solitary mammal apparently swore a vow of celibacy and took up permanent residence. Fungi, the dolphin, became a tourist attraction, and there's even a statue of the creature in town. Perhaps the locals were just happy to see someone moving to Ireland instead of emigrating abroad.

We headed out of town along the well-marked Way. The guidebook said the first five miles might be boring and suggested taking the bus as far as the hamlet of Ventry, but Rosemary was feeling guilty over yesterday's bus ride, so we walked. In 1939, a German submarine, the U-35, put ashore twenty-eight Greek sailors at Ventry's harbor. The sub had sunk the sailors' vessel, the *Diamantis*, off the English coast but apparently held no animosity toward its crew. Although sympathetic with the Allies, Ireland was officially neutral during WWII. Allied planes did fly over Irish air space, however, and thousands of Irish lost their lives fighting in the British army.

Once beyond Ventry, the scenery became truly spectacular as we walked along a beach before heading for higher ground. We spotted some large, white seabirds circulating over the ocean. They were the size of geese, mostly white, but their wings were black with a pointed tail.

"They're Northern Gannets," Rosemary said. Her quick identification was impressive, considering it's a species neither of us had ever seen before. We stopped and watched as the birds wheeled majestically before plunging into the sea for fish, totally submerging themselves in the process.

Across the field, we saw some peculiar, large, vertical rocks. They were ancient gravestones. The guidebook said they dated from as far back as the fourth century. These *Ogham* stones were thought to be pre-Christian. These standing stones were an archaeologist's dream with weird writing composed mostly of broad slashes that were not fully deciphered until the twentieth century.

Farther on, we saw some more remnants of the past. The circular rock foundations called *clochains* were the remains of pagan or very early Christian dwellings. On the hillsides, we noticed that certain areas had been disrupted by plowing but had become overgrown. The guidebook explained that 160 years ago they were potato fields, but around 1840, the potato crop began to fail both from blight and exhausted soils. The famine led to the infamous Irish famine. The crisis had been anticipated a century earlier by Irish satirist Jonathan Swift, who had suggested in his *A Modest Proposal* that the poor sell their children to the rich to be eaten. Over two million Irish immigrants ignored Swift's advice and came to America instead.

In one sense, Ireland had never recovered from the famine. It may be the world's only nation whose present population (four million) is actually less than it was a century and a half ago (seven million). America never fully recovered from the famine either—especially if you've been to Boston on St. Paddy's Day.

We downed our lunch of soda bread, Kerry cheese, and a can of Guinness while overlooking Coumeenoole Bay at Dunmore Head. There was a picnic area, the sky was clearing, and the north Atlantic Ocean was actually blue rather than its usual ominous gray. There was a stone commemorating the filming of *Ryan's Daughter* nearby.

"So, this is the most western point in all of Europe," I reminded Rosemary. "It's only a short hop from here to New York." But my spiel was surprisingly challenged by a young Irish woman who was also enjoying the view. We had exchanged greetings when we first stopped.

"Excuse me for interjectin', but some of us Irish do not consider ourselves to be Europeans, for certain not culturally, and preferably not geographically. Ireland is part of the British Isles, but the 'British' in the term is strictly geographical not political."

"Really?" I said. "I've never heard that. This isn't Europe?"

"No," she said, "at least as far as I'm concerned."

The brief exchange was enlightening for me. Like most Americans, I had never considered it. When we were alone again, Rosemary reminded me of an Irish father's instruction to his two small children that we had overheard in a restaurant in Madrid a couple of years earlier. "We're not in Ireland here," he had told them. "We're in Europe."

In the distance, we could see Great Blasket Island, one of four larger islands that make up the windswept archipelago. They're uninhabited, but you can take a ferry over for the day. The last residents gave up trying to carve out a living on the desolate islands in 1953.

The coastal villages, weather, and scenery on the outer edge of the Dingle Peninsula reminded us of Iceland, although we'd never been there. The homes and shops are painted bright blues, pinks, and yellows. It was spittin' rain and the Atlantic was rough. We spent the evening in a pub in a village with the unique name of Ballyferriter. The pub was huddled on the coast with an ocean view right from the bar. We hunkered down for the evening with a Guinness and a Smithwick's. And ordered mussels.

Out the front window, facing the street, we noticed a scattered parade of young women passing by, walking or on bicycles. Two women parked their bikes against the front of the pub and walked inside. They couldn't have been much over eighteen, maybe in their early twenties. They both ordered a vodka and tonic. Two more entered and ordered the same drink. About as fast as two or three departed and headed off down the street, two or three took their place and repeated the routine.

"Do you mind if I ask what all you guys are doing out tonight?" I asked a dark-haired vodka drinker.

"Oh, we're just college students taking Celtic dancing classes here for two weeks. We're required to do it so as to appreciate our culture."

"What's up with the vodka?" I asked. "Is that part of the culture?"

"Oh, no, but we've got to fortify ourselves for the dancin,' and the teacher won't smell it. We're not supposed to be drinkin'."

"A Kerry footballer with an inferiority complex is
one who thinks he's just as good as everyone else."

John B. Keanne
1928-2002

An obvious advantage of traveling in Ireland is the ability to read the daily newspaper. The front page of the next morning's edition was filled with news over the latest sexual abuse scandal in the church. This one involved an overly testosteroned priest near Dublin. It was comforting to learn that such scandals were not restricted just to the United States and that Irish clerics were finally getting involved.

As more and more such scandals had surfaced in recent years, I'd been taking a hard look back at my own years as an altar boy in the 1950s, especially when some of the financial settlements were announced. I could recall spending considerable time alone with our parish priest in the rectory before and after mass when I was nine or ten, but for the life of me I could not remember a single incident of sexual impropriety by the priest. I've tried really hard to come up with something.

"You know, Rosemary," I said. "I'm thinking of filing a claim against the church. I mean all these altar boys were being fondled and molested back then, and now they're all getting big bucks from the church as settlement.

"Maybe you just weren't sufficiently attractive," Rosemary said over her morning tea.

"That's just my point. I should sue the church for loss of self-esteem. It's downright humiliating."

We decided to take a detour that day to see the Gallarus Oratory. The rock-built structure was over 1,000 years old and was used as a private chapel by early Christians. The structure was no Notre Dame Cathedral but was remarkable in its simplicity. It looks like some sort of inverted boat made from flat rocks fitted tightly together without the use of mortar. The building was still water tight.

Our destination for the day was the village of Feohanagh, and if we were feeling strong, we'd head on to Ballycurrane, but we became confused and found ourselves unable to locate the Dingle Way.

We've learned from previous experience that when asking directions in rural Ireland, there are certain criteria to be met. Peter McCarthy in his *McCarthy's Bar* explained the process. "The preferred approach is to turn the encounter into a social occasion," he told readers, "...on a par with what goes on when two strangers meet and get chatting at a party or a wedding reception."

An elderly man was walking our way.

"Good day to you," I began.

"And to you. It's a fine day for a walk outside. Where are you two headed?"

"Oh, we're going west on the Dingle Way but lost the path," I told him.

"Well, now, so you're walking the Dingle. I've done it myself a time ago. It was a grand experience. My daughter walked with me, but now she's off to school in Dublin. Going to be a nurse she tells me, but the phone rings last week and it's a teacher she wants to be. That's a fine profession, but mum and myself were wishing she'd want to be a technical type like an engineer. Just where are you from?"

"We're Americans," I told him.

"It's America, is it? My sister married a Yank she met in London, and they moved to Kansas. He's got something do to with horse racing or wagering."

"Do you mean Kentucky?

"Oh, I get those mixed up. Is that where the Darby is? Then that's the place. I mean to go visit her, but she tells me there's not much room in her house, but it's lying she is because they had three kids in the house, but they're grown and gone, so there must be an empty bed or two. With the price of a mortgage, it's a wonder they can keep it."

At this point, Rosemary and I knew that we'd best be careful. The conversation could lapse into a wide-ranging discussion of the world's economy, Clinton's sexual adventures, botany, Afghanistan, the price of meat or the advantages of cottage cheese over yogurt.

I held up my map and pointed to Feohanagh, rather than trying to pronounce the name of the place.

"That's a tiny village, and the scenery is as fine as in all of Ireland. You'll be headed that way if you avoid the next turn, but if you take it, then don't bother with the next because it's too far from your direction unless you go to the right."

"Thank you, sir," I responded. "Enjoy your walk."

"And you two as well," he said.

"That was really something. But I felt I ended the conversation too abruptly. How come they talk like that?" I asked Rosemary.

"It's stream of consciousness," she answered.

I still don't know what that means, but the conversation with the stranger was memorable. The problem with the Irish is that they're too damn likeable. They want you to like them, and they seem to genuinely care about you. Money seems to be a low priority in their lives. They've got the demeanor of a warm puppy with spunk and wit to boot.

We ended up spending the night in a B&B in the hamlet of Cuaso. We were happy with our location since it was the closest B&B to the shoulder of Brandon Mountain—the toughest uphill slog on the Dingle Way. It's also the place where Brandon Creek flows into the Atlantic. Why is that important? Because this was the spot where Brendan the Voyager (AD 484-577) set sail and discovered America—nine centuries before Columbus.

According to legend and tainted Irish history books, Brendan and seventeen monks hop-scotched across the Atlantic with stops in the Outer Hebrides, Iceland, and Newfoundland before landing on the east coast of what is now the United States. He did it in a boat made of leather stretched across a wooden frame, thus making Captains Bligh, Cook, Columbus, and Shackleton look like real pussies.

Tommy Makem offered more details in his *Secret Ireland*. Writing with a straight face, Makem wrote:

> "Resting for some time in Newfoundland, he started out once more and sailed down the east coast of Canada and the United States. He stopped at a number of places, including what is now St. Augustine, in Florida, before returning to Ireland."

Understandably Brendan was made a saint for his efforts. A book in Latin detailed the voyage several centuries later. It was entitled *Navigatio Sancti Brendan Abbatis*. If your local library doesn't have it, ask them if they could get it through inter-library loan. Better ask with a smile on your face.

Okay, laugh if you must, but consider this: In 1976 Irishman Tom Severen and his buddies built a boat similar to Brendan's and set out across the Atlantic in an attempt to prove Brendan's sixth-century voyage was possible. They succeeded in sailing to Newfoundland. His book, *The Brendan Voyage*, was a big success (at least in Ireland) and made St. Brendan naysayers stand up and take notice. A monument to Severen's voyage stood along Brendan Creek.

As we headed up Brandon Mountain the next day, Rosemary began singing a little Bob Marley. "One world, One love, Let's get together, It'll be all right."

I couldn't blame her for feeling good. The sky was a bright blue, and there was a breeze off the emerald green Atlantic in the distance. The mountain landscape was breathtaking. It couldn't have been any more lovely. It's time to go on record and just say it. Ireland has the world's prettiest countryside. Sure Switzerland's got bigger mountains, and Spain has hilltop castles, but with thatched cottages, grazing sheep behind rock walls, pastel villages, and mind-boggling greenery, Ireland takes the prize. Is that Maureen O'Hara walking our way?

We considered deviating from the Way to climb 3,126-foot Mt. Brandon. It's the second highest in Ireland, but we thought we didn't have the time. We ascended a narrow col, and a stile got us over a fence. There was nearby *Ogham* stone along the track. In the distance, we saw Brandon Bay, the Slieve Mish Mountains, and Ireland's highest highway, the road over Connor Pass between Cloghane and Dingle town.

We didn't say anything to one another, but we both were thinking the same thing. The Slieve Mish was the range we first saw when we left Tralee days ago. We know we're going to complete the Dingle Way. Before descending into Brandon village, we took a detour to the left to Brandon Point. Far below, we could see white caps on the Atlantic. And directly below us, on the cliffs, there were strange birds. They looked like large ravens with orange feet and orange bills.

I dug out my *Field Guide to the Birds of Great Britain and Europe* from the bottom of my pack. The book said the birds are choughs. I pointed to the picture in the book but didn't dare attempt to pronounce the name. Rosemary scanned the cliffs with a pair of binoculars. "Look at these a second," she said. "I'm not sure what they are, but you need to check them out. I think they're puffins."

She was right. The birds were unmistakable with their colorful triangular bills and clown faces. They were the same species that inhabit the cliffs of North America from Maine to Newfoundland. We were excited to see our first puffins and watched them as they flew back and forth from their rocky nests down to the ocean. They returned each time with a mouthful of small fish for their chicks. It was good to know that I was not the only one that had an appetite for anchovies.

"A gentleman is one who never hurts
anyone's feelings unintentionally."

Oscar Wilde
1854-1900

The tiny hamlet of Brandon sat on Brandon Bay, a subsidiary of the North Atlantic. Wags like to describe these sparsely populated Irish towns as being "so small they have only four pubs and three churches," a testament to the two primary activities of the communities. Tired as we were, we kept walking toward Cloghane. There was a strand just beyond Brandon but there wasn't a soul on it.

Suddenly we witnessed a peculiar phenomenon. The sun broke out from behind the clouds and began warming the afternoon air. Within minutes of its appearance, six or seven people from the surrounding homes showed up and began lounging on the beach. It happened so fast they must have been wearing their shorts and studying the clouds in anticipation of the sun's arrival. Their rapid response would have made any fireman envious.

We walked another few minutes, and the sun disappeared again. I turned to look and sure enough, the beach was empty. "Do you think they spend all summer doing that?" I said to Rosemary. "No wonder there are so many pubs."

"So you're doing the Dingle, are ya?" the bartender at Cloghane's pub asked us. "When ya first walked in, I thought you might be one of those Americans lookin' for their roots. We get them in here all the time."

"No, I'm Polish and my wife's Italian. We're sure we have no roots in Ireland," I replied.

"Well, there are certain advantages to that. I didn't have any trouble finding my roots. They're buried across the road behind the church. I've never investigated them. Judging by my inheritances, I don't think any of 'em amounted to much."

"Maybe your ancestors weren't great achievers, but Ireland's got a rich legacy of talent like Yeats, George Bernard Shaw, Brendan Behan, and Bono," I reminded him.

"Sure, we're great with poems and songs but lousy at technology. For many of us, rosary beads and shillelaghs are high-tech. The only famous Irish inventor I ever heard of was John Holland. A fella in Dingletown wrote a book about him."

"Who's that?" I say. "I never heard of the guy."

"He invented the submarine. No kidding; you can look it up. But I'm not certain if he did it on purpose or was just a bad boat builder."

It was raining hard the next morning as we ate breakfast. There were three other couples in the dining area. We overheard two of them discussing the fact that they may have to cancel their planned hike up Mt. Brandon because of the weather. We were supposed to make the long walk from Cloghane to Castlegregory after breakfast.

Continental breakfasts in Italy and France with their coffee and croissant are just an excuse to pad the bill by a few euros. Want proof? Next time you're in France, tell the proprietor you don't want their breakfast and to reduce the bill accordingly. "No, no, Monsieur. We cannot do that," will be the guaranteed response.

But a full Irish breakfast, best served in a B&B, can be legendary, and this one was no exception. Along with expected juice, eggs and toast, there are usually bangers (sausages), rashers (bacon), bosty's (pancakes), and fried tomatoes. (Why anyone would want to fry a lovely red tomato is a mystery locked beneath the Blarney Stone.)

Our breakfast that morning also included salmon. Typically there is something called black and/or white pudding, but it's not a pudding at all. Black pudding is slices of congealed beef or pork blood mixed with filler such as oats. It's usually fried. Mmmm! For the squeamish, there's white pudding that is a bloodless variation. Black pudding has got to hark back to the days of Ireland's famine when discarding any animal protein was simply not done. I ate my portion but Rosemary abstained. On most days along the Dingle Way, our full Irish breakfast was enough to get us through until the evening.

We felt guilty about lingering so long over breakfast, so we were happy to see another couple show up. Their arrival meant we could hang around a little longer, waiting out the rain and not be the last to depart the dry comfort of the place.

We exchanged greetings. The man and woman were from Boston and were walking the Dingle Way in the opposite direction as Rosemary and I were. "My father and mother did it a couple of years ago, and they raved about the experience. He was always proud of our family's Irish roots. He died this past winter, so we thought we would kind of do it in his memory," the woman explained.

"He's happy to see you here, I'm sure," I said, making certain to use the present rather than the past tense.

The two told us that they had left Castlegregory yesterday and that there was a delightful seven-mile stretch along the beach that adjoined Brandon Bay. "You guys should enjoy it," the man told us.

Thus properly motivated and dressed from head to toe in rain gear, we headed north while sharing our single umbrella. We crossed the Owenmore, Scorid, and Glennahoo Rivers before we reached the sandy shoreline. Fermoyle Strand is the longest beach in Ireland, and the rain subsided sufficiently to allow us to enjoy the experience. The beach was home to all kinds of shorebirds. Our walking interrupted the hunt for food by orange-billed oystercatchers, sandpipers, and large flocks of sanderlings who ran ahead of us, only having to repeat the process a few minutes later.

I glanced over my shoulder and noticed two beach walkers gaining on us. A man and a woman were carrying full backpacks. They began to pass us and we exchanged greetings. Their language was English but with a strong German accent. One looked familiar. "Aren't you the fellow we met in Tom Crean's South Pole Pub in Annascaul?" I asked.

"Oh, yes," he said. "I remember you guys. That was just after the two of us split up," Werner said.

"Well, it's nice to see you guys together again." I told Werner's girlfriend, "He was kind of upset because he told us he left the tent with you and didn't have anywhere to sleep. We were impressed that he did that."

Werner's girlfriend was candid. "The truth is he was upset that night. He could have had the tent. As soon as he was gone, I folded it up and checked into a B&B. I had the credit card."

Apparently it was two or three nights later that the two reunited somewhere around Dunquin. Rosemary and I didn't have the courage to ask Werner where he slept during their estrangement, and I did not ask the nature of the disagreement. There's nothing like a bit of melodrama when doing the Dingle Way. Werner and his significant other walked faster than we did and soon disappeared around a corner of the beach.

"How come you always get to carry the credit card?" I asked Rosemary cautiously.

Our last official night along the Dingle was spent at Castlegregory. Our plan was to walk from there on to Camp in the morning, then catch the bus into Tralee and beyond. There was a Bank of Ireland caravan (trailer) on the edge of Castlegregory. I'd seen this phenomenon before in Scotland. The bank simply moves the caravan from small town to small town throughout the week on a scheduled basis. The concept makes perfect sense, thus providing banking services without having to commit to the construction of a building.

Americans would never stand for such an approach, being deluded into old-fashioned thinking that if the bank doesn't have a big brick building, it can't be a safe place to put money. That belief was thoroughly disproved by the banking and mortgage crisis a few years ago. Most religions have a similar approach. If the church building isn't a massive rock or brick structure, with soaring buttresses and round windows, the religion inside can't be trusted. There's no reason religious services couldn't be held in a travel trailer. It would be God's Airstream.

Castlegregory was a seaside village on the narrow neck of land that divides Tralee Bay from Brandon Bay. We checked into the first B&B we saw. The landlady had no trouble sizing us up once she saw our backpacks. "You're walking the Dingle, are you?" she said.

"We're about finished," I answered. "It's been a good walk."

There was a photograph of the pope in the hallway, probably replacing the one of John Kennedy that was so prevalent across Ireland a generation ago. For a change, the double room was almost large enough for two people. There were clear plastic protectors covering the mattress. We'd seen this feature before but chose not to think of the reasoning behind it. The usual crucifix hung above the bed. A crucifix in that location can be a bit intimidating, but in Ireland it comes with the territory.

Before we left on the trip, an Irish Catholic friend had summed things up for us. "My mother told me when I was a child that when you're Irish, you're Catholic. And if you're not Catholic, you can't be Irish. Until I was thirteen, I thought Jesus was Irish. That's just the way it is." Rosemary and I put our religion on hold and slept soundly, practicing Catholics or not.

I found irony in the fact that only a few miles away in Annascaul, Tom Crean's Inn has photos hanging on the wall of gaunt Antarctic explorers in a battle for their lives. In Castlegregory, we saw photos of surfer dudes riding the waves of the Atlantic as they crashed on the beaches of the Dingle Peninsula. Castlegregory was home to the World Surfing Championships in 2000.

That evening, over Guinness and chips in Jimmy Fitzgerald's Pub, the unavoidable subject of St. Patrick himself made its way into the conversation with a flat-capped local. He was gregarious, talkative, and tipsy. I decided to quiz him about a couple of things.

"What about all the sheep we saw everywhere? They're all over the countryside. It seems like anyone with an acre has got a few. But I seldom see mutton on the menu," I told him.

"It's true. There are a lot of the foul bastards. We raise 'em because of the government subsidy. They encourage us so we'll have something to sell to the Arabs. If it wasn't for the subsidy, you wouldn't see a one," he explained.

Encouraged by his willingness to discuss important issues, I moved on to more sacred things.

"I read somewhere that a few years back the church eliminated some of the saints from its official list because there was no proof that they actually existed. I think St. Christopher was one of them. What about St. Patrick?" I asked.

"No, no, last I checked he's still a saint. They'd never do that. It would be too much trouble to change the name on half the churches in the country," he replied.

"What about the snake thing? Is there any truth to that?"

"Now that *is* a bunch of malarkey. My son did a paper on that very subject in school. Turns out there weren't any snakes in Ireland in the first place, and the scoundrel took the credit for drivin' 'em out. He might just as well as said he drove out the elephants."

"Maybe the church should start checking on all the miracles attributed to the Divine. A lot of them are probably just bunk," I said.

"Of course they are, but that's not going to happen either. The church can't afford to lose any more credibility."

I ended the conversation with a question. "Have you lived in Castlegregory all your life?" I asked.

"Not yet," he replied.

And with that, we headed out the door. The best thing about walking in Ireland is the people you meet, but the problem with the Irish is that they're just too damn likeable.

8

The Annapurna Circuit

Searching for the Himalayan Yeti

Nepal
128 miles

In the midst of ascending Thorung La Pass, the realization struck me that maybe at sixty-six years old, I was biting off more than I could chew. The pass was 17,760 feet above sea level. Only the day before, I had had an attack of altitude sickness. "Are you okay, sir?" our porter Hakkim had asked as he saw me drop my trekking poles, weave out of control, and stagger a few feet off the trail. I kept it to myself that the brief attack of acute mountain sickness (AMS) had nearly made me to pee my pants. Like others in our group, I had been suffering from a constant headache for the past few days but was not taking Diamox. I started popping the pills immediately.

It wasn't as if my attack was unexpected. There were plenty of signs along the trek, warning of the dangers of AMS and advice on its prevention, including drinking plenty of liquids and not climbing too high too fast. Porters along the Circuit also did their best to protect their customers from having problems. For the past few days, we had been told

Bmarr 12

to gain an extra thousand feet or so of elevation at the end of the day, before descending back to the teahouse for the night.

"Climb high. Sleep low" was the mantra. I figured the last thing the porters wanted was to hassle hauling an old white guy back down the trail to safety. In the sixties and seventies when the Himalayan trekking boom began, as many as ten trekkers died each year from AMS. That number had dropped considerably to about two a year now. A couple of days earlier, we had spotted a wind sock and a helicopter pad outside of the village of Manang. I figured the helicopter was there for guys like me, just in case. Considering the expense, locals were probably expendable. The village of Manang sat at 11,614 feet above sea level and most trekkers spend two nights to rest and acclimatize before continuing over the big pass. There was also a daily AMS lecture by the Himalayan Rescue Association, but Bob and I didn't attend.

We had been trekking six or seven days by the time we reached Thorung Phedi (14,600). It was a bleak place composed of a couple of lodges solely for those about to tackle Thorung La in the morning. The pass was the highest point on the Annapurna Circuit. There wasn't much around except the wind, the cold, and the Himalayas. We forced ourselves to tack on the recommended additional 1,000 feet of altitude before returning to eat and sleep. "We'll wake you at four in the morning," our guide Hira told us. "Don't forget to wear your headlamps."

I had been sufficiently intimidated by the pass to ask one of the guides in our group about the possibility of a getting carried over on the back of a horse, although I didn't see any horses in the corrals at Thorung Phedi.

"Do you want a yak?" he asked me. I didn't know if he was serious or not.

"Do people ride yaks?" I asked Bob, my trekking partner. His knowledge of yak riding in the Himalayas was negligible. We were already awake before the knock on the window came. We headed for the lodge's kitchen for the usual hot tea and mystery porridge. About ten of us were huddled around the wood stove, all more intent on obtaining calories than on having an enjoyable breakfast.

The scene as we ascended was memorable. It was still dark. There were about a dozen or so headlamps zigzagging up the pass in front of me and an equal number behind. Apparently the various guides and porters were in sync, and all groups from both the lodges began the climb simultaneously. Your place in the line snaking up the pass was determined by your pace, not by the group you were in or the porter you hired. The scene was eerie. The track was snow covered. I kept my head down, trying to stay with the group but couldn't. It was slightly more than a 3,000-foot gain from Thorung Phedi to the top. I've climbed that much in a day before but never at this elevation. The thin air began to take its toll.

I eventually adopted a routine of ten steps, followed by a rest stop of ten breaths. Others overtook me but there was no shame in that. There was little conversation among us. Everyone was focused. I found comfort in seeing that there were a few trekkers even slower than I was. Without a bush or rock to hide behind, the early morning light revealed a woman relieving herself just off the trail. There was no shame in that either. Hakkim, our porter, was just a few trekkers behind me, carrying our forty-pound GoLite pack. He could probably jog to the top but felt a sense of responsibility to keep an eye on my progress. There was no sign of Bob. He was a decade younger than I and in much better shape. I assumed he was way ahead.

A couple of places along the way had major vertical exposure. Although the track was two or three feet wide, a careless moment or an attack of AMS dizziness could have serious consequences. Later that day, I suggested to Hira that it might be a good idea to construct a protective rope railing at these dangerous places. His response was quick. "Who is going to pay for it?" he said. "Will you pay? This is Nepal."

Just before reaching the top, a trekker pointed out a headstone in a ravine below. One of the guidebooks said it was the final resting place of a trekker who apparently died climbing Thorung La. "Tony and Jean Allen ask that passing trekkers check that the stones on their son's cairn are still in place," the book said. There were no other details.

Most of the other trekkers were already taking photographs and shaking hands by the time I made it to the top. There was every reason to celebrate. This was one of the world's highest passes. Only serious mountaineers will ever stand at a greater elevation. A sign marked the saddle. It was covered with colorful prayer flags.

CONGRATULATIONS FOR THE SUCCESS!!!
HOPE YOU ENJOYED THE TREK IN MANANG
SEE YOU AGAIN!!!

I'd planned for this moment and dug out a small plastic blue and white Continental Divide Trail marker from my pack and hung it among the flapping prayer flags. Bob and I thought it would be funny to see a directional sign from one of America's landmark long-distance trails hanging on a Himalayan Pass.

The other trekkers were mostly from Europe and didn't get it. They'd never heard of the CDT. That's okay. I've also carried a State of Wyoming banner with its buckin' bronco logo and had my photo taken holding the flag.

It was a cloudless morning, and the Kali Gandaki Valley was visible thousands of feet below. Two peaks, Yakawa Kang and Khatung Kang, rose like sentries on each side of the pass. Each was over 21,000 feet high. Bob shook my hand. "Congratulations," he said. "Pretty good for an old guy."

"Yes," I answered. "You did good. I was worried about you."

Rosemary and I spend the winters in the Southwest, and if it hadn't been for my New Mexican friend and neighbor, Bob, I probably wouldn't have gone to Nepal. Initially my son had said he'd go but ultimately backed off. "I kind of think my boss would question my commitment to my banking career if I told him I was going trekking in the Himalayas for three weeks," he explained.

By that time, I was well into planning for the trip, but the more I learned, the more reservations I had. Apparently Nepal's Maoists were attempting to take over control of the country. There were frequent reports of Maoists aggressively demanding money from trekkers to finance their revolution. There was an election scheduled about the time I was going to be in Nepal, and experts were warning that violence could erupt if the vote didn't go their way. Even the State Department was telling Americans to avoid Nepal.

"What kind of Maoists are they?" Bob commented sarcastically. "They can't be very dangerous if they're involved in an election. Do you think Lenin or Stalin was elected? Nepal's Maoists must be pussies."

"Yeah, but what about the State Department warning?" I asked him.

"You can't go by those guys. George Bush pissed off the entire world. Everyone's mad at us. I heard the State Department is about to warn Americans not to travel to Canada or any of the blue states. Oregon is especially dangerous," he explained with a smile.

I persisted with my fears. "Do you know about the royal massacre? I read that in 2001 the deranged son of the King of Nepal pulled out an automatic weapon and mowed down nine members of the royal family including his father and mother, the king and queen. Nepal is not a normal country, Bob."

"What do you care? Are you a member of Nepal's royal family?"

Bob did nothing to relieve my fears, but I decided to go anyway.

"Don't forget we're going to have to get shots," Bob told me a few days later.

"See, I told you if we went to Nepal, we'd get shot." I said.

The guy at my local university's International Travel Health Center asked me where I'm going, and he brought up a map on his computer. Nepal was in red. I didn't know if that has anything to do with the Maoists. "You'll definitely have to get a hepatitis shot," he told me. "And we recommend a rabies shot too. You probably don't need a malaria shot since you'll be at higher altitudes," he explained.

"Rabies? Isn't that in case I'm bitten by a rabid dog?" I asked him. -

"Yes, you'll be walking through many small villages, and there's a possibility that you could be bitten by a rabid dog."

"Hell, if that's your reasoning, I probably need one here in New Mexico. What's the difference?"

He ignored my reply and nailed me twice in the arm. As I rolled down and buttoned the sleeve of my shirt, he gave me one more caution. "You know there's a report of outbreaks of human rotavirus in Kathmandu. I assume you're going to Kathmandu."

"Are you going to tell me I need a shot for that too?" I ask him.

"No, rotavirus mostly is found in children. But be careful over there. Wash your hands a lot."

Bob and I loaded up on a cornucopia of medications just in case. We took along some prescription drugs named after ancient Roman generals. There was Cipro, Diamox, Azithromycin, and Norfloxacin. Bob assured me that he knew which one is supposed to do what. We packed an MSR pump and iodine tablets for water purification. We also had a couple bars of soap. The soap was a smart move. In nearly three weeks, the only soap we saw was ours. Hygiene was not a priority in Nepal. We stayed in some very marginal places, and our food was prepared in kitchens without even a perfunctory nod to sanitation. A trekker told me that she saw a baby's diaper being changed on the table where food was prepared a few minutes later.

It was a relief to see my misspelled last name written on a piece of cardboard and being held by our hotel driver when we got through customs and walked out of Kathmandu's airport. Finding our hotel in the chaos of Kathmandu would have been a challenge. That night's room was the only reservation we had made prior to arriving. There was a lot of conflicting information on whether to book a guide or porter in the United States before going trekking in Nepal. We did not, and it worked out. That evening, we walked the streets of Thamel, Kathmandu's tourist section. We walked the streets because Thamel had no sidewalks. Numerous signs announcing TREKKING INFORMATION hung from hotels and shops. It reminded me of Mexico. Tell anyone what you want, whether it be a donkey, car, blanket, or excursion, and they'd make it happen. The Nepalese may be poor, but they do not lack ambition.

We ended up hammering out a trekking deal on the third-story deck of our hot-waterless hotel. We had decided beforehand that we were going to do the Annapurna Circuit. The trek is on every list of the world's great treks, although its purity is threatened by the construction of roads on both sides of the Annapurna massif. We sipped beer poured from one liter bottles and negotiated our big trip with some local guy the hotel had contacted. Bob did most of the talking. I was too taken with the whole scene around us to pay too much attention to the details.

There were some honest to gosh prayer flags flying overhead, and I might have been able to see the Himalayas in the distance if it weren't for Kathmandu's dense pollution. Most of all, I was enthralled by the beer. It was not the beer so much as the label. The brand was Everest beer! And sure enough, there on the label was picture of Nepal's national hero, Tenzing Norgay, standing on the summit of the world's highest peak, ice axe and all. Some small print added to the label's mystique: IN COOPERATION WITH THE NEPAL MOUNTAINEERING ASSOCIATION. Drinking this beer was a grand adventure. Coors with its Rocky Mountain logo just wasn't in the same league.

Bob interrupted my beer-sipping adventure fantasy. "Get out your Visa card," he announced. "We have to pay now. We leave the day after tomorrow. They'll pick us up here at the hotel that morning."

Of course, it was a leap of faith to hand over our credit cards to a total stranger whom we had met only an hour earlier in a peculiar country far, far away from my known world. I couldn't help but think that we'd never see this guy again. For $750 each, we were promised a ride to the trailhead at Besisahar, all the necessary permits, thirteen nights' accommodations along the trek, a porter/guide to carry our one loaded backpack, three meals a day, and an airplane ride at the end of the trek over the Annapurna massif from Jomsom to Pokhara. We'd have to take the bus back from Pokhara to Kathmandu. We'd been told that that there was no shame in flying out from Jomsom back to semi-civilization, and it would eliminate a boring four-day downhill slog. "After two weeks walking, you'll have had enough," one guidebook said. It turned out it to be good advice.

"Just as you wish."

Tenzing Norgay
1914-1986
(replying to Edmund Hillary as they neared Everest's summit as to whether it was too dangerous and perhaps they should turn back)

When Tensing Norgay joined Hillary on the summit of Mount Everest May 29, 1953, he simultaneously became world famous and a symbol for Nepalese nationalism. According to Maurice Isserman and Stewart Weaver's masterpiece on the history of mountain climbing, *Fallen Giants,* those bent on maintaining an independent Nepal distinct from India and free from foreign pressures, especially the British, jumped on Tenzing's notoriety. The problem was that Tenzing was not Nepalese. He was born in Tibet and had been living the past twenty years in India. "They wanted me to say that I was a Nepali, not an Indian," Tenzing said after his triumph on Everest.

He was also pressured to say that it was he, not Hillary, who first reached the top of the mountain. Nepalese nationalists wanted the word to believe that it was one of their own, not some citizen of the British Empire, who first reached the world's highest point. (Hillary was a Kiwi.)

Adding to the nationalists' argument was the fact that there was no photograph of Hillary standing alone on the summit. That may be due to Hillary's innate modesty or maybe because Tenzing did not know how to use a camera. There was, however, the famous photo of Tenzing.

It was Hillary who reached for his Kodak and snapped the photo of Tenzing holding his ice axe draped with the flags of India, Britain, Nepal, and the United Nations over his head. In their book, Isserman and Weaver stated that the image was one of the most famous photographs of the twentieth century. They may be right; after all, it's on the label of Everest Beer.

During the first few chaotic days after their triumph, a confused Tensing actually signed a statement saying that he was the first to summit, a statement he could not read since he was illiterate. There's little doubt that technically Hillary was the first to summit, but a joint statement was released for the sake of propriety that the two had made it on Everest's summit "almost together." Word of their triumph reached all of London on June 2, the same day of Queen Elizabeth II's coronation. Hillary, the New Zealander and son of a beekeeper, died in 2008 at the age of eighty-eight. Norgay Tenzing died in 1986 in India at the age of seventy-one.

Bob and I had a day to kill before leaving on our trek, so we decided to go to Bhaktapur, a World Heritage site, on the edge of Kathmandu. We took the bus. Bob proved to be very good at figuring out public transportation in third world countries. Our hotel man gave us a rough outline of the bus route and where to find the bus station. Bob led as we snaked our way through Kathmandu's labyrinth of humanity and traffic. We walked by the royal palace, the same palace where the royal massacre occurred. It was a somber place guarded by soldiers toting automatic weapons. There were no tours and no daily changing-of-the-guard ceremonies. Inside, the latest king, Gyanendra, was packing his bags, getting ready for the expected Maoist election victory.

I had already decided that I didn't like Kathmandu. "What's to like?" I told Bob. "It's really polluted, really noisy, and really congested." Adding to the chaos was the fact that the power went off for five hours every afternoon. "We sell power to India," our hotel man explained "Nepal needs the money from India."

"But what about Nepal?. Don't your people need the power during the day to keep the country productive?" I challenged.

"No, we need money more than electricity," he told me.

"But the people probably don't get the money. Just the government benefits and the people are stuck with no power," I answered.

Bob signaled me to shut up, lest I be suspected of being some sort of troublemaker or maybe even a Communist. Of course, being a Communist in Nepal isn't necessarily bad. There are lots of them, and most people believed they would win the upcoming election. Sounding off now might get me a cushy government job in the new Communist government, and then I'll get some of the money from selling the electricity. The irony of the power shortage really came home as we walked the Annapurna Circuit. As you might expect, cascading water was everywhere. Where there are snow-capped mountains, there are waterfalls. And where there are waterfalls, there are hydroelectric plants—just not in Nepal. Breaking the cycle of poverty in third world nations is not easy.

The bus to Bhaktapur accentuated everything I had come to dislike about Kathmandu. At least 3,000 people jammed into the bus, which had no more than thirty seats. There were people hanging on the side. There were some kids on the roof.

"I may be too old and too white for this," I mumbled to Bob as we squeezed on to the bus, presumably setting a new Nepalese bus-stuffing record. Bob and I were the only white guys among the passengers, and we were also the only ones over five feet tall. Later that day, we bumped into another American as we toured Bhaktapur. I told him about the bus. "That's nothing," he said. "If you think it's crowded here, don't go to India. It's got more people than dirt." My time in Kathmandu and the film *Slum Dog Millionaire* sated my need to ever go to India.

Our visit to Bhaktapur was a big success, however. Vehicle traffic was banned in the city, and we walked along timeless, cobblestone streets amidst centuries-old, medieval temples, courtyards, shrines, and ancient squares. We saw woodworkers, potters, and weavers. Women dressed in colorful saris turned grain into flour. Durbar Square was the focal point of Bhaktapur, and women filled bright pots with water from a communal fountain in the shadow of copulating elephants carved from rock. It's as if a time machine had thrust us back into the sixteenth century. I can't say enough good things about Bhaktapur. It almost erased the memory of Kathmandu.

We met our porter, Hakkim, the next morning at 9:00 a.m. He was a slightly built, young man of about thirty. His English was poor, but I credit him for making every attempt to communicate with us in English throughout our trek. The hotel man, who put our trip together, had explained that Hakkim was a combination porter/guide. There's no requirement to hire a guide or porter to do the Annapurna Circuit. And like all famous treks, once you reach the trailhead, you can just follow the German girl in front of you. There were always other hikers doing what you're doing. And for a lousy $16 a day, Bob and I figured hiring someone to carry our one large pack would give our trek a little prestige. After all, how many times were we going to go trekking in the Himalayas? It was part of the experience. British explorer Sir Richard Burton wasn't carrying his pack when he discovered Lake Tanganyika and Liz Taylor.

Our road trip to the start of the Annapurna Circuit was in a dilapidated Toyota Corolla driven by a friend of Hakkim's. Hakkim put our GoLite backpack in the trunk, which was held shut with a rope. Bob gave the car a jaundiced look. "At least we won't be mistaken for one of those high-priced National Geographic Society adventure tours," he commented.

It proved to be a six hour, hair-raising, bone-jarring, almost dangerous ride through Kathmandu and rural Nepal to Besisahar. It took two hours just to get out of the city. As far as we could tell, Kathmandu had no traffic regulations, no stop signs, no signal lights, not even a traffic cop. It was vehicular mayhem.

One major intersection was particularly chaotic. The car horn was the main weapon used to make forward progress, and the bleating cacophony attacked our ears. Vehicles and animals of all kinds—trucks, donkeys, cars, bicycles, mopeds, cows, unicycles, carts and pedestrians—played a game of chicken in an attempt to get through the congestion. And since traffic moved so slowly, opportunistic vendors walked among the congestion, selling brooms and bread, beads, and belts.

Bob and I sat dumbfounded in the backseat taking in the scene. One sight stays with me, even today. Along the roadside, a woman stood in front of a rickety table, selling produce. She was holding a baby. What struck me was the fact that she had only three or four small melons for sale. That's it. She would stand there all day, waiting for someone to buy a melon for a few rupees. She seemed oblivious to the traffic and stared blankly ahead. Poverty was everywhere in Nepal, and so was unrealistic hope.

Ultimately we emerged from the chaos of the city on to a rural road. It was paved, maybe thirty years ago, and has had no maintenance since. It was narrow, potholed, and serpentine. Pedestrians and cows appeared in the middle of the road out of nowhere. Our driver never waited for them to cross but instead wound around them. At one point, Hakkim decided we needed a little entertainment and reached into the glove compartment for some music cassettes.

"What kind of music you like?" he asked. His question brought me to laughter. Here we were in the back-o'-beyond in a bucket of bolts, dodging cows, carts, kids, and road craters, and an Asian man asks us to choose our music. I just couldn't imagine that Buddy Holly's *Peggy Sue* or Tony Bennett's *I Left My Heart in San Francisco* was on any of the tracks.

"You pick something," I told him. Seconds later, some sort of Indian Bollywood rock filled the car. It was all pretty bizarre. "We're having fun now, Bob," I said. Bob pretended to be asleep.

We started actually walking at Besishar. Hakkim dutifully asked for our passports and presented them, along with our trekking permits, to the officials at the Annapurna Conservation Area office. Everything seemed to be in order. A bus from Kathmandu arrived, and some other trekkers and their porters filed out.

"It was a ride from hell," a man from Holland told us. "We left at 6:00 a.m. It took forever to get here."

Bob and I were glad we opted for the Toyota Corolla. Hakkim would carry our big GoLite pack weighing about forty pounds. Bob and I each had small daypacks. Compared to many of the others along the Circuit, we were traveling light. I had read that many trekkers abused their porters by taking way too much stuff, and we did see instances of porters being overloaded. In the days ahead, we witnessed porters carrying hard-cover books, extra hiking boots, camera tri-pods, electric hairdryer, unnecessary tents, and large cans of foodstuffs like peanut butter, marmalade, and peaches. One English trekker had his porter carrying two bottles of whiskey and even lacked the decency to transfer the booze into lighter Nalgene bottles.

Both Bob and I had sleeping bags. They may not be actually necessary along the Circuit, unless you're camping. (But we never saw anyone tenting.) Every teahouse we stayed in offered us heavy quilts at night. It seems that one could do the Circuit with a very lightweight summer bag or just a sheet, and pile on the quilts when necessary. Every trekker we saw, however, had a down bag.

"Let's get after it," Bob announced.

"Give me a second to get my trekking pole out of the big pack," I asked motioning to Hakkim to take it off so I could retrieve the pole. It was tightly wedged into the bowels of the pack, and I had difficulty getting it out. I grabbed the end, gave it a yank, and my MSR Denali III separated. I stood sheepishly holding half a trekking pole. It was an inauspicious beginning to my trek of a lifetime.

"You can always use it as a backscratcher," Bob said.

Today an estimated 60,000 international travelers journey every year to Nepal to walk in the Himalayas. In addition to the classic Annapurna Circuit, other popular treks are the Annapurna Sanctuary, Everest Base Camp, The Royal Trek (Prince Charles did it the 1980s), and the Jomsom Trek, which is actually the last few days of the Annapurna Circuit done in the opposite direction.

The father of all this adventure trekking may be the American Jimmy Roberts who, in 1964, began advertising guided overnight hikes in the Himalayas. He called his venture Mountain Travel Nepal. In 1965, according to *Fallen Giants,* three middle-aged American women took Roberts up on his offer and became the vanguard of the hoards that were to follow. The 1960s also saw the arrival of hippies and flower children to Kathmandu, motivated by beat poets like Allen Ginsberg, seeking their personal karma.

By 1975 there were more than seventy trekking agencies in Nepal. It may be just a question of time until the Nepalese government, in order to provide employment for its people, makes the hiring of trekking companies mandatory. Peru has taken that step for anyone wishing to walk the Inca

Trail to see Machu Picchu. Roberts' real ingenuity was coming up with the term "trekking" to describe his services. It had the sound of genuine adventure rather than simple, soft tourism.

In 1973 two young Brits, Tony and Maureen Wheeler, wrote a pamphlet called *Across Asia on the Cheap*. That early entrepreneurial effort evolved into more that 650 separate *Lonely Planet* guides, and at least one is in every backpack anywhere in the world. Their guides helped make it possible for nearly anyone to venture into the world's recesses. The couple sold the business in 2007 for an estimated $100 million.

The idealistic Shangri-la of Nepal soon succumbed to the onslaught of Western culture, and today Snickers bars and Coca Cola are available along the entire Annapurna Circuit. That intrusion, however, does not dampen the experience. We were told early on that the Circuit was as much a cultural experience as a mountain experience, and that was an accurate assessment. All along the route, we stayed in Gurung villages, visited Hindu and Buddhist temples, passed stupas, pagodas, rows of prayer wheels, and walked under colorful prayer flags, all accented by five-mile-high peaks. We visited *gompas* where orange-robed monks meditated and studied the teachings of Buddha. We experienced a culture that was decades removed from the twenty-first century.

The desire by the Nepalese to cater to the international trekkers even has them serving baked goods like chocolate cake and apple pie along the Circuit, which has been nicknamed the "The Apple Pie Trail." Bob and I were aware of the trail's association with apple pie, and when we saw the dessert on a menu, we each ordered a slice at a rundown restaurant along our trek. Our request was followed by a bit of shouting from the kitchen until a boy ran out of the café and down the track. A few minutes later, he reappeared with apples. Apple pie on the menu did not mean there was an apple pie on the shelf in the kitchen. More than an hour later, still warm from the oven, we were served our pie. The Nepalese are not ones to miss the opportunity to make a few rupees.

For a few miles that first day, we wandered up a dirt road, which soon became a narrow dirt track. Our starting point, Besisahar, had an elevation of 2,690 feet. For the next nine days, we hiked up the Marsyangdi River Valley. Our goal was Thorung La Pass, an elevation gain of 15,000 feet. From the top of the pass, the Annapurna Circuit track descended the arid Kali Gandaki Valley back through Jomsom to lush Pokhura. But that first day, the landscape was almost tropical. Women planted seedlings in rice paddies and didn't give us a second glance as we walked past their fields. Three or four groups, totaling about fifteen trekkers, walked with us that first afternoon. They were scattered along the track. I recognized the Dutchman who got off the bus in Besisahar.

There were also the two young Brits who we had shared a beer with us two days earlier in Thamel and a German threesome who had stayed at the same hotel as us the night before we left Kathmandu. Also walking with us was a group of four or five American college kids from California. One of them told us that they were doing the Annapurna Circuit as part of their studies and would get college credit for the experience. In four years of college in the 1960s, I never did anything but sit behind a desk and listen to an old man drone on, and on, and on. Bob and I trekked with all of these people for the next twelve days.

We soon fell in with a couple of school teachers. They were upbeat and chatty. Charles was a Californian and Jawnee was from Christchurch, New Zealand. They taught in a private school in London. Charles was gay and Jawnee was straight. (Not that there was anything wrong with that.) "It's a perfect arrangement for those wanting the company of the opposite sex without the tension and drama," Charles explained a couple days later.

The two hired a porter and a guide. Hakkim knew their guide, Hira, from previous trips, and the two of them made a decision that we would all travel together. Hira's full name is Hira Prasad Lamichhane, and he had full command of English. He was bright, loquacious, and engaging. Hira melded so well with Bob, Charles, Jawnee, and me that at times we forgot who was the guide was and who was the client.

We reached our first teahouse early that evening. After a very long day, which had begun in Kathmandu, the promise of a bed was welcome. We didn't seem to be in a particular town. There was tiny store selling candy bars and beer, and a teahouse. Every evening's routine was almost the same. We would take a nap, be presented with a menu by Hira or Hakkim, and then have dinner. All teahouses seemed to have a kitchen. We were expected to eat our meals at our assigned teahouse, and when we entered each village at the end of a day of hiking, Hakkim chose our accommodations. That was okay with us. For the most part, they all looked the same.

Apparently there was some sort of arrangement between the guides and the teahouses along the Circuit. We learned to do what we were told. Despite their euphemistic name, the word "teahouse" was a bit of a misnomer on our trek. Any hopes we had that they would be similar to those idyllic Japanese teahouses astride mountaintops, with geishas, manicured gardens, and spotless, padded dining areas were quickly crushed. Although we did stay in one or two that were decidedly superior to most, the majority were composed of ten or twelve Spartan rooms with little furniture. They were often painted in garish Mexican pink or aquamarine and had the look of a 1940s Iowa motel. There was usually a kitchen with a wood-burning stove and some sort of dining area. The rooms had paper-thin walls easily permeated by the voices in the adjoining room.

"This place is kind of dumpy," I told Charles and Jawnee that evening. "Our room is just two mattresses propped up with boards. There's not even a table or a closet. It reminds me of one of those rooms where Americans are kept when they're kidnapped and held for ransom by terrorists in the Middle East," I complained.

"Embrace it, Ric," Jawnee replied. "Embrace it."

Teahouses along the Annapurna Circuit do not have sit-down toilets. Rather there's a large, shallow, dish-shaped square metal or porcelain receptacle on the floor with a hole in the middle. There are two small raised islands for one's feet. It's all about the squat.

"Geez," I reacted after exiting one particularly nasty bathroom. "Don't we give these countries billions in foreign aid? What do they do with it all? The least they could do is buy some toilet seats. What about the Peace Corp? What have they been doing all these years? And where's the soap? What about soap?"

"Embrace it, Ric," Jawnee told me. "Embrace it."

The teahouses did have rather comforting names like Hotel Hill-Ton, Shangri-La Guest House, and Xanadu Lodge. All had two amenities, which came as complete and welcome surprise—electricity and beer. There was electricity along the length of the Annapurna Circuit. The Nepalese didn't seem to actually use it, however, to make their lives better. All heat and cooking was derived from burning wood. Consequently there were considerable ill-health effects in Nepal caused by smoke-filled rooms as the locals (and trekkers) crowded around the stove to keep warm.

Wood was the principle energy source, and women along the trail carried bundles of sticks for heating and cooking. In many places, the trail was denuded of trees and shrubs along the hillsides by generations of wood gatherers. A few teahouse rooms did have a single electric bulb hanging from the ceiling, but the principal use of electricity was by the trekkers who lined up in the morning in front of the rare outlet to charge their digital camera batteries.

Some porters and guides appeared to carry cell phones, although getting a signal along the Circuit was rare. In third world regions like Nepal, the cell phone has allowed rural areas to take one giant step forward in two-way communication without ever bothering with the first step—land lines. In the West, we still have one foot in each.

There was also bottled beer at every teahouse. That $2.00 liter of Everest in Kathmandu rose in price as we ascended. At the midway point, it sold for $5.00. Bob and I usually paid the price whatever it was. It struck me as odd that the beer was sold in heavy bottles, not cans. Everything along the upper reaches of the Annapurna Circuit was brought in by humans or donkey train. Every day, we passed young men carrying enormous loads, often towering three or four feet above their heads, on their backs. Many wore simple flip flops on their feet.

We soon saw the first of numerous signs asking trekkers not to give candy, pencils, or rupees to the small children who pestered us for handouts along the track, especially in the villages. "We do not want a nation of beggars," the signs said. A pamphlet handed to us at the beginning of the Circuit by the Annapurna Conservation Area authorities explained the policy. "Begging is a negative interaction that was started by well-meaning tourists."

Nonetheless it was difficult to turn my heart to stone when I would see a small child, nose running, wearing worn sandals, and threadbare clothing holding his dirty little hand out to me.

The track rose steadily each day, and we crossed our first suspension bridge over the deepening gorge of the Marsyangdi. We waited patiently until a group of Nepalese coming our way finished crossing. The bridge was too narrow to accommodate two-way pedestrian traffic. And just how much weight the bridge could support was anyone's guess.

The abutments at the end of the suspension bridges often had a plaque with an inscription crediting the organization responsible for its construction. The first one listed the date of its construction and its sponsor, THE MOUNTAINEERING ASSOCIATION OF SWITZERLAND. We saw other bridges with similar accreditations. Apparently their cost was too much for Nepal to bear, so international organizations became involved. Who knows what the local villagers did prior to the building of theses swinging bridges over the insurmountable gorge that separated them? For centuries, their interaction may have been limited to a simple wave across the chasm.

On day four, we entered Chame, the headquarters of the Manang District. The track passed through a wooden archway draped with red hammer and sickle flags. Apparently this town was under the control of the Maoists who had recently declared a truce—at least until the upcoming election results. For this kid raised during the Cold War, and who reached adulthood during an era when the Communists were hated and feared, it was an eerie feeling. "Where are we?" I asked Bob, communicating my xenophobia with the isolated place. Just inside the gate there was a large *mani* or wall of prayer wheels. Buddhists always pass to the left of a *mani* and so did we. Hira told us that it is not discourteous for non-Buddhists to spin the prayer wheels, so I did but respectfully.

Two or three hours beyond Chame on our seventh day, we passed a small sign with an arrow pointing to a trail leading to the north. It said

TIBET. "I've got a feeling we're not in Kansas anymore, Todo," Charles said. There were plenty of other sights and signs along the Annapurna Circuit to let you know that we weren't in Kansas. I watched a man standing on a log, cutting it lengthwise with a large handsaw. It took a great deal of effort to make a simple board. There was an elderly woman using a spinning wheel right out of the eighteenth century, turning goat hair into thread. A man stood on a lonely stretch of the trail attempting to sell a yak skull to trekkers. He just wanted a few rupees.

Every shop in every village sold the same six or seven objects. Trinkets, candy bars, Cokes, maybe some hand-woven socks, perhaps some pirated CDs. All the shops were run by women, who flashed you a smile as wide as the Himalayas when you entered. On one occasion, a woman chased me down after I left the shop without buying anything. "I make special price for you," one told me. Despite her earlier smile, she had a look of desperation.

Later that day, we saw our first major mountains of the Himalayas. We reacted the same as had thousands of trekkers before us. "They're huge," Charles said. "I didn't have any idea just how massive these mountains were. They're like nothing I've seen before or ever imagined." Bob and I agreed.

The mountains formed a jagged ridge along the southern horizon. The Annapurna massif is thirty-five miles long and has six peaks over 7,200 meters, including Annapurna I (25,540 feet)—the first peak over 8,000 meters to be summited. They are considered the most dangerous in the world to climb. Everest is to the east and is not in the massif. Hira pointed out Annapurna II and IV. Annapurna III didn't come into view until the next day. Annapurna I is to the west. (The peaks are numbered sequentially by their height.)

The climbing history here is the stuff of legends. Most notable was the 1950 ascent of Annapurna I, the world's tenth highest peak, by Frenchmen, Maurice Herzog and Louis Lachenal. Their accomplishment was monumental because the mountain was reconnoitered and climbed all in one single effort.

Typically, summit attempts on major peaks, including Everest, were made only after several preliminary expeditions. The Nepalese government gave the French a permit to climb either Dhaulagiri (26,795 feet) or Annapurna I in the spring of 1950. The two mountains are only twenty-one miles apart and separated by the gorge of the Kali Gandaki River. After considerable exploration of a possible route up Dhaulagiri, and a prophetic pronouncement from a Buddhist monk who told them, "Dhaulagiri is not propitious to you, it would be best to give it up and turn your thoughts to the other side," the Frenchmen focused on Annapurna.

They ultimately made a dash for the summit, wearing light boots and no supplemental oxygen. (They were among the first climbers to use nylon ropes.) Herzog lost his gloves on the summit, and their two-week retreat back down the mountain using one sleeping bag for themselves and two members of the support team was a triumph over near catastrophe.

All of Herzog's toes and fingers and all of Lachenal's toes would eventually be amputated. Back in France, Maurice Herzog dictated what is considered the most successful adventure book in history. Over eleven million copies of his *Annapurna* were sold. Herzog went on to become the French Minister of Youth and Sport, a member of the International Olympic Committee, and the mayor of Chamonix. He's still living as of this writing.

Hira and Hakkim kept us on schedule—their schedule. There was usually a knock on our door in the morning, and they brought us tea. "The

British did a fine job of educating these porters," Bob commented, making reference to the fact that although Nepal was never a part of the British Empire, it did fall under Britain's influence with its proximity to nearby India.

Hakkim incorporated the preparation of the day's drinking water into his routine, using my MSR pump, and usually helped fill our Nalgene bottles. Most other trekkers used iodine to purify their water. One morning, I walked down to the village pump to filter water. My behavior created a bit of a crowd as locals paused to watch me repeatedly squeeze the handle of my strange device, pressing water through the filter. Probably they couldn't understand why their water supply was safe for them but not for me.

We always stopped for as long as two hours for lunch at a restaurant along the way. Periodic breaks were mandatory. "We stop here now and rest," one of the guides would announce. I got the impression that the breaks were as much for them as for us. After all, this was their job, and the porters' packs were heavy.

At one lunch break, I became anxious to get going again. I was conscious that I was the oldest and slowest in our group and worried that my pace would slow down the others, so I start walking before Hira or Hakkim gave their official go-ahead. "I'll see you guys in Pisang," I told Bob and walked off without Hakkim or anyone else noticing that I was heading up the track.

It proved to be a mistake. Hira had told me that we would be staying the night in Pisang, so I was surprised that they did not overtake me before I reached the village a couple of hours later. I waited an hour or so on the main street, but they did not show. I became worried. Suddenly I heard my name being shouted across the Marsyandgi Valley. A thousand feet above me was a small settlement, and I spotted familiar figures waving their arms. I checked my map. Nobody told me there are two Pisangs.

Our group had turned off the main track just before Pisang and climbed to Upper Pisang. Bob never looked so good when we reunited an hour later. Hakkim was not amused. "You stay together with group," he told me sternly in perfect English. Apparently losing one of your customers along the Annapurna Circuit does not look good on a guide's resume.

Upper Pisang was a desolate place with extraordinary views of Annapura II. The atmosphere was medieval. Prayer flags flapped everywhere in the wind. It was cold, and spitting snow. We spent the evening crowded around a wood stove, sipping hot tea and some sort of soup. Normally the guides and porters disappeared in the evening to their own amusements, but Upper Pisang was too small for them to find a bit of privacy, so they joined us around the fire. At this altitude, everybody was equally chilled regardless of education, ethnicity, or income.

The guides and porters never slept in the rooms reserved for the Western trekkers even if some were vacant but found a flat place somewhere on the floor. That night, they slept on the floor in the kitchen. Before heading out in the morning, we climbed to a temple above the village. The inside was a rainbow of red, blue, and green. There was a terracotta statue of Buddha.

In the morning, for the first time, the altitude began to take its toll on our pace, and things got a bit slower. A young woman on horseback, without a saddle, galloped past us. Her horse was decorated with colorful woven braids hanging from its bridle, and her self-confidence in her riding ability would have earned the respect of any Wyoming cowboy. We went higher.

Our destination was Manang at 11,514 feet. On the hill to our right was the village of Ngawal. It was a rabbit warren of flat-roofed stone buildings out of the Dark Ages and could have been used as a backdrop set in *The Lord of the Rings*. Ladders provided access to the living quarters above the stables. Somewhere along the trail, we saw a sign announcing that we were entering the HIMALAYAN SNOW LEOPARD PROTECTION AREA. During lunch, we discussed the sign. None of the porters and guides had ever actually seen one of the endangered cats, but they assured us that they were out there.

At one point, Bob reported that he thought he may have seen a creature even more exotic than the snow leopard. "Earlier today, I saw a pair of big, hairy, erect creatures walking along a ridge. They might have been Yetis."

Bob's usually at the front of our group, so he would understandably have the most opportunity to see the famous abominable snowman before it hurried out of view. "Did you get a picture?" I asked him.

"No, I didn't have time to reach for my camera. It all happened so fast. I think they were a male and a female. They were holding hands as they went over the ridge."

"That's a homophobic reaction," Charles said smiling.

Hira enjoyed Bob's report and laughed. "I saw one last year and got some great pictures, but I left them at home."

In 1960 *World Book*, maybe in an effort to fatten up the "Y" volume of its encyclopedia set, actually sponsored an expedition to search for the yeti in the Everest region. In an attempt to give the venture some credibility, the venture was led by none other than Sir Edmund Hillary. The Everest conqueror was publicly skeptical of the existence of the creature, but *World*

Book reaped a great deal of publicity from the effort. No abominable snowmen were found, probably because neither Bob nor Hira was along.

Later that day, many of us did spot an exotic mammal. The porters stopped suddenly as we were passing through a forested area and pointed to an animal scurrying among the branches in the trees overhead. "Monkey, monkey," one of them shouted. I had a pretty good look at what the guidebook said was actually a long-tailed grey langur. The creature had a long tail, long limbs, and a black face. At an elevation over 10,000 feet, monkeys were the last thing I expected. The creature is considered holy and protected because of its association with the monkey-god in the Hindu epic, *Ramayana.*

In order to acclimatize before heading up Thorung La Pass, we spent two nights in Manang. It was a fair-sized town with some 200 structures. Most of the town seemed to focus on providing goods and services to trekkers. Like every teahouse along the Annapurna Circuit, there was a big sign outside our teahouse advertising HOT SHOWERS. Some others in our group had attempted to shower along the way, but they reported the water was lukewarm at best and more often cold so I had been avoiding the experience.

Despite the fact that I had just showered only eight or so days earlier, another body cleansing, however unnecessary, seemed appropriate. Showering along the Circuit was challenging because there was no consistent hot water source. Teahouses typically had a couple of fifty-five-gallon drums sitting on their roofs. If it was a sunny day, and it was late in the afternoon, there was a chance for a hot shower. But the odds were against it. It wasn't going to happen because there was always someone just a bit braver, and dirtier, who would beat you to it. And chivalry dictated that it was always "ladies first."

My shower attempt was a failure. The water was cold, really cold. I lasted maybe fifteen seconds before I abandoned my attempt. 'What's another week?' I told myself.

That evening, I complained about the situation to our group. "When we get out of here, we should contact the Better Business Bureau in Kathmandu about the false advertising of these hot showers. They don't actually exist. I nearly froze to death taking that shower."

"Embrace it, Ric. Embrace it," Jawnee said.

Although they should get failing grades in the personal cleansing department, most teahouses did a pretty good job with the food. There was always plenty of hot water for teas, and the flavors could include peach, apple, lemon, and jasmine. Any menu usually had a couple of soups, usually tomato or some sort of bouillon.

The most common entrée was daal bhat, Nepal's national dish. We soon realized that we would not have any trouble ordering it. In fact, it was difficult to avoid. The quality and quantity of daal bhat was variable. Supposedly it was an "all you can eat" thing. Typically it consisted of a plate of rice with a bowl of lentils and some sort of mystery vegetable. Meat was never included. Our guides and porters ate their daal bhat Nepali style with their hands. Westerners were given utensils. Two or three restaurant menus advertised yak meat, but we never could get it.

"We don't have it today," we were usually told if we saw yak on the menu. Meat was a rare thing along the Annapurna Circuit, although Bob and I did have an actual chicken dinner. We saw it on a menu and ordered it. "Chicken, chicken? You want chicken?" Hakkim asked us again to be certain.

Ten minutes later, we saw him walk back into our teahouse carrying a live chicken. "At least, we know it'll be fresh," Bob said. The word "Lazygne" or "LaaZanya" appeared on a couple of menus. We had no idea what it could be. We decided to give it a try. We got the feeling Hakkim didn't know what it was either, but he gave our request to the kitchen. Turned out it was Italian lasagna. Only the spelling was unrecognizable. It wasn't bad either. The Nepalese did try to please, and most places offered pizza and hamburgers made with some sort of veggie patty. There was even chocolate cake for dessert at some teahouses.

Manang was coated with a couple inches of fresh snow the next morning, and we had a long, lazy breakfast of tea and porridge made from some unknown grain. We were planning on just hanging out for the day, but Hakkim and Hira had other plans. "Today we visit holy lama for his blessing to get over Thorung La," Hira announced. It was a 1,500-foot climb to the *tsamkhang*, the monk's hermitage, known as Praban Gompa."

The lama and his wife lived in a cave. Six of us—Bob, Charles, Jawnee, Hira, Hakkim, and I—dutifully trudged up the side of the mountain that afternoon. The blessing *(puja)* was important, but we got the idea that our climb is all part of the "climb high, sleep low" conditioning process needed to get over the 18,000-foot pass safely in two days. We formed a line outside the curtained entrance of the cave where the lama sat cross-legged on a ledge just slightly higher than those being blessed. He wore a pointed maroon hat. We instinctively kowtowed before kneeling in front of him. He prayed and touched each of us on the head. Nobody smiled.

The lama placed a beaded necklace over each of our heads. (Actually, each necklace had only a few beads and lots of exposed string.) At the conclusion of the ceremony, the monk's wife passed around hot tea and a plate for our donations. We all contributed a few rupees.

"Well, that was an experience," I told Bob as we descended back to Manang. "Do you think that the lama was Hira's relative, and he gets a kickback for bringing us up there?"

Bob chastised me for my cynicism. "Don't be so critical. It's all part of the experience. Besides at your age, you'll need all the help you can get getting over Thorung La." He was right.

It was only seven-and-a-half miles from Thorung Pedi, over the Thorung La and down the other side to dusty Muktinath, but we didn't make it over and down until mid-afternoon. The descent from the pass was steep. We leaned on our trekking poles and kicked our heels deep into the gravel or packed snow to keep from slipping and falling. All of us, who had started up at daybreak, were now scattered along the tracks on the backside of the pass and down into the upper Kali Gandaki Valley below—the Mustang District. Just below the top of Thorung La, we passed within a couple hundred feet of a large glacier, and Hira pointed out the world's seventh highest peak, Dhaulagiri, to the west.

During my descent, I was overtaken by a tall man whom I not seen before. Apparently he spent the night at Throung Pedhi's only other lodge. He was English and used an old, wooden-handled ice axe to help him down. I knew that it was old because metal and fiberglass handles replaced wood in the late 1960s.

"It was my father's," he told me when I commented on the axe. "He loved the mountains and gave it to me before he died. I brought it on this trip in his memory. He told me that it was made by the same Swiss manufacturer as the ones used by George Mallory and Sandy Irvine." He showed me the name Willish of Tasch on the metal head.

"I looked into it," he explained. "Irvine's ice axe was found lying in the snow on the approach to Everest in 1933. It's in the possession of the

British Alpine Club," he told me. "But it had this brand name on it. It's Swiss. So this axe could have been made decades ago."

Most climbing buffs know Englishmen George Mallory and Andrew "Sandy" Irvine were last seen tantalizingly close to the summit of Mount Everest on June 8, 1924. Then they disappeared forever. Mountain-climbing romantics hope they made it to the top and died on the descent. Nothing has ever been proven, although significant clues have surfaced. In 1933 Irvine's ice axe was indeed found lying in the snow.

On May 1, 1999, a major effort, the Mallory and Irvine Research Expedition, actually found a climber's body just below the point where the two climbers disappeared. G. MALLORY was clearly visible on the jacket's collar. A climbing rope was found around Mallory's waist. Inside the jacket were a watch and a knife, some lozenges, and a pair of scissors. Unfortunately the Vestpocket Kodak camera, which the pair took with them on that final day, was not found. Somewhere amidst the ice and snow below Everest's summit lie the body of Sandy Irvine and the camera. If they made it to the top of Everest, they would have taken the photographs that would answer the great mystery of Mallory and Irvine's disappearance.

> "All of a sudden a patch of white, different from the snow and as bright as marble, caught my eye. As I got closer I realized it was a person. Bleached white skin. A hobnailed boot. A braided climbing rope. Not nylon."
>
> *Conrad Anker upon discovering*
> *George Mallory's body.*
> *May 1, 1999*

The Englishman's appreciation of his father's gift and his knowledge of its significance were impressive. "If you fall on our way down, let go of that ice axe," I chided. "It'd be a shame to lose it."

Muktinath was the location of the Jwala Mai Temple and one of the principal religious sites for Nepal's Hindus and Buddhists. Throughout my time in Nepal, I remained confused over the odd blending of Buddhist and Hindu temples. Mixing religions is unheard of in the West but not here. The next day, we took off our shoes and toured the temple. The center of focus was an eternal blue flame upon a pool of water energized by natural gas escaping from a fissure in the earth. Hindus believe this fire was an offering made by Brahma. In the courtyard of another temple on the same grounds was a peculiar wall of some 100 stone rhinoceros with water flowing from of their mouths. We watched as Hindu pilgrims washed themselves with the flowing water. "I suppose it would be in poor taste if I did that just to get clean," Charles said, only half kidding.

The next day's destination was Kagbeni, and we walked through the most environmentally hostile terrain of our entire trip. The land was dry, dusty, and barren. There was little vegetation, and when the wind blew, a few of us wrapped handkerchiefs around our faces to keep from breathing the dust. We saw laborers working on the new road that would soon run all the way up the Kali Gandaki to Muktinath. It was all being done by hand. There was no heavy equipment.

There was some excitement during our lunch break when Hira and most of the other porters begin cheering and clapping. One of the porters had made cell phone contact with the outside world (or at least Kathmandu) and received word that the Maoists had won the election. To celebrate, Hira reached into his pack and produced a bright red hammer-and-sickle flag. The Nepalese began waving it and singing.

"Our guide and porters are roaring Communists," Jawnee said. "Funny, they don't look like Communists."

I snapped a photo of the flag-waving celebration. It was one of the most memorable photos of my trip. Despite being red-blooded, flag-waving, God-fearing, democracy-supporting capitalists, we were happy with the news of Commie victory. There had been warnings from foreign sources that an election loss by the Maoists could result in demonstrations and even violence in Kathmandu at about the time we returned to catch our flight home. On the other hand, considering the chaos we had experienced in Kathmandu, I wasn't certain a riot or two would have made much difference to the overall demeanor of the place.

Kagbeni was a medieval-looking place of mud and brick. There was a stable below each little house, which lined the narrow and dusty streets. Kagbeni was the nearest town for trekkers wishing to visit the mysterious quasi-independent Mustang Kingdom. Access was strictly limited by the government of Nepal, and it had imposed a stiff entry fee up to $70 a day per person. Employing a trekking agency to visit the Mustang Kingdom was mandatory. Signs announced the Mustang border just north of Kagbeni. Upon my return to the United States, I learned that once it had consolidated its power, the new Maoist government of Nepal dissolved the Mustang monarchy.

The Kali Gadaki riverbed widened below Kagbeni, and we repeatedly got our feet wet, crossing its many shallow channels. The wind was nasty, and we once again wrapped our handkerchiefs around our faces to avoid eating and breathing the airborne sand. The lack of vegetation was surreal. I saw a horse desperately scrounging in the gravel for something, anything, to eat. The creature's situation was dire, but did anyone besides me care?

We were a day ahead of schedule when we arrived in Jomsom where we would catch our plane down to Pokhara, so we walked an extra three hours downhill to the village of Marpha where we spent the night in one of our trek's better teahouses. Marpha labels itself THE APPLE CAPITAL OF NEPAL, and the fruit trees surrounding the town were in blossom. Bob and I each devoured a couple of apples from last year's crop. It had been two weeks since we'd had any fresh fruit. Hakkim also seized the opportunity and bought a couple dozen apples to take back to his family in Kathmandu.

"They're not so much money here," he told us. The next day in Jomsom, Hira took me aside. "I would like to work in the United States," he said. "I need a letter of recommendation to help me get a visa."

Of course, I agreed to write the letter on his behalf, and we exchanged addresses and phone numbers. Hira, like thousands of other educated Nepalese, knew that there was little future for him in his native land. But it was difficult for him to get through the bureaucracy needed to emigrate to a nation with better opportunities. Ten days later, back in the United States, my phone rang at 3:00 a.m. Hira was oblivious to the time difference and had called to remind me to write the testimonial letter for him. Hira, like the horse in the Kali Gadaki riverbed, wanted to improve his lot in life.

Flying back to Pokhara from Jomsom, we had great looks at the Annapurna massif. Hakkim pointed out Annapurna I. "Do you think Maurice Herzog's French tricolor is still flapping in the wind?" I asked Bob.

"Maybe but not for long," Bob replied. "The Maoists are probably planning on replacing it with their hammer-and-sickle flag."

9

The Coast to Coast Walk

Walking in the footsteps of Alfred Wainwright

England
192 miles

Coincidently the American artist, Thomas Kinkade, died while Rosemary and I were hiking northern England's Coast-to-Coast (C2C) Walk in April 2012. You may not recognize his name, but you'd recognize his work. It's sometimes hard to avoid. In its obituary of Kinkade, Britain's *The Week* magazine wrote that the artist was the most collected artist in the United States. Critics hated his work, blasting it as being syrupy and trite. His paintings of babbling brooks, pastoral scenes, and cozy cottages would make one believe that he was inspired by the picture-perfect peace and beauty of the moors and dales of this region of England. Despite the fact that Kinkade even stole his trademark "the painter of light" from Britain's great nineteenth-century landscape artist, J.M.W. Turner, Kinkade never visited England's expansive north with its signature rolling hills, grazing sheep, and Georgian buildings.

The reality of actually walking the C2C is not quite so pluperfect. There was mud and more mud. An endless series of stiles over rock walls wears on the walker. There were enough navigational challenges through mountain passes and across rectangular sheep pastures to befuddle even Captain Cook. But for us, the constant rain was our biggest nemesis. If the Eskimos had thirty words for different forms of snow, the British surely had that many for the many forms of dampness that can plague the C2C walker. A fog would turn to mist, a sprinkle to drizzle, and a shower to sleet, hail or rain.

We carried an umbrella and used it routinely. At times, the rain forced us to seek the protection of a sheep shed or barn, so we could read our guidebook, lest it deteriorate into a collection of soggy pages. Interestingly, despite the rainy climate, few English structures seemed to have gables. We usually looked in vain for a place to hunker rain-free against a building, but inexplicably many roofs in rural England do not extend beyond the walls of the home, barn or church. You're either inside or outside. There was no middle ground.

We knew the weather would be an issue when we chose to do the C2C but naively went ahead with our plans, figuring that it can't rain all the time. Sure enough, it didn't rain all the time, but it did rain most of the time.

The reality of the damp climate hit us while we were still in the Manchester Airport. We walked by a long line of Brits waiting in line for their departing flight. The sign, announcing the flight's destination, said it all—MALTA.

"That ought to tell us about what to expect," I commented.

Actually many departing flights from Britain's airports probably need not be designated with a specific destination. A flight labeled simply

SUNSHINE would probably have them queuing to get on board. Whether the flight was headed to Italy, Spain, Greece, or Malta would be irrelevant.

Most serious British walkers have the C2C on their "must do" list. In a sense, it's their Appalachian Trail, although not nearly so long. The walk has no official status. Unlike the government-sanctioned Pennine Way or the Cleveland Way, trail signs were hit and miss, despite the fact that it passed through three national parks. The path was frequently arbitrary with numerous variations. As they hike across the country, it is common for walkers to make their own alternatives to the recommended route.

Most walkers hike from west to east beginning at the village of St Bees on the Irish Sea and ending at Robin Hood's Bay on the North Sea—a distance of 192 miles. By the second day, the walk enters the Lake District National Park, then through Yorkshire Dales National Park, and finally into North York Moors National Park.

If you're an American, leave your preconceptions of a national park at home. Don't expect large mammals, towering waterfalls, or giant trees. The C2C is more about lonely vistas, rolling hills, and perfectly preserved nineteenth-century stone villages that will make you think you are a character in a Jane Austen novel. The Lake District of the C2C offers the most dramatic scenery, and its mountains are serious. As you climb over 2,000-foot passes, the surrounding peaks will remind you of Colorado, only not quite as expansive.

The Coast to Coast Walk was created by England's Alfred Wainwright (1907-1991) who was sort of a blending of America's John Muir and Colin Fletcher. Wainwright acquired a love for the Lake District while still in his early twenties and expressed his affection for the region in his *Fellwalker*, published when he was just twenty-three.

His most famous work was his seven-volume *Pictorial Guide to the Lakeland Fells*. The series, published over an eleven-year period, was characterized by his detailed line-drawings of England's loveliest mountain region. They quickly became classic coffee-table picture books. His *A Coast to Coast Walk* appeared in 1973. Laid out by Wainwright, across the narrow neck of northern England, the walk is a combination of country roads, footpaths, and existing national trails. Wainwright broke the Walk into twelve stages, but the decision as to how far to walk each day is obviously up to the individual.

The C2C is hugely popular. About 10,000 walkers make the trek annually. Wainwright's guide, or some version of it, is carried by most walkers, us included. There's even a Wainwright Society. We were three days into our walk before we figured out that our guidebook entitled *The Coast to Coast Walk* was written by *Martin* Wainwright, who admitted in the preface that he was not related to Alfred. *Martin's* book described *Alfred's* route. Who'd a thunk it?

For us, each day's walking usually ended in a pub. These British icons of socialization and imbibing were exactly as we hoped. Traditional, small, warm, friendly, and with pig bristle dartboards on the wall. There was no obnoxious music. All proudly offered cask-conditioned "real ales," hand pumped from the cellar with no extraneous gas. They were naturally carbonated. The rural pubs were a highlight of the C2C.

The walk may not be for everyone. One sarcastic veteran of the walk summed up his experience:

> "For the trekker seeking an escape from sunshine, some of the world's most unimaginative food and over-priced B&B's, the C2C may be just your cup of tea."

His cynicism is a bit extreme, but after concluding our trek, Rosemary and I agreed he had a point.

We took the train from Manchester to the seaside town of Whitehaven four miles north of St Bees, then a cab to the Queen's Hotel. This was where we would begin our walk. Sadly it was another Whitehaven taxi driver that was the perpetrator of one of the most heinous tragedies in the history of modern Britain. In 2010 an unstable Derrick Bird, fifty-two, lost control of his faculties and drove his cab through Whitehaven and the neighboring communities, randomly shooting pedestrians. He killed twelve people and wounded at least fifteen before taking his own life.

"I knew Derrick," our taxi driver told us. "He seemed normal enough to us. There was nothing in his behavior before that day that made us think he might be having problems. He just lost it. He drove right down this street, shooting," he told us as he pulled in front of our hotel.

Our train tickets to Whitehaven, bought in advance, were less than $25. The brief taxi ride into St Bees cost us nearly as much as the train ride from Manchester did. I felt we were being overcharged but said nothing. History considered, it was unwise to argue with a Whitehaven taxi driver.

"The taxi was expensive because today is a bank holiday," the pub's proprietor told us that evening. "They're allowed to charge nearly double on bank holidays."

Bank holidays are a pain in the ass if you're a traveler in England. We soon learned that banks are not the only thing closed on bank holidays. All public buildings are shut, and trains and buses run on reduced schedules. England seems to have lots of bank holidays. If it's a Monday, there's a good chance it's a bank holiday.

That evening, we walked down St Bees' main street to the beach and the Irish Sea. It was raining and I broke out my umbrella. It's a tradition to pocket a stone from the beach before heading east on the C2C. Upon completing the walk, trekkers throw the stone into the North Sea. We forced ourselves to walk out on to St Bees Head, despite the rain and the overpowering urge to return to the pub and enjoy our first real ales. Puffins were supposed to be visible along the sea cliffs, but the bleakness and the fading daylight prevented us from spotting any of the clown-faced creatures. We did spot a few guillemots. The black-and-white cliff dwellers resembled flying penguins, and we appreciated the sighting.

Our goal the next wet morning was the village of Ennerdale Bridge, fourteen miles east. I was a bit intimated by the lousy weather and the distance to be covered, so we decided to eliminate about four miles by immediately heading east rather than beginning the walk along the shore of St Bees Head. "Besides, we walked some of that yesterday evening," I rationalized.

We were well into the morning before we saw any designation of the C2C. We finally spotted a Coast to Coast Way marker, but our confidence was destroyed when a local walker informed us that we were on the C2C cycling route, not the walkers' C2C. He was helpful but appeared somewhat unfamiliar with the area. We left the paved walkway and headed down a narrow roadway somewhat confused but aiming for the hamlet of Cleator. We were disappointed that there were no other walkers, so I had to actually use my guidebook, rather than just falling in with other trekkers.

We stumbled into Cleator, a small village lined with sandstone buildings. We were desperate to get out of the rain, so we entered a small shop selling groceries and sundries, more interested in the shelter the store offered than its merchandise. Feeling guilty, I bought a couple of candy bars and prolonged our protection from the rain by eating them inside the shop.

"How far is it to Ennerdale Bridge?" I asked the teenage girl minding the store.

"Oh, I'm not sure. It's over in the next valley. The path begins just down the way. Make a right and go over the Blackhow Bridge and up to Dent Fell," she said almost as if by rote.

"You sound like you're familiar with the C2C," I said.

"Lots of walkers come in here asking, so I've memorized what to tell them. I've never been on the path, but my Mum did go over to Ennerdale once. Of course she didn't walk; she drove," she explained.

We thanked her and reluctantly headed out the door into the rain. I found it strange that she'd never been to a neighboring village that was only six or seven miles away. "She sounded like I was asking her directions to the dark side of the moon," I commented sarcastically to Rosemary.

Soon enough, we were headed up our first mountain of the walk. Dent Fell was a minor hill, probably no more than 700 feet above sea level, but as we climbed, the rain and foggy dankness increased and our visibility deteriorated. We were relieved to see the large pyramid cairn, which designated the hill's summit, but we couldn't make out the descent into the next valley. We were a bit worried. For the first time in all my trekking travels, I had to resort to using a compass.

The guidebook pointed us east (I think), so we put our trust in our compass and headed off in that direction. A beaten trail appeared and we felt better. A couple of hours later, we reached a small river bottom, but we really had no idea whether to turn upstream or down. It was supposed to be the Nanny Catch Valley, but who knew?

We hadn't seen another soul in hours, and the guidebook offered us little solace. It only confused us further. We were now genuinely lost, so I tossed a coin in my mind and we headed downstream. We were tired, soaked, and worried. An hour further on, we rejoiced at seeing two young men on dirt bikes that thankfully stopped when they saw me waving my arms like a drowning sailor.

"You're heading the wrong way if you're goin' to Ennerdale Bridge," one said.

We didn't argue but placed our trust in the local teenagers and turned around. Two long hours later, we saw the sign for Low Cock How Farm on the outskirts of Ennerdale Bridge. I could have kissed it. It was our reserved B&B destination for the night. It had been a very difficult day, and it was the worst of the trip.

Our first B&B was actually a thousand-acre working farm. The owners had added a small six-bed dorm and a couple of private bedrooms a few years ago to accommodate some of the many walkers who passed by here. It proved to be one our better lodgings with a kitchen, private bath, and a welcome roaring fire in a central room with a stone floor. Unlike the more traditional B&Bs that were yet to come, it was designed for weary and wet walkers. There were no frills, just open space, comfortable furnishings, and wool blankets.

A female hired hand wearing muddy rubber boots introduced us to our quarters and then disappeared. That evening, the man of the farm, a crusty, elderly character, stopped by to make certain we were comfortable, but mostly he came to talk. We had difficulty understanding him. His thick Cumbrian dialect was made even more incomprehensible by his new dental work.

"These damn new dentures are giving me lots of problems," we think he said. "My wife doesn't even bother trying to listen to me, anymore, but then she hardly bothered before I got 'em."

The discussion turned to politics and the hoof-and-mouth disease, which had threatened Britain's livestock industry some years ago. He was succinct in his criticism of the way the government handled the crisis. "Instead of shooting the diseased cows, they should have shot Tony Blair," he told us.

The next morning at breakfast, we met an English couple and their lanky twelve year old. They had been shuttled here by car and planned on doing four days of the walk through the Lake District. The wife did not appear particularly enthused about the family adventure, especially after we told them about our logistical problems yesterday.

"We're doing it," the husband said adamantly. Their son, Jason, avoided the discussion and focused on the eggs, bacon, and cooked tomatoes on his plate.

The farmer's wife, our hostess, was matronly and sturdy and kept the food coming. I asked her about Alfred Wainwright. She admitted that his walk was a boon to B&Bs along the C2C but did not treat him kindly.

"He was an old curmudgeon," she told us. "He didn't speak to anyone and always slept outside under a tree."

As we walked through Ennerdale Bridge in the morning, we saw other walkers emerge from the hotels and B&Bs in the village and join us in a scattered line along the C2C. We counted over a dozen.

"Where were they yesterday?" I asked Rosemary.

We can only assume that in our urgency to get an early start and by not hiking the entire Bee's Head, we ended up far ahead of the others. Too bad. We could have used their guidance in staying the course instead of spending time route finding and backtracking. I'm no Daniel Boone, and whether it's Spain's Camino or Patagonia's Paine Circuit, I'm perfectly content to fall in with fellow trekkers or at least keep them on the horizon and trust in them to stay the course.

Not an hour into the morning, we were passed by another couple and exchanged greetings. She was an American, but he was a Brit. We told them we were from Wyoming. "So are we," the woman, Deb, told us with little obvious amazement at the coincidence in her voice. "We spend six months of the year in Pinedale, Wyoming," I said.

"Oh. Sure. I know Pinedale. We're from Jackson," she said. The two communities are less than seventy-five miles apart. What are the odds? Deb worked at the Jackson Post Office, and Robert, her partner, born in England, worked at Jackson's mandatory breakfast stop—Pearl Street Bagels.

"Robert wanted to show me that Wyoming may have the Tetons, but England has some pretty decent mountains too," she explained. Deb further surprised us by saying that they were actually tenting along the C2C. There were some campgrounds along the walk but not many. Most tenters simply asked permission to camp from a farmer or pay to camp behind a hostel. "We camped behind a hotel in Ennerdale last night. They felt sorry for us and let us use the shower in an empty room this morning," Deb said.

Deb and Bob were strong walkers and soon outdistanced us. As rainy days followed rainy nights over the next few days, we wondered how their tenting experience, and their relationship, along the C2C was progressing.

Wainwright's itinerary suggested walking from Ennerdale Bridge to Rosthwaite and the Barrowdale Valley, a distance of fourteen miles, on the second day. That would take us into England's mountainous Lake District National Park. We knew that since we were in our seventh decade, it would be a difficult day. We were not disappointed. We passed along the shore of Ennerdale Reservoir, through a man-planted forest, and began our ascent to the Black Sail Youth Hostel. The hostel, England's most famous due to its location, sat high up the River Liza Valley amidst serious mountains at the base of Tongue Beck and near Honister Pass. It was a 1,500-foot elevation gain from Ennerdale Bridge to the top of the pass.

The Black Sail was nothing more than a modest, rough cabin that once served as a sheepherder's bothy with a small kitchen and a dorm and about sixteen bunks. Surprisingly, two bunks were still available. We were tempted to spend the night, but since we had booked rooms at B&Bs for nine nights all the way to Richmond, we would face a logistical Gordian Knot of cancellations and re-bookings if we varied from our schedule. So we marched onward and upward.

The climb to the top and down the other side into the next valley proved to be almost as arduous as any we had ever tackled in the American West. We were relieved that the rain was limited to a few scattered showers, and our visibility was pretty good. We followed a series of cairns as well a couple of other trekkers. As we gained elevation, we saw some steep ridges to our left. They were the Haystacks. Alfred Wainwright's ashes were spread among those rocks—one of England's wildest places surrounded by his beloved becks, pikes, and fells.

English geographic terms are confusing. Mountains are fells or pikes. Streams are becks or gills. A ridge is a gable (I think). A dale is a valley, and a moss is a moor, which is a swampy area. A tarn is a small lake, but a pond is an artificial lake. Thankfully, a hotel was a pub.

As we approached the village of Rosthwaite, we kept our eyes to the south, searching for Scafell Pike. At 3,204 feet, it's *England's* highest point. We had been told it was visible from here. It was not *Britain's* highest mountain, however. That distinction belonged to Scotland's Ben Nevis at

4,408 feet. We couldn't pick it out, however. There were just too many pikes and fells on the horizon, and none seemed to distinguish itself.

Our room for the night was in the tiny hamlet of Rosthwaite. We were dog tired but couldn't resist turning in to a pub before searching for our B&B. Rosemary had a Jennings Cumberland, and I got a Jennings Bitter. By this point in our journey, we were developing some sort of appreciation for these hand-pumped real ales. As compared to American craft ales, they tended to be less hoppy and had a lower alcoholic content. They seemed to be designed more for sipping than quaffing. We complimented our ales with an order of chips. Rosemary, a self-appointed French fry gourmet, knew what she wanted.

"Please make them extra crispy," she told the server. We savored the fries and the moment because, all in all, it had been a successful day of multiple miles and a serious mountain pass. We really hadn't anticipated the C2C being so arduous, especially the altitude gain, but we now felt confident we could handle it. The next day's itinerary was even more serious than today's with an ascent of nearly 2,000 feet.

We found our B&B down the street. There were couple of cows penned in the backyard. Nook Farm was fairly typical of the B&Bs we encountered along the C2C. It was snug, clean, and a bit over-priced. Despite the fact that owners repeatedly told us that the overwhelming majority of their guests were walkers, every B&B we stayed in seemed more designed to accommodate Victorians arriving by horse-drawn coach. The bedrooms were usually cluttered with vestigial furniture and knickknacks. In most cases, in order to find a place for our personal items, we were forced to clear the dresser tops and end tables of useless decorative junk like pitchers, plates, vases, and stuffed animals. We stacked the stuff on the floor in a corner.

Rosemary and I are minimalists. We carried everything we needed throughout our walk in our backpacks but we were in the minority. Most walkers hired shuttle services to advance their luggage along the C2C. They typically had many more belongings than we had. God only knows where they found find room for it all once they stepped into their B&B bedroom. I may be walking on thin ice by lambasting the iconic British B&B, but common sense seemed to have been thrown out the window, probably because there was no place to put it.

Just as frustrating was the obsessive penchant for crocheted cozies, doilies, and filigree. There was a doily under every lamp, and a cozy covered anything that can't escape. Lace was king. Lampshades were decorated with dreadful dingle berries hanging from their underside. The lamp may not function, but the dingle berries were de rigueur. Purple was the most common color of lampshade dingle berries. Most B&Bs we encountered needed a good Saturday morning garage sale.

The saving grace of the B&Bs, of course, was that they were located precisely where they were needed. Typical days along the C2C ended in small villages where the only choices were a room above the pub or a B&B. The proprietors were not ignorant of the fact that they had a monopoly, and walkers wasted their time, shopping the village for a lower price. Rates were pretty standard, and it was obvious that the owners of these establishments had colluded. We paid on average 60£ to 70£ for two of us per night. That converted to at least $100. That may be reasonable for older adults who are in the midst of their careers or even retired, but it was prohibitive for the college-age set. Remember walkers doing the entire C2C were not in need of *one* night's accommodation but at least *ten.* It adds up.

We had investigated hostels, but their rates were not significantly lower. For two of us, they averaged 50£. We had attempted to reserve a couple of hostels, but they were booked solid, even though we had contacted them a month in advance of our trip. England's Coast to Coast Walk is relatively expensive compared to other world class treks, so savor the experience.

The saving grace of the B&Bs was the extensive breakfast. Our hostesses seemed determined to serve as much artery-clogging fare as the heart allowed. A Full English Breakfast usually included eggs, beans, toast, potatoes, sausages, bacon, and mushrooms, juice, and coffee or tea. Seasonings were rare and consisted only of pepper imprisoned in a clogged shaker and England's national condiment—HP Brown Sauce with its picture of the House of Parliament on the label. We decided that breakfast would be our main meal of the day and usually carried a little cheese and for lunch. Along the way, we often made an effort to purchase England's only significant contribution to gourmet cuisine—the legendary Stilton cheese. Typically in the evening, we had a plate of chips with our beer at the pub for dinner. We were never hungry. That's the reason Guinness is sometimes called "a meal in a glass."

Responsibilities for the operation of the B&Bs were not shared equally between the English husband and wife. It was the woman who greeted us at the door, asked us to remove our boots, pointed us to our upstairs room, and cooked and served the breakfast. Then she made up the room for the next guests.

The husband's role appeared to be one of sitting in the living room, watching television and changing positions often enough to prevent his wife from placing a doily on his head. The wife also collected our money as we departed. Credit cards were not accepted. It was a cash only, no taxes on this income, thank you. In the backyard of one simple farm house B&B, we spotted a spanking new Volvo and at another a cool blue Peugeot. The kids better not even think of moving back in with their parents and sleeping in that upstairs bedroom. The least the B&B operators along the C2C can do is erect a statue to Alfred Wainwright.

Wainwright's recommended itinerary suggested walking 14.6 miles from Rosthwaite to Patterdale on day three. After yesterday's difficult 14 miles over a serious mountain pass, we were glad we had the sense to break this segment into two and planned on ending end our day at Grasmere, a 7.6-mile distance. It included a climb of nearly 2,000 feet between two of the Lake District's loveliest valleys, Barrowdale, Far Easedale and the River Rothay. It was no sin to disrupt Wainwright's schedule. Many C2Cers recommend it. For instance, the leg from Patterdale to Shap is 15 miles—an unreasonable distance for many.

We began our ascent following Stonethwaite Beck and then Greenup Gill toward the divide. We stopped to chat briefly with a lone walker who had paused to admire the view behind us. It was a quintessential English pastoral scene of Rosthwaite and its surrounding peaks and valleys. "Lovely, isn't it?" the man said. We couldn't help but agree. We're glad we came.

"The lady at my B&B told me that Prince Charles himself sometimes stayed at her place," he told us. "When he needs to get away, he comes here."

"Does his wife, Camilla, come with him?" I asked.

"I don't know. She didn't go into detail, but maybe it depends on what he's trying to get away from," he said with a smile.

We discussed our hiking plans for the day and told him that we were going to quit tonight at Grasmere.

"Who the heck wants to walk fifteen miles from here to Patterdale over two passes in one day?" I comment authoritatively. "It's just too much."

"Me," he replied, as he tipped his cap, and walked on.

We trudged upward, following the Greenup Gill toward the top. The small stream tumbled down alongside the trail, its course interrupted by small and frequent waterfalls. Pinnacles and rocky points on either side, with names like Eagle Crag and Sergeant's Crag, rose above the gill. We reminded ourselves that despite the topography's similarity to America's Rocky Mountains, this was England. This was the heart of the Lake District, and only those naysayers who had never been here would not take these mountains seriously. "Come on. They're in England. They can't be that spectacular," they might say, but they would be wrong.

We became confused at the top and searched for the way across the pass. There seemed to be numerous choices leading down into a valley. A wrong decision wouldn't be fatal but could mean a walk of many additional miles into Grasmere. We saw a group of three hikers ahead, who were studying their map. As we got closer, we recognized them as the English family that we had met at breakfast on our first morning at Ennerdale. We exchanged greetings and discussed trail options. Since they were sort of locals, we placed our confidence in them and after some searching, stumbled on a line of cairns leading downhill.

As we walked with the family, we fell into a discussion of Beatrix Potter. She is credited with using the profits from her books, including *The Tale of Peter Rabbit,* to preserve much of the land in the Lake District from development.

"Her genius was in giving her animals human qualities. They spoke to one another. No author had ever done that before," I said with certainty.

The mother of the family instantly rebutted my statement. "What about Aesop?" she countered. "Didn't the tortoise and the hare talk?"

"Oh, I forgot about them," I answered sheepishly.

Three hours later, we entered the village of Grasmere.

"Come forth into the light of things,
Let nature be your teacher."

William Wordsworth
1770-1850

After three days spent walking in rural countryside and mountainous terrain, Grasmere was a shock. It apparently is one of England's most visited tourist traps. The attraction was the town's setting with its surrounding mountains, streams, and forest. As we entered, the sun was shining, and we saw a bizarre scene of pseudo-hikers strolling around the village green with a trekking pole in one hand and an ice cream cone in the other. It was doubtful that any more than a handful of these pretenders ever actually got out into the surrounding mountains. The town was filled with silly shops offering teddy bears, chocolates, birdhouses, jams, and gingerbread. The whole scene reminded us of a summer day on the square in Jackson Hole, or was it Vail?

Poet William Wordsworth spent a lot of time in Grasmere and referred to it as "the loveliest spot that man has known." We located the churchyard where he and his wife Mary were buried beneath a yew tree that was planted by the poet himself. As we stood in front of his grave, Rosemary, an English major, couldn't abstain from a critique of Wordsworth's work.

"It's real flowery," she said. "His poems are corny. I always thought they were bad and avoided them in college." Take that, Wordsworth, bard of the lakes.

We were booked for the night at Town Head Farm, a B&B that advertised itself as being just ten minutes north of Grasmere. It may be ten minutes if you're traveling by car at 60 mph, but for us it was a two-mile walk along the busy A591 highway. That's one of the risks of reserving ahead based on Internet information. B&B Web sites use the words "at," "near," "by," and "in" interchangeably. You can't know exactly where your B&B is located until you find it.

"Maybe we shouldn't have had that second pint in Grasmere," I told Rosemary against the roar and rush of vehicular traffic.

The next day's walking offered yet another grunt over a mountain pass. We followed Tongue Gill around a mini-mountain labeled the Seat Sandal on our map. There was a delightful waterfall just below the saddle. Our guidebook suggested picnicking at the fall, but, despite the clearing sky, we didn't want to tarry at the high altitude. We looked over our shoulders and were heartened to see a line of six or eight other hikers heading up toward us. We trusted them more than our map-reading abilities.

The top was inexplicably labeled Grisedale Hause, and we began our descent along Grisedale Beck into Patterdale. Just below the pass, the track circled alongside a picturesque mountain tarn that reminded us of many we'd seen in Wyoming's Wind River Range. There was little vegetation, just stark rock. As we hop-scotched across the rocks at the lake's outlet, a young woman appeared headed toward us. She was doing the C2C solo from east to west. On our entire walk, she was the only person we ran into doing it in the unconventional direction.

"I cheated a couple of times," she admitted to us. "I rode the bus from Glaisdale to somewhere near Clay Bank and also bussed from Ingleby Cross to Richmond."

As a way of making conversation, I asked her where she had gone to college. "Cornell," she told us.

"That's an Ivy League school. You must be smart. That's why you had the sense to use public transportation," I said, glancing at Rosemary and hoping she was getting the message. I quizzed her about bus connections, and the three of us vowed never to repeat the details of our conversation to anyone.

Actually Rosemary and I knew from the start that we would have to resort to the bus if we were to complete the C2C, at least in principle. We did not have sufficient time to walk the entire 192 miles. We had agreed that at a minimum, we would do the Lake District and at least try to walk to Richmond in Yorkshire before selling our trekking souls to the devil.

"Besides," I reminded her, "What about Rosy Ruiz?"

Rosemary knew about Rosy Ruiz. "Isn't she the woman who used the subway to win the Boston Marathon?" she responded as quickly as any *Jeopardy* contestant.

"And then there's the most famous long-distance cheater of them all," I continued.

"Who's that?" she asked.

"Ferdinand Magellan, but he cheated too. He was killed by the natives in the Philippines. The only reason he made it back to Spain was because his crew pickled his body in a barrel of saltwater and sailed home with it."

"I'd rather not go to that extreme," she said. "But the subway was a pretty creative idea."

High up in the valley, we passed a hut used by climbers and hikers in these mountains. The door was locked but there is a plaque on the outside wall:

RUTHWAITE LODGE
Restored by the maintenance team of
Outward Bound Ullswater
And dedicated 26-3-93 to the memory of
RICHARD REED AND MIKE EVANS
Tutors from O.B.U. killed on Mount Cook
New Zealand 31-1-88

Our first stop upon reaching Patterdale was the White Lion Hotel. The three-story structure hugged the village's main street. The pub was intimate with three hand-pumped real ales. We chatted with the bartender who told us that our B&B, Noran Bank Farm, was just up the street.

There was a newspaper on the bar with an article about a man from the nearby city of Penrith who was arrested for being drunk and disorderly. The article said that as a consequence, he was put on something called "Pub Watch" and was prohibited from entering twenty-eight specific pubs in the Penrith area for three months. Improbably one of the pubs included the one he owned. I was dying to know more about the man's peculiar sentence, but the bartender was busy, and Rosemary, sensing my urge to excessively question the bartender, signaled that it was time to leave.

The next morning while stocking up on lunch munchies at Patterdale's small shop, we bumped into Deb and Bob, the couple from Wyoming. They, like us, were pondering the day's walk, which the guidebook said was a fifteen-mile haul over the highest point on the C2C—the 2,560-foot Kidsty Pike, then along Haweswater Reservoir and ending at Shap. None of us was enthused about the long day ahead and quizzed the helpful shop owner about alternatives. Deb and Bob decided to cut out a few miles by taking the tourist boat up Ullswater Water and getting off about halfway up the lake.

Rosemary and I eliminated even more miles by taking a bus to Pooley Bridge at the head of the lake. We then hiked east across open country to the River Lowther Valley, which we followed south to rejoin the official C2C at Rosgill. A highlight near the end of the day was the ruins of Shap Abbey. Built around 1200, the medieval monastery, and others like it, was dissolved by the multi-married Henry VIII in 1540 and became a casualty of his war on the power of the pope. Henry, not wanting to push things too far, granted all out-of-work monks comfortable pensions. Over the centuries, most of the stone from the abbey had been cannibalized for constructing other buildings, but the surviving West Tower gave an indication of the Abbey's former glory.

Shap marked the eastern edge of the Lake District. We knew we were making easterly progress because the village had a fish and chips shop. It was the first we'd seen, but we didn't eat there. This was still Cumbria, and it was Yorkshire, a couple of days ahead, that claimed to have England's best fried fish. We headed east toward Orton and Kirby Stevens. We walked through countless sheep meadows lined with rock walls.

It was lonely country and we saw no one. Many walkers apparently quit at Shap, satisfied that they had walked through the Lakes, the most dramatic portion of the C2C. On the horizon, we saw the summits of England's backbone—the Pennines. The trail was indistinct and poorly marked. Other paths intersected the C2C and caused us confusion. Many of our directional decisions were more a leap of faith than actual knowledge obtained from our guidebook.

We spotted a slender column in the distance, marking the spot in 1651 where Charles II stopped to refresh his army on his way to defeat Oliver Cromwell at the Battle of Worcester. We had never heard of the battle, but seeing the monument that's mentioned in the guidebook meant we were headed in the right direction. Then we looked in vain for a pile of stones that was supposed to be the final resting spot of Robin Hood.

"This could be anything except the grave of Robin Hood," Alfred Wainwright famously commented in his guide. Rosemary pointed to a nondescript rock pile up a draw and decided that it was Robin's grave.

"We'd better say we saw it," she said. "Just in case we don't ever come this way again." Legend said that Robin Hood shot an arrow from his deathbed a multitude of miles away, and he was buried on the spot where the shaft landed. Truth be told, there was little historic legitimacy to the whole saga of the man in green, and it had about as much veracity as Paul Bunyan or the tooth fairy. Still, it made a good movie or two.

The village of Orton was dominated by the gleaming white limestone tower of its Anglican church. It was a delightfully preserved place. Except for the few cars and power lines, it had the look of the eighteenth century. We checked in to the George Hotel where we were the only paying guests. On-line Internet advisers had suggested that we make advance reservations along the C2C, and we followed their recommendation. But in reality, it proved to be unnecessary. There were vacancies at every stop probably because it was early April, and the mad rush along the C2C had not yet fully begun.

That evening, we strolled through the town, taking in the Georgian architecture and atmosphere. If we had seen Lord Darcy and Elizabeth Bennett walking hand in hand, it wouldn't have surprised us.

We chatted with an elderly couple stacking firewood and compliment them on their lovely home.

"Oh, this isn't my home. This is Janet's home," the man said. "I live down the road. I'm just giving her a hand with the wood."

"Sure," I replied, "That's the thing about small towns. People helping their neighbors."

"Well, we're not just neighbors; we're a couple," he explained. "We've been together for forty years, but we've always lived separately. That's why we've been together for forty years."

From Orton, the C2C traced its way through well-kept sheep meadows and across a moor dotted with heather. We saw swans and ducks on the Sunbiggin Tarn, a designated nature reserve. There were pheasants too.

They were Chinese ring-necked pheasants, frequently seen on pastures everywhere along the C2C. Some Brits may be bothered over the dilution of their Anglo Saxon heritage by Pakistani and Indian immigrants, but these feathered Asian immigrants were more than welcome.

By this point in our trek, we knew that on any given day walking the C2C, we were bound to become disoriented. Today was no exception, but we pushed on in a general easterly direction. Part of the problem was that our guidebook made references to such things as sheepfolds, grouse butts, Pillow Mounds, mires, and Severals. We'd never heard of any of those things and wouldn't recognize a sheepfold if we were standing in it. Somehow we stumbled on a curved stone arch over a small stream. We instantly recognized it as a bridge and assumed it to be the Smardale Bridge over the Scandal Beck. A farmer on an ATV told us that our assumption was accurate.

Kirkby Stevens (the second 'k' is silent) was a real town. Not too touristy, not too hard scrabble, not too Georgian. All in all just right. There was an assortment of shops, restaurants, and pubs, including a fish and chips take-out. Again we decided to hold off on the deep fried cod until we reached Yorkshire or even better—the North Sea. There was even a tourist information office. The helpful ladies knew every nook and cranny of their town but turned stone cold when we asked them about the C2C beyond Kirkby Stevens toward Keld.

The town's focus was its market square and its monument to the soldiers who died in the Great War (1914-1918). Typically most English towns had another monument not far away from the first honoring those who lost their lives fighting in World War II. Rosemary and I did the math. An eighteen year old in 1918 would have been forty in 1940.

"I wonder how many of those guys fought in both wars and survived?" Rosemary asked me somberly. "And during World War II, many of their cities were bombed repeatedly. Right? Thousands of civilians died."

"Yeah, I guess we can question their allegiance to tea and the monarchy, but these guys have paid their dues," I added.

As we walked back to our B&B, we saw and heard a squawking flock of four or five colorful birds flying low over the town. "What the hell are those?" I asked the first person I saw who was also looking at the birds.

"They're parrots. A few years back, a couple of scarlet macaws escaped from their cage and nested, reproduced, and survived. We keep thinking our cold winters will be their death, but they hang in here," he said. "I kind of like 'em, but some people think they're destructive since they chew on anything that might be food, like the rubber around windshields or shoes left on the doorstep. And of course nobody likes being hit by parrot shit."

Rosemary mentioned the parrots as we headed to bed and the fact that some people would actually complain about the spectacular macaws and their droppings. "Maybe their grandparents should remind them about the German bombs," she said.

We left the parrots to their mischief and headed out of town in the morning along Stoneshot Lane to Keld. The street was so narrow that a town legend holds that bank thieves drove down the lane driving a Mini and escaped when the pursuing police car became wedged between two buildings.

The C2C quickly became rural. A highlight along this leg was the appearance of the mysterious Nine Standards—a line of rock cairns along a ridge. Some were fifteen feet high and could be seen from a great distance. There were all kinds of theories as to their purpose including medieval boundary markers or decoys meant to fool the advancing army of Bonnie

Prince Charlie into thinking they were a line of marching soldiers. (Prince Charlie forgot his telescope.)

With a glance backward, we said goodbye to the green fields of Cumbria and entered the bogs and drab-colored grasslands of Yorkshire. At the top of a rise, a sign announced that we were entering YORKSHIRE DALES NATIONAL PARK. This Pennine divide is not topographically impressive, but it did represent the point where rainwater either flowed west to the Atlantic or east to the North Sea. This was the headwaters of the River Swale. The C2C followed the river's course for miles all the way to Richmond and beyond, widening as it flowed into a broad valley checker-boarded with pastures. We followed a lonely, narrow, paved road for most of the afternoon.

A green Range Rover was parked along the roadside. The man inside was wearing olive-green clothing and seemed to welcome a bit of conversation.

"Are you military?" I asked him.

"I'm a gamekeeper," he explained. "I'm looking for red grouse. The hunting season opens next week."

Rosemary pulled out our *Birds of Western Europe.* "That's it," he said, pointing to a picture of a large, sage, grouse-size bird. It was distinctively rust colored. He was impressed that we were carrying a bird book, and he let us to use his binoculars. We both saw one of the birds perching on a clump of gorse a couple of hundred yards away. We listened carefully, and we could hear the bird cackling and clucking across the undulating grassland. I was appreciative that he took the time to show us the bird, but I couldn't resist teasing the young guy.

"Wasn't Lady Chatterley's lover an English gamekeeper?" I asked him with a smile. "Has anything like that ever happened to you?"

He knew the literary reference and answered with a chuckle. "Not yet. Maybe today."

The interaction with the gamekeeper and the red grouse was time well spent on the C2C.

The countryside became stark. There were no signs of permanent human habitation, only the occasional derelict farmhouse abandoned decades ago. The terrain was apparently too rugged for the plow. A particularly forlorn structure across the valley grabbed our attention.

"I think that could be Wuthering Heights," Rosemary said. "The story was set in rural Yorkshire. Maybe that's the house that inspired Emily Bronte."

"I successfully avoided that book in college. Was it any good?" I replied.

"Well, it was a big bestseller in the nineteenth century. The most famous character was Heathcliff. He was adopted into a rural family living in a dank house out in the middle of nowhere. Kind of like that place over there. His new family had a daughter about his age, and the two of them grew up exploring these moors and dales. When puberty kicked in, they started exploring each other," Rosemary told me.

"It sounds corny. Who'd read that stuff?"

"Remember," Rosemary said. "Back then, they didn't have television."

Besides the grouse, we saw shorebirds nesting in the soggy moors. There were curlews and even oystercatchers. Their large bright orange bills were clearly visible against the drab surroundings. We'd seen them many times before on rocky ocean beaches but didn't realize until now that the birds nested so far inland.

A couple of miles outside of Keld, we struck up a conversation with an English couple, David and Ann, who had stopped their car to take a photos of the scenery. They offered us a ride into town, and we accepted with not much guilt. We'd walked about nine miles.

"You know that the highest pub in Britain is just up here. It's only a couple of miles off this road. Do you want to go?" he suggested.

"It would be a shame to be so close to such a national landmark and not see it," I answered.

So off we went, riding in the backseat of a comfortable car on our way to a pub that surely must be in *Guinness World Records*. Life was good. A large sign hanging above the pub's door proclaimed the pub's claim to fame: TAN HILL INN. BRITAIN'S HIGHEST INN. 1,732 FT. ABOVE SEA LEVEL. David and Ann bought us pints, and we talked like old friends. Afterward they drove us on to Keld. It's nice when you're traveling and strangers go out of their way to make you welcome in their country.

"That was a great day," I said as we walked the little town, looking for our room. "And remember that was the highest pub in Britain so that includes Scotland and Wales too."

"But our house in Wyoming sits at over 7,000 feet," Rosemary replied.

"I'm glad you didn't mention that to them. They might have been offended."

Keld wasn't much, just a cluster of 150-year-old buildings along the River Swale, and a pub on the hill. We stayed at the Keld Bunkhouse, which was our most sensible accommodation along the entire C2C. The modern facility had a couple of private rooms, a small dorm, a common room and a kitchen. There were even a couple of large, empty tables where we spread out our belongings. It was a refreshing change from the overdone B&Bs. The isolation and charm of Keld and our lodging was a highlight of our adventure.

Edwin, a quiet man in his late fifties, was doing the C2C solo. He arrived in the early evening and took a bunk upstairs. Before he retired, he showed us how to prepare a proper cup of English tea.

"I've seen Americans just put a teabag in a cup and fill the cup with boiling water," he said. "That's dreadful. I'm English. The correct way to do it is to always use a teapot, and first warm the inside of the pot with hot water. Let the tea seep. And it's best to cover the pot with a cozy. Don't rush the experience."

It's at Keld that the C2C is bisected by one of Britain's most famous official tracks—the 267-mile Pennine Way. The trail traced its way through the heart of England and was part of the main route for those trekking Britain from one end to the other. In the summer of 2003, Britain's most infamous walker, Stephen Gough, forty-three, wearing nothing more than boots and a rucksack, probably passed this way while walking from Land's End in the south to John O'Groats at the tip of Scotland. Known as the "Naked Rambler," Gough was arrested several times along the way and served four months in prison before finally reaching John O'Groats. In June 2005 he again set off naked from Land's End, this time with his girlfriend, Melanie Roberts, who was also naked. They were photographed naked in pubs and in grocery stores. He was quoted as saying that what he missed most when walking naked was pockets. "Somewhere to put my hands."

Their walk was interrupted by their arrest in Scotland and a two-week jail sentence. The pair finally reached John O'Groats in February 2006. The couple broke up, but Gough kept insisting on his right to be naked even when released from prison and at subsequent court appearances. As of April 2012, with the exception of brief freedoms between jail terms, he had been imprisoned for six years. He refused to clothe himself in prison.

"The human body isn't offensive," Gough told a reporter for Britain's *The Week* magazine. He has been found mentally stable.

Late the next afternoon, fully clothed, Rosemary and I entered the village of Reeth. We had followed the widening Swale Valley through two or three villages of stone houses that resembled scenes from *Pride and Prejudice*. We had to look hard to find any sign of this or the last century. There was no need for movie-set facades when filming here. Directors simply covered the main road with dirt, asked the locals to park their cars out of town, and shouted, "Action!"

Downtown Reeth encircled a large, open village green. There were three pubs, the Black Bull, the King's Arms, and the Buck. Pub names are not to be taken lightly. Unlike American bars, pubs in England never take the name of its owner like Bill's Bar or a generic title such as The Lucky Lounge. Most common are attention catching handles like the Whistle and Duck or the Castle and Cat.

Bill Bryson wrote in his *Mother Tongue* that "the present quirky system dates mostly from the Middle Ages, when it was deemed necessary to provide travelers, most of them illiterate, with some sort of instantly recognizable symbol." Bryson said that many pubs adopted royal names associated with particular monarchs. "The one obvious shortcoming of such a system was that names had to be hastily changed every time a monarch was toppled," Bryson explained. "But pub owners quickly realized that the most cost-effective approach was to stick to generic names…" Thus there are hundreds of pubs called the King's Head, the Crown, and the Queen's Head. Bryson credited Richard II with ordering all pubs to have a sign.

There was a small, three-sided shelter on the green, which housed the legendary Reeth Parliament where locals sit and solve the problems of the world. Parliament was not in session the day we are there. We did strike up brief conversations with two local women. The first was a shopkeeper who was stacking some Union Jack flags on a shelf in preparation for Queen Elizabeth II's Diamond Jubilee celebration in a couple of months.

"We love our royals," she said when I asked if the Jubilee would be celebrated even in rural Reeth.

"What about Prince Philip, the queen's husband?" I asked her. "I've always kind of wondered about him. Is he equally loved?"

"Let's not go there," she replied. "The Jubilee is about the queen."

Later that evening, while walking across the green, we engaged another woman, and the subject of the monarchy surfaced again.

"That whole royal thing is a bunch of rubbish," she began. "When the ridiculous Jubilee comes on the television, I'll be in my garden, avoiding it. But the royals do have a lot of influence and most people support it. If you don't, you'll be isolated."

It was a ten-mile walk from Reeth to Richmond. It rained every moment, and we hunkered in cowsheds to get relief from the weather. At one point, we were so close to a line of feeding Holsteins that a cow managed to slap her tongue over a page of our guidebook. For awhile, we walked with a single woman from Australia. Like us, she was using an umbrella. She was the only other trekker along the entire C2C, besides us, that we saw using one. Go figure.

Richmond was the largest town along the C2C, so we played tourist and visited Richmond Castle. Construction on the impressive structure by the Normans began shortly after the French invaders defeated the Anglo-Saxons at the Battle of Hastings in 1066. The conquerors were intent on maintaining their hold no matter how much they were hated. The Normans were responsible for the introduction of over 10,000 new French words into the English language including *en suite* and *Gerard Depardieu.* During World War I, the castle served as a prison for a handful of the thousands of conscientious objectors who refused to fight. The imprisonment of the "Richmond Sixteen" became a subject of national attention and despite their strong moral principles against fighting, public sentiment was mostly unsympathetic. In 1916 the men were secretly taken from the prison against their will and shipped to the French front. When they refused to fight, they were court-martialed and sentenced to death. The last-minute intervention by the liberal MP, Arnold Rowntree, of the chocolate dynasty, resulted in their sentence being reduced to ten years of hard labor.

We had been walking for nine days and were running out of time, so we were forced to resort to public transportation, especially if we hoped to walk into Robin Hood's Bay. Shamelessly we jumped ahead by bus and train to Grosmont. Connections were so good that we were back on the C2C that same day and found ourselves trudging uphill from Grosmont through the heather of North York Moors National Park.

"Do you think anyone noticed that we cheated?" Rosemary asked as we reached the day's destination, the hamlet of Littlebeck.

"Don't talk about it," I answered.

In the morning, we headed south along a stream that shared its name with the hamlet before the C2C turned abruptly north. The track undulated across the moors, and the countryside reminded me a bit of Pennsylvania with cultivated farmland along the valleys and forested lands on the surrounding hillsides. Not far beyond the village of High Hawsker, we got our first glimpse of the North Sea. We passed by a couple of trailer parks that provided summer getaways for city dwellers. Abruptly the trail ended in a junction with the Cleveland Way, which headed north and south along the sea cliffs. The junction was midway between Whitby and Robin Hood's Bay.

We had heard good things about the port of Whitby and decided to add a day to our walk in order to tour the town.

Late that afternoon in Whitby, we queued in front of The Magpie, Britain's legendary fish and chips shop. "You must do The Magpie," we had been told repeatedly throughout our trek. A sign listed the day's catch and even the fishing boat that caught it:

> Today's Haddock was landed by the
> *Leinbris* and today's cod was landed by
> the *Bjorgvin* and the *Arctic Warrior*

We both got the take-out cod and chips but passed on something called mushy peas. "Don't ask," I told Rosemary.

We ate on a bench by the Whitby Harbor beneath a partly cloudy sky with seagulls everywhere. Rosemary gave her assessment. "This cod is good, but it's not on par with Spain's bacalao. There's too much batter. The chips, however, are excellent."

"Maybe we should have ordered the mushy peas," I suggested.

Whitby was delightful. It was a bit touristy, but the setting was on the North Sea with real fishing boats in the harbor. The town also had enough sights to fill a day. We walked past a nineteenth-century home with a plaque explaining that it was the residence of the inventor of the crow's nest. Wow!

The town had plenty of seafaring history including the Captain James Cook Museum. Cook, England's greatest maritime adventurer, was an apprentice in Whitby and got his sea legs here in the merchant navy. Early in his career, he explored the mouth of the St. Lawrence River and was present at the siege of Quebec and the subsequent battle with the French on the Plains of Abraham. His career climaxed with three world-encompassing voyages taking him from the South Seas to Antarctica and north of Alaska to the Arctic. All three voyages began in Whitby, and his ships the *Endeavor*, *Resolution,* and *Enterprise* were constructed on a site now occupied by a large supermarket.

'Do you think the women pushing their shopping carts down the grocery aisle have any idea those famous ships were built there?' I asked myself.

On a bluff on the edge of Whitby, there was a statue of Cook gazing off into the North Sea. A live sea gull was standing on the captain's head. He didn't mind. He was focused on the horizon.

For those with a literary trivia bent, there is a lot of it in Whitby. It was where Bram Stoker's *Dracula* came ashore from a ship that had run aground and began his blood-sucking adventures.

It was a seven-mile walk along the sea cliffs from Whitby to Robin Hood's Bay. We retraced our steps from two days ago before again meeting the junction with the C2C, which at this point heads due west. Early on, the track passed the impressive remains of Whitby Abbey. Like Shap, the abbey was another casualty to Henry VIII's war on Roman Catholic monasteries. The abbey was inadvertently shelled by a German battle cruiser in WW I.

The view from the site was impressive as it looked down on Whitby Harbor and the North Sea. Due east, across the sea, was Denmark. The walk on the bluffs by the edge of the sea proved to be one of the few days without any trace of rain, and Rosemary and I savored the blue sky and the sight of waves crashing on the beaches below. We were on the home stretch of the C2C. As we approached Robin Hood's Bay, we saw a group of hikers using their binoculars to study the surf. They were excited about a large shark feeding near shore and shared their binoculars with us. The thing was huge. Easily twenty feet or more. A woman in the group explained that it was a species known as a basking shark, and it could grow to over forty feet. I made a note to add the creature to my big animal life list that I kept in mind.

And suddenly in the distance, hugging a concave bend in the shoreline, was the village of Robin Hood's Bay. It was a pretty sight, even if you hadn't been walking for days across England. Supposedly the town once served as a refuge for Robin Hood himself who lived a simple life of a fisherman here when not harassing the sheriff of Nottingham.

The village had a rich sailing and fishing history as well as a legendary role in rescuing crews whose ships became grounded along this stretch of coast. In 1881 the ship *Visitor* crashed on rocks offshore of the village, and strong seas made it impossible to launch the closest lifeboat from Whitby. A team of fifty pairs of horses dragged the lifeboat over the snow along the cliffs, where we had just walked, to Robin Hood's Bay. The small boat was slipped into the sea and rowed out to the *Visitor*, saving its crew of six.

The walk passed newer vacation homes before descending steeply into the old town and meeting the sea next to The Bay Hotel. A sign on the hotel's wall announced to C2C hikers that their trek is finished.

THE END
Coast to Coast Walk
St Bees to Robin Hood's Bay
192 miles

Three men had arrived just ahead of us and were congratulating each other on completing the C2C. They asked us to take their photo in front of the sign and then returned the favor. Each of them reached into a pocket and, in turn, tossed the stone he had picked up on the beach at St Bees into the North Sea. Good thing they did, otherwise Rosemary and I might have forgotten to do the same.

Inside the hotel, at the appropriately named Wainwright's Bar, Rosemary and I toasted our accomplishment with pints of Theakston Best Bitter. The bar was crowded, and nobody seemed to care about our accomplishment until a familiar face smiled at us from across the room. Edwin, the trekker in Keld, who had shown us how to properly prepare a pot of English tea, completed his walk only a couple of hours earlier. He seemed surprised to see us.

"You two did it. Well done," he said. "You almost beat me here. I've been walking pretty quickly and had some really long days. I'm surprised you're here so soon."

"We cheated a little," I admitted without hesitation. "We skipped a few miles by using the bus and train to get from Richmond to Grosmont."

"You call that doing the Coast to Coast Way?" he said disapprovingly.

"I know. I know," I said. "But I figured it out. We did walk about 120 miles, not counting an extra six miles we added by walking to and from Whitby. That's more than half of the Coast to Coast."

"I have to admit it was a little boring crossing the fields in the North Yorkshire Moors," Edwin said, extending us his hand. "And you did more of it than 99 percent of the people in England. Not bad for a couple of Yanks. Congratulations!"

10

The Wind River Range

Finis Mitchell was a friend of mine

Wyoming
85 miles

Some may challenge the traverse of Wyoming's Wind River Range being included in a list of the world's great treks, but that's probably because they've never experienced these mountains. Let's cut to the quick. All things considered, the range arguably offers the finest pure wilderness backpacking experience in the United States. Here's why: Even in the most popular areas, hikers, by their second day, can enjoy genuine solitude. Second, the Wind Rivers are not a national park. No permit or reservation is needed. Just get your butt to the trailhead and start walking. As long as you don't camp along a stream or lake edge, you can pitch your tent anywhere you want. Nobody is going to tell you where you must camp.

There's more. You can take your dog and forget the leash. Fishermen will find that catching trout is relatively easy. Barring intermittent fire restrictions, you can make a campfire. Finally, and most important, the scenery competes with any other mountain region on Earth. Running along a southeast-northwest axis, the Wind Rivers form the most spectacular portion of America's Continental Divide and the Greater Yellowstone Region. They are the most heavily glaciated area in the contiguous states.

Geologically the Wind Rivers run from South Pass to Union Pass, a distance of ninety-five miles. It's the longest continuous range in the Greater Yellowstone. The Continental Divide follows the crest of nearly the entire chain. Most of those who traverse the range begin at the Big Sandy Trailhead on the southwest corner and finish at Green River Lakes—a trail distance of about eighty-five miles. A few purists add about ten miles to their traverse by starting (or finishing) at Sweetwater Gap farther south.

The Continental Divide Trail travels exclusively across the west side of the Wind Rivers within the Bridger Wilderness. But CDT Trekkers who insist on sticking to the designated route will miss most of the real gems of the range including Deep Lake, the Cirque of Towers, East Fork Valley, Titcomb Valley, Peak Lake, and Cube Rock Pass. And, unless they know precisely where to look, they'll never see Gannett Peak, Wyoming's highest mountain. Taking that approach is akin to touring Paris and skipping both the Louvre and the Follies Bergeré. Most hikers doing the CDT take five to seven days to do the trek and are more focused on completing the traverse than seeing the range's treasures. That's too bad.

CDTers intent on seeing the best of the Wind Rivers should begin their trek at the Sweetwater Gap entrance at the range's southern end, proceed past Little Sandy Lake and over Temple Pass past Deep Lake, down to Big Sandy Lake, then over Jackass Pass to Lonesome Lake and the Cirque of Towers. The next leg takes the hiker across the Lizard Head Trail, around Grave Lake, and back over the Divide via Hailey Pass to the exquisite East Fork Valley.

A rarely used pass between Mt. Bonneville and Raid Peak leads to the Bonneville Lakes and the Fremont Trail over Hat Pass, Lester Pass, and down to Island Lake, and the magnificent Titcomb Valley. Trekkers then should climb up Knapsack Col, hike through the seldom visited Peak Lake Valley before beginning their descent across Vista Pass, past Squaretop Mountain, and down into the Green River Lakes.

Three designated wildernesses—the Bridger on the west side and the Fitzpatrick and Popo Agie on the east—protect the range from extreme human impact. The central portion on the east side receives protection by being part of the Wind River Indian Reservation and is designated as the Wind River Roadless Area. Backpackers tend to avoid "The Res" either because they don't know they can get a permit to access the area, don't want to spend the money on the permit, or are afraid of Indians. But for those seeking great fishing and solitude, that portion of the range, which lies on the reservation may be their nirvana.

Combined, the three wilderness areas total 729,000 acres. The Bridger Wilderness (428,000 acres) is the largest. (Wind River Mountain enthusiasts will be disappointed to learn that the Bridger Wilderness is not the largest in the contiguous states. Both the Boundary Waters Canoe Area in Minnesota (1.1 million acres), and the Frank Church River of No Return in Idaho (2.3 million acres) are larger.)

A comparison of Wyoming's more renowned Teton Range to the Wind Rivers shows the latter to be both more extensive and higher. In his *Teewinot*, author Jack Turner sets the length of the Tetons at a maximum of fifty-five miles to no more than twenty miles, depending on one's demarcation points. "...only peaks above 11,000 feet are well, *real* mountains. These high mountains stretch for only twenty miles from Prospectors Mountain (11,355) in the south to Ranger Peak (11,355) in the north," Turner wrote.

Applying Turner's criterion to the Wind Rivers, the distance from Square Top (11,695) at Green River Lakes Rivers to Wind River Peak (13,192) near the range's southwestern end (13,192) is fifty miles as the crow flies.

Nine of Wyoming's ten highest peaks are found in the Wind Rivers, including Gannett Peak (13,804), the state's highest. The Grand Teton (13,771) ranks second in the state in height.

But it's neither the length of each range nor the height of the peaks that really distinguishes the two. The difference lies in their accessibility. To appreciate the Teton Range, a visitor need only drive along Highway 89 through Grand Teton National Park. The peaks jump from the sagebrush plain. The view is unimpeded by pesky foothills and the panorama is sublime.

But to see the wonders of the Wind Rivers, one must abandon their vehicle and walk into the interior of the range. Isolated locations like the Brown Cliffs, Peak Lake, or Deep Creek Lakes will remain with you for life. With the exception of the Green River Lakes trailhead, just driving to the range's access points will be insufficient to understand why the Wind River Range is so special. For years, I've watched motorists in a rush to the Tetons and pass quickly through Pinedale, thus choosing to remain ignorant of the splendors of the Wind Rivers just on the horizon. Let them go.

My first exposure to the range was in 1967. My wife and I had landed teaching jobs at the high school in Riverton, Wyoming. In the school's library, I stumbled upon Orrin and Lorraine Bonney's *Guide to the Wyoming Mountains and Wilderness Areas.* First published in 1960, the book detailed the human history, trails, and mountain peaks of all of Wyoming's wild areas. It was the first guidebook to do that, and for many of us older Wyomingites, it remains our backcountry bible. The Bonneys devoted the largest segment of the work to the Wind Rivers. Their book opened the portals of the range to me, and forty years later, it still occupies a special place on my bookshelf and in my heart. And I am not alone.

"I've used the Bonney and Bonney guide since high school days in the 1960s," Phil Roberts, who authored the *Wyoming Almanac* along with his brothers David and Steve Roberts, told me in an e-mail in 2012. Roberts, a University of Wyoming history professor, mentioned his affection for the book. "…it was extraordinarily valuable for a kid to use exploring the Absarokas out of Cody. It's a monumental effort long before there was GPS as well as all of the other labor-saving aspects in the publishing department."

Orrin Bonney, who also recorded numerous first ascents in the Wind Rivers, died in 1979, but Lorraine still spends her summers in Kelly near Jackson. "I typed every word of that damn book," she told me when I stopped by a few years ago to tell her how much I admired their guide.

The book has undergone four revisions. Orrin would be pleased to know that there are some of us who still treasure and use their work. In 1983 The Federal Board of Geographic Names honored his climbing and route-finding achievements by officially designating the pass between Titcomb Valley and Dinwoody Glacier as Bonney Pass. The 12,800-foot pass over the Continental Divide is the most frequently used access for those attempting Gannett Peak from the Elkhart trailhead near Pinedale.

With the passing of time, Bonneys' guide has fallen out of favor and has been replaced by Joe Kelsey's deservedly popular guidebook, *Climbing and Hiking in the Wind River Mountains.* (The fact that Kelsey overlooked the renaming of Dinwoody Pass can be excused until his next edition.)

"I hate golf."
Joe Kelsey

Kelsey, who grew up in New Jersey, first visited the Wind Rivers in August 1969. In the past four decades, he has summited over 200 peaks and made over twenty technical route first ascents including three new routes, one on Bollinger Peak and two on Pingora. He has climbed Wolf's Head eleven times and has stood atop Pingora more than forty times.

"There is nothing like the Cirque," he told the *Jackson Hole News & Guide* in 2009. "That first morning I woke up in there, I thought 'I am home.'" It is the rare backpacker or climber who ventures into the range without photocopies of a few pages from Kelsey's guide.

My first forays into the Wind Rivers were on the Lander and Dubois side of the range. The traditional east side approach to the Gannett region is via the arduous Glacier Trail just east of Dubois. In 1969 I climbed Gannett with my friend Larry Amundsen. We were both in our twenties and accessed the peak using the Ink Wells Trail, which begins at the end of a dirt road that leaves Highway 26/287 at the hamlet of Burris. That route is about eight miles shorter than the Glacier Trail and is the quickest route to Wyoming's highest point.

It passed through Indian land, and then, as today, access required an Indian permit. We shamelessly skipped the permitting process by having my wife, Rosemary, drive us to the trailhead in the wee small hours and set off at first light. We counted on the Indian wardens not being around at that hour. I recall there was some discussion between us about getting caught but decided there probably was no jail on the reservation.

"I think the Indians use the county jail in Lander," Larry said.

"Good. I'm not crazy about fry-bread," I replied.

For the next few years, Larry and I explored the east side of the Wind Rivers, adding Mt. Warren, Mt. Sacajewa, Mt. Theodore Koven, Dinwoody Peak and Doublet Peak to our list of climbing accomplishments. Bonneys' guide described an imbedded piton on one of the three pinnacles named Les Dames Anglaises between Doublet and Warren. I was thrilled when we actually discovered the piton and were able to remove it from the rock. I still have it.

In 1998 the USFS banned the use of bolts drilled into rock or pitons hammered into a crack. Not everyone was happy with the decision including one climber from Jackson Hole who called it illogical. "I don't know how you could get off Pingora without using a sling. It's pretty rare that on anything that ends in a true summit, you can descend without fixed anchors."

The decision was based on a provision in the Wilderness Act of 1964, which stated that there will be "no structure or installation" within wilderness. Sophisticated bridges, however, appear to be exempt from the mandate. There are several bridges across streams within the Bridger Wilderness, as well as many other wilderness areas in the United States.

The late 1960s and early 1970s marked the beginning of the backpacking/climbing explosion, and we were part of it. In about 1971 Larry and I backpacked from one side of the range to the other via the Ink Wells Trail, Elsie Col, through Titcomb Valley and the Seneca Lake Trail to Elkhart Park. We thought we were hot stuff. The idea of hiking the *length* of the range never crossed our minds. Nobody's counting, but today at least a hundred or more trekkers traverse the Wind Rivers every summer, and the traverse does appear on lists of the world's great treks. More important, the range is on every serious American backpacker's "must do" list. I have continued to backpack throughout the range. During the past four decades, there are probably only a handful of locations in the Wind Rivers that I've missed.

The first recorded penetration by a white man into the Wind Rivers was by Captain Benjamin Bonneville. Washington Irving, the same guy that gave us *The Legend of Sleepy Hollow*, used Bonneville's journal to pen the *Adventures of Captain Bonneville*, published in 1837. Irving gave a detailed account of the captain's 1833 attempt to cross the interior of the range, probably at its southern end, heading up a tributary of the Popo Agie and reaching the summit of an unknown divide peak.

Exactly which peak Bonneville climbed is open to speculation since Irving's description of Bonneville's view from the summit is ambiguous. Historians have suggested that it may have been Wind River Peak, Mt. Chauvenet, Lizard Head or even Gannett. Orrin Bonney, apparently basing his decision on the fact that Irving quotes Bonneville as seeing the Tetons and the Green River from the top of his peak, credited Bonneville with summiting Gannett.

Kelsey doubted that Bonneville summited Gannett and pointed out that Gannett would not be approached via the Popo Agie and that Bonneville mentioned seeing the Sweetwater River, which is not visible from Gannett. The Roberts brothers in their *Wyoming Almanac* agreed with Bonney and list Bonneville as the first person to climb Gannett.

A detailed account of Bonneville's adventure into the interior of the Wind Rivers can be found in Thomas Turiano's *Select Peaks of the Greater Yellowstone.* Turiano dissected Irving's version of Bonneville's attempt to cross the range from Dickinson Park into the north fork of the Popo Agie to Deep Creek Lakes and then the ascent of a major peak, "The summit they chose to climb…is not entirely clear from Irving's account," Turiano said. "…but if the aforementioned presumptions about their approach are correct, then there is little reason to doubt that they climbed Wind River Peak."

Only the Bonneys and the Roberts brothers credit Bonneville with being the first to climb Gannett. Turiano, Kelsey, and everyone else gives the honor to Arthur Tate and his guide, Floyd Stahlnaker, with being the first to ascend Wyoming's highest point. Tate was a mechanical engineer from Connecticut whose accomplishments included climbs in Glacier National Park, the Cascades, Yosemite, and the Alps. Stahlnaker had arrived in Dubois about 1910 from Casper where he served as a guide into the surrounding mountains. The two reached the summit of the highest mountain in the Greater Yellowstone on July 25, 1922.

Nine years after Bonneville's likely ascent of Wind River Peak, Lieutenant John C. Fremont led a government expedition, which included Kit Carson, to explore as far west as South Pass. Fremont, influenced by opinions that the Wind Rivers were home to the highest peak in the Rockies, led a party past Boulder Lake and Seneca Lake, then down to Island Lake into Titcomb Valley. (Fremont named Island Lake.) They then made their summit assault on their peak probably from the slopes above Mistake Lake.

On August 15, 1842, Fremont, along with five others, stood atop what he assumed was the highest peak in the Rockies. They raised the Stars and Stripes and a sketch of their achievement later appeared on the cover of *Scribner's Magazine.* By today's climbing standards, Fremont Peak is considered a "walk-up." Scores of people, along with their kids and dogs, climb it every summer. But Fremont's ascent was significant for his day. David L. Roberts in his *A Newer World Kit Carson, John C. Fremont, and the Claiming of the American West* called the ascent a "bold feat of exploration, the hardest climb yet performed by Americans in the West."

Of course, Fremont Peak is not only *not* the highest peak in the Rockies; Colorado's Mt. Elbert (14,443 feet) has that distinction. Fremont Peak (13,745) is obviously not even the highest in the Wind Rivers. Gannett is 13,804. Fremont must have seen Gannett's snow-capped summit four miles up the range. Did he assume it was lower than the one on which he was standing, or did he choose to simply ignore the big mountain on the near horizon fearing his achievement would be voided?

Fremont continued to explore the American West. He was the first U.S. citizen to see Lake Tahoe and named the Golden Gate (not the bridge, but the narrow strait). In 1856 he was the Republican Party's candidate for president but lost to James Buchanan. The American flag he unveiled from atop Fremont Peak is somewhere in the collection of the Autry National Center in Los Angeles. The flag, which was hand sewn by his wife, belongs in Pinedale's fine Museum of the Mountain Man. Inexplicably, the museum gives short shrift to Fremont and gives no mention of Fremont's climb and the mountain named in his honor.

"His climb really doesn't fall into the era of the mountain men," the director of the museum told me a few years ago. In 1898 the U.S. Postal Service was scheduled to release a stamp commemorating Fremont's scaling of Fremont Peak, but the Spanish-American War interrupted the stamp's issuance. The five-cent stamp, showing the explorer waving the American flag atop his mountain, was reissued in 1998.

There are, however, a couple of historians of the Wind River Range who said that it was not actually Fremont Peak that the lieutenant climbed on August 15, 1842. The Bonneys, in their *Guide to the Wyoming Mountains,* based their argument on Fremont's description of the climb and sketches done by Charles Preuss who was with him. They concluded that it was actually Mt. Woodrow Wilson (13,502 feet), which sits at the head of

Titcomb Valley, about three miles north of Fremont Peak and one mile south of Gannett. The Bonneys cited Fremont's precise description of the climb including its latitude and the difficulty of the ascent.

"Woodrow Wilson is at least a Class IV climb, much more difficult than Fremont Peak, up which one can walk," the Bonneys said. "Clearly, definitely, his description of the climb fits no other peak," they concluded. We'll probably never know the certain truth.

Interestingly, David L. Roberts in his *A Newer World* devoted some ten pages to Fremont's climb but did not mention the Bonneys' assertion that J.C. Fremont climbed Mt. Woodrow Wilson. This, despite having endorsed the Bonneys' argument that Bonneville was the first to climb Gannett as stated in the *Wyoming Almanac*, which he co-authored. (Perhaps the brothers' opinion on the subject was divided.)

If all this history sparks your interest and you've wandered among the ranges surrounding Yellowstone National Park, Turiano's *Select Peaks of Greater Yellowstone* belongs in your library. His account of the topography, climbing history, and climbing routes in the Wind Rivers, Wyoming Range, Absarokas, Gros Ventre, Tetons, Gallatins, Beartooths, and the Madison Range makes great reading for any lover of these mountains.

Fremont's endeavors were followed a couple of decades later by more extensive government explorations of the Greater Yellowstone. In the 1860s and 1870s, surveyors led by Ferdinand Hayden, crossed South Pass and camped along the Wind Rivers. These expeditions included photographer William Henry Jackson, and artists Thomas Moran and Albert Bierstadt. (Fremont Peak's neighbor, Jackson Peak, is named for the photographer, who photographed the range and climbed Fremont Peak. The town of Jackson is named for the early fur trapper, Davy Jackson.)

Their landscapes opened the eyes of those back East to the natural wonders of the American West. Bierstadt, an American born in Germany, was probably amongst the very first group of white men to visit Big Sandy Lake where he sketched the scene. In his subsequent landscape, *The Rocky Mountains, Lander's Peak,* Bierstadt exercised a bit of poetic license by enhancing Rapid Creek waterfalls, adding a few buffalo and an Indian camp complete with teepees. The painting can be found in the collection of the Amon Carter Museum in Fort Worth, Texas. Colorado's Mt. Bierstadt (14,065 feet) preserves the artist's legacy.

Every day in July and August, there's a line of hikers walking the six short miles to Big Sandy Lake who are oblivious to Bierstadt but not to the scenery. Upon reaching the lake, most turn left over Jackass Pass and the incomparable Cirque of the Towers, the range's most iconic sight. Some, however, turn right at the upper end of Big Sandy Lake and head downrange toward Clear and Deep Lakes. This mile or so walk along the uppermost reaches of the Big Sandy River between the two lakes is arguably the finest in the Wind Rivers and a hallmark to the concept of wilderness preservation.

A thin layer of water, at times a hundred yards in width but only inches deep, slides down across the smooth granite, heading toward its confluence with the Green River fifty miles away. The hiker that stands on the shore of Deep Lake experiences a 360-degree view unparalleled in the range. Straight ahead, to the south, is East Temple Peak, and to the left is the massive Haystack Mountain with enough faces, ledges, and slabs to keep a rock climber busy for life. Between Haystack and East Temple is the exquisite Steeple Peak, one of the few Wind River peaks that has no easy climbing route to its top. It's perfect. Hidden against the face of East Temple is the tough-to-see Lost Temple Spire. There's a 200-foot notch separating the two. On the right is the mountain that Angus Thuermer, editor of the *Jackson Hole News and Guide,* dubbed the Wind River Range's southern bookend—Temple Peak. (It's complimented by the range's northern bookend—Squaretop Mountain.)

Behind, to the north, Warbonnet and Mt. Mitchell guard Jackass Pass. In the distance, across the divide, is the Cirque of the Towers and Pingora, the rock tower that for many is the Wind River Range's exclamation point.

As early as 1878, members of the Hayden Survey suspected that Fremont Peak was not the highest peak in the Wind Rivers, but it was not until 1906 that Gannett's elevation was determined to be fifty-nine feet higher than Fremont. Wyoming's highest mountain was officially designated Gannett Peak in 1922 in honor of Henry Gannett, mountain climber, member of the Hayden Surveys, chairman of the U.S. Geographic Board, and one of the founders of the National Geographic Society.

The second successful ascent of Gannett was made by Louis McMichel of Dubois and Dr. C.T. Jones of Lander in 1923. Guidebook author Orrin Bonney along with Frank and Notsie Garnick reached the summit via the east face in 1936. The two Garnick brothers were among the earliest modern climbers in the range. They, along with Bonney, were the first to summit Pingora.

The Garnicks were born in Slovenia before their family emigrated to Diamondville near Kemmerer, Wyoming, where their father found work in the coal mines. "We were just young kids looking for a little adventure," Notsie told me when I found him living in a small apartment in Pinedale in the 1980s. "We'd get bored hanging around Kemmerer and started heading into the Wind Rivers during our summers."

Notsie was surprised that I had bothered to look him up. "You're kind of famous to some of us," I told him, acknowledging his first ascents.

"You and your brother were far ahead of your time." Notsie died in 2004 at the age of 100.

Frank died in 2012 at the age of 96. He was quoted in his obituary, "We were there when it was the best," Frank said referring to the two brothers' early climbing days in the Wind Rivers. Garnicks' Needle in the upper Titcomb Valley was first climbed by the brothers in 1939 and serves as a monument to their memory.

"We don't stop hiking because we grow old.
We grow old because we stop hiking."

Finis Mitchell
1901-1995

But for most lovers of the Wind Rivers, the individual most associated with the range is neither Fremont or Bonneville. It's Finis Mitchell, a Union Pacific Railroad worker from Rock Springs. Today, on any summer afternoon, the trails of the Wind Rivers are filled with yuppie hikers and climbers wearing overpriced Patagonia apparel, using titanium trekking poles, carrying Black Diamond ice axes and college degrees.

Finis didn't need any of that stuff when he first started exploring and climbing the Wind Rivers in the 1920s. Over the next sixty years, he would make some 250 ascents, wearing a plaid flannel shirt, bib overalls with rolled-up cuffs, high top lace boots, and using a crooked hiking stick.

Like the Garnicks, he too was ahead of his time. In the years prior to World War II, there was little reason for local Wyomingites to head into the Wind Rivers except to hunt elk. Admittedly most of his early climbs were non-technical and primarily in the range's southern end (although he did occasionally don crampons). But what makes Finis Mitchell unique is that he was the first to explore the range and climb its peaks just for the fun of it. There was no climbing cult in blue collar Rock Springs.

In 1919 at the age of eighteen, he stumbled upon the Cirque of the Towers and made the first ascents of Watch Tower and Warrior I in the Cirque. Other first ascents included Big Sandy Mountain (1933), East Temple Peak (1933), Washakie Peak (1930), and Mitchell Peak (1923). He climbed Mitchell Peak no less than eleven times and, apparently not trusting his legacy to his children, carried a bronze plaque to the peak's summit listing his ascents of the mountain that would soon be named in his honor.

In June 1930 he and his wife, Emma, set up a fishing camp at Mud Lake where the present Big Sandy Lodge is now located. Unfortunately very few of the lakes in the Wind Rivers actually contained any fish. The Mitchells set out to rectify that situation by gaining the trust of the Wyoming Game and Fish Department, which supplied hatchery trout to the couple. Mitchell explained it all in his homey 1975 guide book, *Wind River Trails*.

> "The hatchery brought fish to us in five gallon milk cans, twelve cans at a time. We would put these twelve cans on a six pack of horses a can on each side and pack them out into the mountains. In the seven years we were there, we packed out two and a half million trout."

From 1930 to 1937, Mitchell stocked over 300 lakes, thus making him a sort of Johnny Appleseed of the Wind Rivers.

In 1982 I ran into an elderly hiker wearing bib overalls on the trail to Big Sandy Lake. We chatted briefly. I shook his hand and took his photo. Like thousands of others who enjoyed the Wind Rivers, Finis Mitchell was a friend of mine.

Today, a photograph of Mitchell hangs in Big Sandy Lodge, standing on the summit of Gannett Peak. The photo was taken in August 1976. He was seventy-five years old. He's obviously among the oldest climbers ever to reach the top of the 13,804-foot mountain. The record for the youngest person to summit Gannett was probably set by a seven-year-old boy from Iowa who shared his first name with the mountain. Gannett Swan climbed the peak on July 30, 1999, along with his family, which included his eight-year-old brother.

Reaching Gannett's summit is not particularly technically difficult. Most make their ascent via the Gooseneck Route, and early in the season, a snow bridge provides access across a deep *bergschrund.* Climbers are typically equipped with an ice axe, crampons, and a rope. The real challenge in climbing Gannett is the mountain's remoteness from the nearest trailhead. It's a twenty-two mile walk using the Glacier Trail beginning at Torrey Lake near Dubois. The Ink Wells trail through the Wind River Indian Reservation to the base of the mountain is about fourteen miles. The most popular access is from Elkhart Park through Titcomb Valley then over Bonney Pass The hump over Bonney Pass is almost as daunting as the subsequent climb up Gannett. The pass rises over 2,000 feet from Titcomb Valley, and it's a sixteen-mile hike from Elkhart to the base of the pass. So just getting to Gannett is a challenge whether you're seven or seventy-five.

On December 26, 1982, in a fit of irrationality, seven of us left Elkhart Park to attempt to put a climber or two on top of Gannett on New Year's Day. We wore skis and took turns breaking trail through the deep snow. It was slow and exhausting work. The snow was not the only obstacle. The bitter cold proved to be our toughest challenge. Inexplicably, we did not make any campfires, and the short days had us in our tents usually by 6:00 p.m.

The nights were excruciatingly long and cold. My "sleeping bag within a sleeping bag" tactic to stay warm was insufficient against the sub-zero temperatures, which reached -30-degrees before the sun's rays broke over the mountaintops. We peed into our water bottles and used them to add a bit of temporary warmth to our sleeping bags. Minor tasks became very difficult including lacing up frozen boots or keeping our hands and feet semi-warm. (Rotating our arms like windmills proved to be the most effective way to force blood into our fingertips.)

Three of us made it to the head of Titcomb Valley where we spent two nights in a snow cave waiting for an opportunity to head up Bonney Pass and on to Gannett. Violent winds and steady snowfall ultimately prevented any summit attempt. Ten days after our departure, we returned to Pinedale where we were greeted warmly by nearly everyone with, "You guys must be nuts."

That was not the only unique attempt on Gannett. Somewhere around 2005, Rob Shaul of Pinedale left Elkhart Park at exactly midnight. With the help of a headlamp to find the trail at night, he successfully climbed Gannett and returned to Elkhart in less than twenty-four hours.

Between 1985 and 2011, Scott Parish of Riverton, Wyoming, successfully climbed all fifty-one peaks in the range with an elevation of 12,500 feet or greater.

"I have been in love with the Wind River Mountains since 1978, and when I get to old to climb, I figure I can walk all the trails I have missed over the years. That should last me well into my eighties or nineties," Parish told me.

Climbing is not the only reason most backpack into the Wind Rivers. For many, it's all about the fishing. Finis Mitchell had hardly begun hauling trout into the range in the 1930s when fishermen started following his tracks in search of cutthroats, brooks, and rainbows. "You've got to be dead" not to catch trout in these mountains," a fly fisherman told me once as he rolled something called a Mini-Me Beetle on the surface of Valentine Lake. Within seconds, a fourteen-inch cutthroat rose to the occasion, resulting in a one-sided tug-of-war. The fisherman usually wins the fight, and the poor fish can only hope that his captor subscribes to the popular "catch and release" philosophy.

In 1979 the Wyoming Game & Fish Department distributed a small brochure, which contained maps of all the drainages on the west side of the range along with the trout species found in each lake or stream. The trout species in over 300 lakes were identified. Far and away the two most predominant species listed were cutthroat and brook trout. Golden trout were listed as inhabiting about thirty lakes. For many Wind River fishermen, catching a wild golden using a fly rod is a fisherman's dream come true.

Goldens are notoriously finicky feeders. Those found in the Wind Rivers today were introduced into the range from their native range in California's High Sierra's. In his *Travels in the Greater Yellowstone*, Jack Turner said the goldens arrived in Wyoming by railroad boxcar in 1929. Mitchell, in the preface to his *Wind River Trails,* listed the exotic and colorful golden trout as one of the species he packed into the mountains.

Unfortunately golden trout hybridize readily with other species of trout, and actually catching a racially pure golden may be asking a lot. Turner reported that the Wyoming Game & Fish Department was attempting to establish a pure brood stock in a few isolated lakes just in case their California cousins experience some unforeseen piscatorial genocide.

In recent years, four or five lakes in the Bridger Wilderness have been identified as the most likely place to catch a golden trout. These include Elbow, Peak, Mistake, Nelson, and Tommy Lakes. There's a time-tested procedure for knowing if a lake has golden trout. If you fish the lake for hours without a hit, never even see a trout rise, and walk away muttering, "There's no fish in that lake," you can then be certain it's full of goldens. In

1948 the world record golden trout of just over eleven pounds was taken from Cook Lake in the Wind Rivers.

Far and away the most commonly asked question from those about to backpack the Wind Rivers is "What about bears?"

"There are lots of black bears and a few grizzly bears in the Wind Rivers," I usually tell people. "Consider yourself lucky if you see one. But don't count on it."

In four decades of tramping through the range, I have seen exactly one bear. People do see bears but not often. The appearance of grizzlies in the Wind Rivers is a new phenomenon. Up until about a decade ago, there was none in the range, but their existence has been confirmed. In 2011 a gaunt grizzly was trapped in the Big Sandy area, and in the same year, the campground at Green River was closed briefly because of the appearance of a grizzly.

In 2012 a Wyoming Game & Fish Department large mammal biologist told me he had seen photos of grizzlies feeding on bear bait taken by automatic cameras placed by bear hunters in the Wind Rivers. The U.S Fish & Wildlife Service estimated there are about 600 grizzlies in the Greater Yellowstone. Exactly how many are roaming the Wind Rivers is anyone's guess. There have been incidents where some kind of bear has entered a backpacker's camp, so toss your food bag over a high limb before crawling into your tent. Bear canisters are not required in the Bridger Wilderness. Meanwhile I'll keep telling anyone who cares that "No bear has ever touched a human in the Wind River Range." I hope I'm never corrected. Your best chance at seeing a bear is by eating sardines in your tent at night.

Many backpackers are disappointed that they do not see large game animals, especially elk, in the range. Rest assured the wapiti are there. There are about 110,000 elk in Wyoming, and the Wind Rivers are home to many of them. Remember elk, moose, and deer are hunted in the range. It's is not a national park. They know it and fear man. You may want to see them, but they have no interest in seeing you.

Moose are not particularly wary of humans, and one of the best places to catch a glimpse of a moose is along the dirt road to Green River Lakes or in the willows at the head of the first lake. There are about 7,000 moose in Wyoming, but if that seems like a big number, consider that Maine has seventy-five thousand. Rocky Mountain sheep can often be seen on Whiskey Mountain just east of Dubois. Try climbing a ridge in the wee hours of the morning or at dusk, and you might see elk.

In August 2009 a young woman climbing Fremont Peak photographed a mountain goat at about 12,000 feet. It was the first documented sighting of the species in the Wind River Range. "He walked about two circles around me, probably eight to ten feet away," Katie Mortenson of Pinedale said. "He was just very inquisitive."

A Wyoming Game & Fish biologist surmised that the goat probably wandered off from an established herd in the Snake River Canyon along the Wyoming/Idaho border about seventy miles away. (Be careful! In October 2010 hiker Robert Boardman was gored by a mountain goat in Olympic National Park. He died from blood loss caused by a severed artery in his thigh.)

There are wolves in the Wind Rivers too, but they are rarely seen. If you're lucky enough to spot one, you may be on a roll and should immediately head to Las Vegas. (In 2012 the U.S Fish and Wildlife Service estimated there were 328 wolves in Wyoming including Yellowstone Park.)

The range is full of birds, and most backpackers will spot juncos, finches, chickadees, and ruffed grouse. There are a few species especially worthy of your attention. Pine Grosbeaks can be anywhere. Harlequin ducks are often spotted on the two Titcomb Lakes. Harlequins inhabit rocky coastlines and swift flowing streams in the Pacific Northwest north to Alaska; the Wind Rivers represent the southernmost extension of their range. Climbers ascending the highest peaks should keep a sharp eye for gray-crowned and black rosy-finches foraging for insects on snowfields and glaciers. Lots of serious birders do not have these species on their life lists since serious birders tend to be senior citizens who are unlikely to don crampons to add a bird to their list.

The best place to see three-toed woodpeckers is in the thick timber of the Lakeside Trail along the west shore of the lower Green River Lake. Williamson's woodpeckers can be seen infrequently in the aspens along New Fork Lake. There are supposed to be black-backed woodpeckers in the range, but you're more likely to see a wolf or even a unicorn.

Not all the four-legged creatures in the Wind River Range are wild. The U.S. Forest Service does grant grazing leases for cows and sheep on the Bridger-Teton National Forest and the Shoshone National Forest including within the designated wilderness areas. Backpackers heading up the dirt road to Green River Lakes will see hundreds of cows grazing in the valley and along the banks of the Green River itself. In terms of cattle numbers, a group of ranchers, joined together as The Green River Valley Cattlemen's Association, holds one of the largest grazing leases on any national forest.

Grazing on national forest lands has long been integral to the "multiple-use" concept of our national forests, and, with some exceptions in the Southwest and California, there has been little grassroots opposition to the practice. It is a long accepted use of public lands. What some do not realize, however, is that the cattlemen do not lease the land itself but rather the right to graze their critters on public lands. Those lands are still very much open to hunting, backpacking, fishing, and camping. Ranchers do, of course, pay for their grazing privileges. But not much. In 2011 the cost was $1.35 for a cow and its calf per month on all National Forest and Bureau of Land Management lands nationwide.

Don't ever suggest to any holder of a grazing lease that the low rate is a subsidy as I once did.

"It's not a subsidy," a rancher authoritatively told me. "It makes no sense to simply let the land go unused. It would be a subsidy if we were actually receiving tax dollars like some of those row crop farmers in Iowa or North Dakota, but we're not."

Most Wind River backpackers will not encounter cattle, at least in the Bridger Wilderness. Unfortunately the same cannot be said for sheep. Every summer, countless domestic sheep graze the Big Sandy area of the range well within the Bridger Wilderness boundaries.

"What are they doing to my mountains!" a friend of mine exclaimed in disgust a few years ago as we watched hundreds of defecating sheep being herded along the shore of Dad's Lake and through one of the lake's feeder streams by a Nepali shepherd.

It's all legal, of course. Every summer hundreds of sheep graze along the shores of Marm's Lake, Mirror Lake, and throughout Sedgewick Meadows. The grazing permit is held by a Rock Springs rancher. The 2011 rate for grazing sheep on USFS and BLM lands nationwide was a $1.35 for every *five* ewes and *five* lambs per month. Let's do the math: 1,000 sheep with 1,000 lambs, divided by 5 is 200 pairs. Multiply the 200 pairs by $1.35, and the U.S Treasury is enriched by $270 each month. Multiply that $270 by five months of grazing and the total reaches $1,350, an amount that most certainly represents a valid tradeoff for the annual defacing of one of the prettiest areas of the Bridger Wilderness.

In 2011 I stopped at the Bridger-Teton office in Jackson and spoke briefly with the USFS official who administered the grazing leases on the Bridger-Teton.

"Have you ever actually seen the sheep wade through the streams and lakes of the Big Sandy area?" I asked him. "It's disgusting. The forest service tells backpackers where they can camp and how to shit in the woods, but the sheep graze and defecate everywhere in that area. It's a sin to allow that to go on within one of the most spectacular areas of the National Wilderness System."

The man was polite and didn't seem surprised by my comments and concerns. Apparently I was not the first to complain about the situation. "Sheep grazing in the Big Sandy area is a complicated thing," he replied.

I didn't push it. There was no sense. He was just doing his job and didn't have the authority to change the status quo even if he wanted to. Besides it had already been explained to me that grazing on public lands was not a subsidy.

Arguably the man who more than any other exposed the wonders of the Wind Rivers to the world was legendary mountaineer Paul Petzoldt, the founder of the National Outdoor Leadership School.

Petzoldt was born in Iowa in 1908 and with his family moved to southern Idaho when he was still a boy. It was there that he saw his first real mountains, the Sawtooths. At the age of sixteen, he hitchhiked into Jackson Hole and summited the Grand Teton. He and his climbing partner, Ralph Herron, were only the fourth party to reach the summit, and the fact that they were just a couple of teenagers electrified the community of Jackson.

Petzoldt gained a reputation as a skilled mountaineer, and when Grand Teton National Park was established, he was granted the climbing guide concession. In 1933 he befriended a wealthy Englishman who invited him to England. From there, he found his way to the Alps and climbed the Matterhorn before returning to Wyoming to resume guiding in the Tetons. In 1938 he was invited to join the All-American K2 Expedition in the Himalayas. He distinguished himself by reaching the 26,000-foot level of the 28,251-foot peak setting a record for climbing to the highest altitude without the use of auxiliary oxygen.

Petzoldt never quite got over his failure to be the first to climb the world's second highest peak. "Jesus Christ," he was quoted as saying in *Fallen Giants*. "We weren't turned back by bad weather. We made up our mind not to climb the mountain. If we'd have brought up a little more food and planned to get to the summit, we would have come back as conquerors of K2."

During World War II, the Wyoming mountain climber served in the U.S. Army's Tenth Mountain Division where he used his expertise to educate the soldiers on tackling the hazards of snow, ice, skiing, and climbing in difficult alpine conditions. Although Petzoldt never saw action, the Tenth Mountain Division fought German troops in Italy and suffered nearly a thousand fatalities.

After the war, he tried his hand at a variety of occupations including raising alfalfa seed on a farm near Riverton. Following that agrarian endeavor, he bought the Ram's Horn Saloon in Dubois before heading to California to sell used cars. In 1963 Petzoldt returned to his roots and became the chief instructor with the newly formed Outward Bound adventuring program in Colorado. He hoped to open a branch of Outward Bound in the Wind Rivers before ultimately founding his National Outdoor Leadership School headquartered in Lander in 1965. Forty-three students showed up in Lander in June of that year.

"The classroom is the entire Wind River Range. Of all the mountain ranges I had visited in the whole United States, it was the best one to teach in," Petzoldt said. At the time of his death in 1999, NOLS had 50,000 graduates; the organization now offers wilderness adventures worldwide.

In 1967 Larry Amundson and I were just beginning our lifelong love affair with the Wind Rivers and were planning a backpack into the middle fork of the Bull Lake Creek drainage and the Milky Lakes. We decided to ask Paul Petzoldt a favor. At the time, Petzoldt was living in a small apartment in Lander. (We looked up his address in the phone book.) He was sitting in a Lazy-Boy, smoking a cigarette and watching TV when we entered. He was a big man, the warm teddy-bear type with large bushy eyebrows and a paunch. We were a little intimidated at first, but he warmed right up when we told him we were going backpacking in the Wind Rivers.

"Paul, we heard that your school kept a couple of canoes at the outlet of the lower Milky Lake. We were wondering if we could borrow one of them to paddle up to the head of the lake," I asked politely. "We'll return it to the outlet a couple of days later when we return."

"Aw, hell, those kids are paying a lot of money to be miserable in the mountains. Don't do 'em any favors. Leave it at the head of the lake."

That's the only time I saw Paul Petzoldt. He was fifty-nine years old at the time and a legend to many. I wished I had taken his photo. The legendary mountaineer died in a nursing home in Maine.

Like all mountain ranges, the Wind Rivers are not without tragedy. Almost every summer, carelessness, bad weather or fate seems to result in a fatality. In June 2003 Ryan Sayers, twenty, of Colorado was struck by lightning on Steeple Peak and fell to his death.

Wyoming State Defender Kenneth Koski, fifty-six, fell and died while climbing 12,585-foot Mt. Bonneville in September 2006. "Talk about getting away—no cell phone, no telephones, no e-mail, no television. Eight days of pure bliss!" Koski had written in an office newsletter, describing an earlier Wind River adventure.

In August 2011 Don Scott, sixty-three, of Boise fell while walking across a snowfield on Gannett Peak and tumbled to his death.

In October 1979 a single-engine Beech Debonair carrying three passengers and the pilot took off from the Pinedale airport on a brief sightseeing trip and disappeared. Two of the passengers had Pinedale roots, Bill and Loretta Binning. Despite an extensive search, the crash site was not discovered for almost two years. In September 1981 three hunters scanning for Rocky Mountain sheep with binoculars spotted airplane wreckage across an enormous chasm in the Downs Mountain area of Fremont County. They did not attempt to reach it since they assumed that it was old wreckage that had been reported and investigated much earlier. They did record the number on the plane's fuselage and after their hunt, they reported their sighting. The number corresponded to the missing plane carrying the Binnings that had disappeared almost two years earlier.

A search party reached the crash and confirmed that it was the plane that carried the Pinedale couple. But it's what was found near the wreckage that went far beyond the bounds of human decency. "There were two wallets sitting unnaturally atop rocks at the crash site," one of the searchers reported. Both wallets contained no currency. A relative of the Binnings told authorities that the couple had made a significant bank withdrawal just before their flight.

Of course what makes the incident so despicable is not the theft itself, but that the individual(s) did not bother to make an anonymous phone call reporting the crash site, which would have provided closure to those who lost loved ones in the accident.

As tragic as these fatal accidents may be, none may be as traumatic as the death of Reverend Mike Turner, a Presbyterian minister from Caldwell, Idaho. In August 2002 Turner, forty-eight, along with his dog, Andy, was hiking off-trail in the Brown Cliffs area on the east side of Indian Pass. He was carefully picking his way across a chaotic expanse of large rocks when a boulder began shifting beneath his feet. He jumped ahead to avoid the moving boulder but slid and fell into a gap as another boulder slammed against him pinning both his dangling legs above the knees. The rockslide left him trapped. His legs were not broken, but after a couple of hours of terror and repeated attempts to free himself, he started to abandon hope. He began writing in his journal.

"About two hours ago, a large rock rolled upon me and trapped my legs. I was very careful, be sure of that, but I am hurt. I am in your hands Lord…I don't know what I face."

The coroner's report, which also relied on Turner's journal, stated that Turner became trapped on the afternoon of August 2 and died on or about August 11 of exposure to the elements, hypothermia, and dehydration. We can only hope that we will not have to face death for such a long duration and under such cruel circumstances as did Mike Turner. His remains were not found until August 31. He had wrapped himself in his tent and other clothing and was able to prepare meals, using his stove and food in his backpack.

"He could eat; he just wasn't able to get water," a member of the Fremont County Search and Rescue said. Turner used his stove to melt snow until the snow was exhausted. He had tied a cord to his water bottle and had attempted to throw the bottle into a nearby small lake but was unsuccessful.

The search for Turner was called off on August 23. On August 28, two hikers emerged from the wilderness followed by Turner's dog. A few days later, the search was renewed and Andy went along. Mike Turner's remains were found by a lone backpacker who had seen posters at trailheads alerting hikers of Turner's disappearance.

"I already knew who it was," Jeff Stewart of San Diego said when he saw the trapped body.

Turner's tragedy, along with quotes from his journal, was detailed in Jeff Rennicke's article "I Cried Out Aloud For You" in the June 2002 issue of *Backpacker*.

Turner's death can be described as a tragic accident of fate. The same cannot be said about the senseless death of Peter Absolon, forty-seven, a renowned climber and the Rocky Mountain director for the National Outdoor Leadership School in Lander. He and his wife, Molly, had one child, Avery. On August 11, 2007, Absolon, along with NOLS instructor Steve Hirlihy, were climbing a new route up the face of Leg Lake Cirque in Upper Silas Canyon. Directly above them, hiking along the rim of the canyon, Luke Rodolph and three others were enjoying the magnificent view. They seemed to have the canyon all to themselves. They began amusing themselves by pushing a few rocks off the edge.

"I picked up a rock and threw it off," Rodolph said. "(I) Looked over just a little further to watch it fall, see where it was going to hit, you know, kinda leaned out further than what I was comfortable normally, and watched it hit Pete Absolon." The rock struck Absolon in the head, and he was killed instantly.

"I threw it," Rodolph told Hirlihy after calling 911 and running the four miles to the canyon's floor to see if anything could be done. The two spent the night together while the rest of Rodolph's group went back to their campsite. Rodolph and Hirlihy walked back out to Lander together the next morning and spoke with Fremont County Attorney Ed Newell. Absolon's body was recovered the next day.

Rodolph, twenty-three, a native of Casper, had served two tours in Iraq as an infantry soldier in the 82nd Airborne Division.

"I never wanted to cause a loss like that, so big for Molly and Avery," Rodolph said. "It's unbearable for them to have to go through this. It's my fault."

Rodolph's fate lay in the hands of County Attorney Newell who announced that he would not prosecute. Newell pointed out that Rodolph was extremely remorseful, took immediate responsibility for his act, did not intend to inflict harm, and had no criminal record. Newell also cited Rodolph's service in Iraq as a factor in deciding not to prosecute.

▲△▲

Over the years, I've seen a lot of backpackers, climbers, nature nuts, and fishermen trekking through the Wind River Mountains. They range from techie yuppies with the latest expensive gear, to old men wearing jeans and carrying hefty cotton Coleman sleeping bags wrapped in plastic. A couple of summers ago, a line of Midwesterners passed me, heading up over Jackass Pass. There were overweight adults, a couple of teenagers wearing shorts and T-shirts, slapping mosquitoes, and too many little kids to count. Taking up the rear was a man in his fifties carrying a long-handled, double-bladed axe.

"What are you doing with that thing?" I asked him.

"I always take my axe," he replied.

"What for?"

"For firewood," he said.

"Geez, there's plenty of wood lying around. Just bust it up."

"Nope, I got to use my axe," he replied throwing rationality to the wind.

Every summer season, there are a handful of backpackers who venture into the Wind Rivers and for a variety of reasons decide they need to be rescued. The use of the satellite-assisted spot locator has made these calls for help perhaps a bit too easy. A flip of the switch can begin a chain of events involving search and rescue organizations and even a helicopter. Most could simply walk out if there were no alternative. Some years ago, Rosemary and I passed a man camped along the trail to Island Lake who was leisurely cooking breakfast. He handed me a note and attempted to give me three or four crumpled twenty dollar bills.

"I talked to someone on Monday about coming to get me with a pack animal and a horse for me," the note read. "I am at Little Seneca Lake. Came down with a head cold. Thought it was an allergy. No lung capacity. Off and on equilibrium problems. Very slow thinking. My name is Steve. Pay whatever. Please help!"

Steve's situation didn't strike us as very serious. I did contact the sheriff's department the next day, but I don't know if they did anything. As I walked on, I looked back and saw Steve sitting on a log, finishing his breakfast. Good thing Steve didn't have a spot locator.

"Maybe you should have taken the money," Rosemary said sarcastically.

Then there was the young man on the Big Sandy Trail, carrying a shotgun and enough slugs across his chest to capture a small town. He was carrying the gun in front of him like a second lieutenant on patrol in the Vietnam War. He was ready. The rest of the people in his group looked normal. He looked stupid.

"What the hell are you going to do with that thing?" I asked him impulsively, forgetting the fact that he had a big gun.

"There may not be any bears, but if there is, I'm ready, and we saw some bear tracks up by Clear Lake," he said. "I'd rather have a gun and not need it, than need it and not have it," he said.

"I hope you won't be too disappointed if you don't get to use that thing," I said with a smirk.

There are lots of loners in the Wind Rivers. These solo hikers seem to seek out the remote nooks and crannies of the range. Joe Kelsey called them "wind freaks." Look for them hanging out with the picas and marmots in places like Peak Lake Valley, Deep Creek Lakes, Blaurock Pass, and Europe Canyon. They tend to be single, disheveled males who have recently told their parents that they are not returning to Brown, Dartmouth, or U.C. Berkeley for their senior year, despite accumulating some $50,000 in student loans. Many seem to be searching for their niche in life and head to the mountains to ponder and wander.

I ran across one of these loners a few years ago above Island Lake in the shadow of Ellingwood Peak. He had a banjo tied to his backpack. It must have been the only large musical instrument ever carried into the Wind Rivers. Records of this type are not yet kept.

"I'll play it this evening," he told me. "I'm going to set the Guinness Record for playing the banjo farthest from a paved road."

"Good for you," I told him. "That's a significant accomplishment. You're bringing real purpose to your life." I kind of admired the guy for doing something so frivolously creative and was sorry I wouldn't be around that evening to hear the theme from *Deliverance* across Island Lake as alpenglow embraced Fremont Peak.

Ellingwood Peak (13,052 feet) is one of the loveliest mountains in the range. Viewed from the trail up to Indian Pass above Island Lake, it's a pyramid of Rocky Mountain perfection. Alas, the mountain's name is the subject of controversy. Originally it was named after Albert R. Ellingwood (1888-1934), one of the great climbers of his day who made many first ascents in the Wind Rivers including Helen, Turret, Warren (all in 1924), Knife Point, and Sacagawea (1926), as well as his namesake peak (1926). Ellingwood was also the first to summit the Middle and South Teton and make the third ascent of the Grand Teton and Gannett (1924).

Unfortunately in 1977 the Sublette County Historical Society petitioned the U.S Board on Geographic Names to name the peak Harrower Peak to honor James Harrower, a former USFS Ranger, game warden, and Pinedale mayor. Perhaps the peak was never officially designated as Ellingwood Peak, or the Board of Names simply erred, but for whatever reason the new name, Harrower Peak, was adopted. Climbing historians were dismayed by the decision and none more so than Orrin Bonney. He wrote me regarding the change.

"James K. Harrower was a fine man, greatly respected locally and deserving of honor, and it is too bad that a tribute to him should be diminished by giving his name to a peak that has long been known for another person. I doubt that Mr. Harrower was ever on the peak, which is now supposed to bear his name," Bonney said. "Mr. Harrower can be really appropriately honored by having a park in Pinedale or a principal street named for him."

Those who care, including Joe Kelsey, still continue to refer to the mountain as Ellingwood Peak.

"At least we're not accountants."

Todd Skinner
1959-2006

Most Wind River climbers, CDTers, and backpackers pass through Pinedale before heading out for one of the three most popular trailheads on the west side—Green River Lakes, Elkhart Park, or Big Sandy where I counted 146 vehicles in August 2012. Sipping a micro-brew on the second-story deck of the Wind River Brew Pub with the distant peaks on the horizon is fast becoming a tradition for those about to begin or have just finished a Wind River trek. Pinedale's a busy place in the summer, and some have figured out that if you want to enjoy Wyoming's wilderness, this is the place to start. (Tourists and the less adventurous keep heading to Jackson.) Taxes from natural gas development south of town have filled the coffers of the school district and the county giving its residents one of the highest per capital incomes in the nation.

Like many small towns, Pinedale and its environs was the birthplace of a few overachievers. Grateful Dead lyricist, John Barlow, was raised on a ranch just north of town. You can see a couple of his gold records hanging on the wall inside the Rock Rabbit bistro on the main drag. Bareback rodeo champion, Joe Alexander, also was raised on a ranch near town. "Alexander the Great" won the world bareback championship five consecutive years, and last I checked, he still holds the record for the best score every awarded to a bareback rider for a single ride.

Few of the climbers challenging the granite walls of the Cirque of Towers are aware that Pinedale is the home to one of the finest rock climbers ever to assault a granite face—Todd Skinner. He was raised in Pinedale where his family operated the Skinner Brothers Wilderness Mountaineering. His real exposure to rock climbing occurred while attending the University of Wyoming. After graduation, he embraced his climbing passion and over the next twenty-five years mastered the most difficult free-climbing routes around the world including 5.13 cracks on the

Gunfighter at Hueco Tanks and Yosemite's The Stigma. Later he went on to pull off big-wall coups on Mount Proboscis in Canada and on the Nameless Tower in Pakistan. These were all free climbs in which the climber ascends, using no artificial aids, only a rope to protect against falls.

He established countless first ascents worldwide including Africa, Greenland, China, and, of course, the Wind Rivers. He settled in Lander, Wyoming, where he opened an outdoor shop and promoted the rock of the Wild Iris area near Lander as a world-class climbing destination.

On October 23, 2006, Skinner fell 500 feet to his death when his harness broke while rappelling when attempting a new free climb on Yosemite's Leaning Tower's west face.

▲△▲

The Wind River Mountain Range has a way of grabbing your soul. One backpacker from Ohio summed it up pretty well for me a couple of years ago as we passed one another atop Shannon Pass. "I keep coming back. I can't ever get enough of these mountains," he told me as he leaned on his trekking poles. "I come here for the vistas, the peaks, the rushing streams, and especially the wilderness isolation. These mountains are world class."

Hundreds of men and women would agree with his assessment, and every year they return again and again to the Wind Rivers to get their fix. Pinedale's Fred Pflughoft is one of those people. Fred's a friend of mine and has been climbing, backpacking, fishing, and photographing these mountains for nearly three decades. He is the author/photographer of *Wind River Range, Impressions* and has a special empathy with the range. Recently he told me of an experience he and his wife Sue once had at the Elkhart Trailhead when they were about to head up the trail. The year was 1985.

"As we readied to shoulder our packs, we noticed an elderly gentleman cruising the parking lot in his International Harvester Travelall and stopping to talk to others who were heading into the wilderness," Fred told me. Fred and Sue decided that the man might be Finis Mitchell. Their guess as to the man's identity was confirmed when the man asked if they were interested in purchasing a copy of his book, *Wind River Trails*. Fred was familiar with the little book and had used it on his very first trip into the Wind Rivers.

"We had seen his name in Wilderness Registers at trailheads several times before, but we had never met the man who was so much a part of these mountains. Talking with him about *his* mountains, you could tell he took great pride in his accomplishments," Fred said, emphasizing that back then no one knew the Wind Rivers as well as Finis Mitchell. Fred told me that there was a touch of melancholy in Mitchell's tone as he quizzed them about their pending backpack trip. "Where are you going?" he asked. "How long are you staying in?"

"Then pointing to a cane at his side, he mumbled something about a bum leg that was keeping him from hiking. You could tell he was pining for the past," Fred told me. Finis Mitchell would be eighty-five that autumn.

It's understandable that Fred would sense Finis Mitchell's affection for the Wind River Range. These mountains had enriched both their lives over many decades, yet both would admit that it would be difficult to put their affection for the range into words. In his book, Fred makes a succinct but eloquent effort to express his feelings.

"After twenty years, I am still unable to explain why the Wind River Range has such an allure for me and countless others I know...But mention the Winds to an avid backpacker or climber and invariably you will catch a special glint in his or her eye or a change in demeanor as to indicate there is something different about this place."

Sources & Further Reading

Chapter 1
Backpacker, November 2010 (Kalalau Trail).

Farcaros, Dana and Michael Pauls. *Corsica* (London: New Holland Publishers, 2008).

Fletcher, Colin. *The Man Who Walked Through Time* (New York: Random House, 1967).

Fletcher, Colin. *The New Complete Walker* (New York: Alfred A Knopf, 1976).

Kaufmann, Kenn. *Kingbird Highway* (Boston: Houghton Mifflin Harcourt, 2006).

Napier, Eloise. *Walking the World's Most Exceptional Trails* (New York: Abbeville Press Publishers, 2002).

Obmascik, Mark. *The Big Year* (New York: Free Press, 2004).

Wyoming Wildlife September 2010 (Cooke City grizzly attack).

The Seattle Times June, 08, 2002 (Fatalities on Rainer).

Delawareonline.com/article 20100729 Matthew Brown, AP July 29, 2010 (Cooke City grizzly attack).

Highpointers Club http://highpointers.org.

Walkopedia the World's Best Walks http://wwwwalkopedia.net.

Victorian Herald Sun (Victoria, Australia) 01/17/11 (Jean Béliveau).

Chapter 2
Brockman, Frank. *Trees of North America* (New York: Golden Press, 1968).

Leadem, Tim. *Hiking the West Coast of Vancouver Island* (Vancouver: Douglas & McIntyre, 2008).

McRae, Bill, and Shawn Blore. *British Columbia & the Canadian Rockies* (New York: Hungry Minds, Inc., 2000).

Vaillant, John. *The Golden Spruce* (New York: W.W. Norton & Company, 2005).

Ver Berkmoes, and John Lee. *British Columbia* (Lonely Planet Publications Ltd. 2007).

Winchester, Simon. *Atlantic* (New York: HarperCollins, 2010).

Chapter 3

Bardwell, Sandra, and Nancy Frey, Jose Placer, Gareth McCormick, Helen Fairbarn. *Walking in Scotland* (Victoria, Australia: Lonely Planet Publications, 2001).

Bindloss, Joe, and Clay Lucas. *Scotland's Highlands & Islands* (Victoria, Australia: Lonely Planet Publications, 2002).

Buchanan, Rob. "The High Hills of Freedom" *Outside* (April 2005).

Burns, Robert. *Burn's Complete Poetical Works* (Boston and New York: Houghton, Mifflin, & Co.1897).

Johnson, Samuel, and James Boswell. *The Journey to the Western Islands of Scotland and The Journal of a Tour to the Hebrides* (London: The Penguin Group).

Obmascik, Mark. *Halfway to Heaven* (New York: Simon & Schuster, 2009).

Quammen, David. "Trek" *National Geographic Adventure* (May, 2004).

Chapter 4

Bergreen, Laurence. *Over the Edge of the World* (HarperCollins: New York, 2003).

Davies, Bethan, and Ben Cole. Walking *the Camino de Santiago* (Pili Pala Press: Vancouver, BC, 2003).

Facaros, Dana, and Michael Pauls. *Northern Spain* (The Globe Pequot Press: Guilford, Conn., 1996).

Hanna, Edward. "Purgatory" *The Catholic Encyclopedia* (Robert Appleton Company: New York, 2011).

Kurlansky, Mark. *The Basque History of the World* (Alfred A. Knopf: Toronto, 1999).

Michener, James A. *Iberia* (Random House: New York, 1968).

Roddis, Miles, and Nancy Frey, Jose Placer, Matthey Fletcher, John Noble. *Walking in Spain* (Lonely Planet Publications: Victoria, Australia, 1990).

Steves, Rick. *Spain 2007* (Avalon Travel Publishing: Emeryville, CA, 2007).

Winchester, Simon. *Atlantic* (Harper Collins: New York, 2010).

Chapter 5

Bergreen, Laurence. *Over the Edge of the World* (New York: Harper Perennial, 2003)

Chatwin, Bruce. *In Patagonia* (New York: Summit Books, 1977)

Jones, Judy, and William Wilson. *An Incomplete Education* (New York: Ballantine Books, 2006)

Roberts, David and Charlie Buffett. "Cesare Maestri, The Legend Roars" *National Geographic Adventure,* Cesare Maestri, (April, 2006)

Chapter 6

Dorn, Jonathan and Dennis Lewon. "New Zealand" *Backpacker* (April 2005)

DuFresne, Jim. *Tramping in New Zealand* Melbourne: (Lonely Planet Publications, 2002).

Dugard, Martin. *Farther Than Any Man* New York: (Pocket Books, 2001).

Harding, Paul and Carolyn Bain and Neal Bedford. *New Zealand* Melbourne: (Lonely Planet Publications, 2002).

Harper, Laura and Tony Mudd and Paul Whitfield. *The Rough Guide to New Zealand* London: (Rough Guides Limited, 2002).

Chapter 7

Alexander, Caroline. *The Endurance* New York: (Alfred A. Knopf, 1998).

Bardwell, Sandra and Helen Fairbain and Gareth McCormick. *Walking in Ireland* Victoria, Australia: (Lonely Planet Publication Ltd, 2003).

Lansing, Alfred. *Endurance* New York: (Carroll & Graff Publishers, 2004).

Makem, Tommy. *Tommy Makem's Secret Ireland* New York: (St. Martin's Press, 1997).

McCarthy, Pete. *McCarthy's Bar* New York: (St. Martin's Press, 2000).

Peterson, Roger Tory and guy Mountfort and P.A.D. Hollom. *Birds of Britain and Europe* Boston: (Houghton Mifflin Company, 1983).

The Dingle News Dingle, Kerry, Ireland October 14, 2009.

Chapter 8

Davis, Wade. *Into the Silence The Great War, Mallory and the Conquest of Everest* (Toronto: Alfred A. Knopf, 2011).

Herzog, Maurice. *Annapurna* (London: Random House, 1952).

Thomas, Bryn. *Trekking in the Annapuran Region* (Hindhead, Surrey, UK: Trailblazer Publications, 2005).

Isserman, Maurice and Stewart Weaver. *Fallen Giants* (New Haven and London: Yale University Press, 2008).

Chapter 9

Bryson, Bill. *Mother Tongue, English and How It Got That Way.* (New York: Avon Books, INC., 1990).

Bronte, Emily. *Wuthering Heights.* (London: Laurel Press, 1987, first published 1847).

Wainwright, Martin. *The Coast to Coast Walk.* (London: Aurum Press Limited, 2011).

The Week. April 21, 2012 no. 865 (Thomas Kinkaide, The Naked Rambler).

Chapter 10

Bonney, Orrin & Lorraine. *Guide to the Wyoming Mountains and Wilderness Areas.* (Chicago: Sage Press, 1977).

Isserman, Maurice and Stewart Weaver. *Fallen Giants.* (New Haven and London: Yale University Press, 2008).

Kelsey, Joe. *Climbing and Hiking in the Wind River Mountains.* (Guilford, Conn.: The Globe Pequot Press, 1994).

Mitchell, Finis. *Wind River Trails.* (Salt Lake City: Wasatch Publishers, 1975).

Rennicke, Jeff. *I Cried Out aloud for You.* Backpacker Magazine, June 2002).

Ringholz, Raye. *On Belay! The Life of Legendary Mountaineer Paul Petzoldt.* (Seattle: The Mountaineers, 1997).

Roberts, Dave. *A Newer World.* (New York: Simon & Schuster, 2000).

Roberts, Phil, and David & Steven Roberts. *Wyoming Almanac.* (Cheyenne: Wyoming Almanac/Skyline Press, 2010).

Turner, Jack. *Travels in the Greater Yellowstone.* New York: St. Martin's Press, 2008).

Casper Star -Tribune. August 15, 2007 (Peter Absolon fatality).

Casper Star-Tribune. September 7, 1998 (Mike Turner fatality).

Jackson Hole News & Guide. September 9, 2009 (Joe Kelsey).

Bureau of Land Management News Release, January 31, 2009 (Grazing fees).

CPSIA information can be obtained at www.ICGtesting.com
Printed in the USA
LVOW13s1042100114

368734LV00002B/281/P